Life at the End of the Tunnel

Christina Black

Clink
Street

London | New York

Dedicated to my children and to Barbara and Dave who were always there for me ever since I was 17 years old.

Published by Clink Street Publishing 2021

First edition.

ISBN: 978-1-913568-92-4 Paperback
978-1-913568-93-1 Ebook

CONTENTS

HER VESTAL GRACE PROVOKES

"It's nerves," my dad said in the car, seeing my eyes brimming with tears. "Just nerves." He repeated it a few times, as if trying to convince himself that that the more he uttered the words, the more likely they were to be true. But the fact was, if he said them a hundred times, a thousand even, it wouldn't make it any truer than it was now – the reason I was shaking so much wasn't anything to do with my sodding nerves.

The shadow of the registry office fell over us and I felt the car slowing down. "Please don't stop, *pleeease* don't stop" I said to myself, hoping the driver, or God, would hear me and get me out of the awful predicament I'd allowed myself to stumble into. Dad stretched his arms forward and cricked his fingers. It sounded like a cockroach being stepped on. "Here we are," he said, feigning the enthusiasm a little too much.

The air hit our faces as we clambered out. I could taste dirt in the air, and the briny stench of the nearby river that Birkenhead could never fully escape. The car had dumped us on a narrow road outside a mud-coloured building that could've passed for a rich merchant's house seventy years ago, the kind of man who'd have left a place like this stuffing into his coat pocket two First Class tickets for the *Titanic*. Overhead, a sky, the same shade of grey as my heart, roiled like a sick stomach. Both rain and tears were forecast, but which would fall first? Sensing my hesitation, Dad put his hand on my lower back and coaxed me forward, like a farmer bringing his most prized ewe to market. "Oh, don't worry, fellas," I could imagine him saying. "This one's good for breedin'."

John was inside already, waiting – the only time he ever would for me in all the time I knew him. He was wearing a creased navy suit more befitting a funeral than a wedding, which was apt, given the circumstances. He threw up the corners of his mouth, which might have passed for a smile in some quarters, but I knew the sparkle in his eyes wasn't for any joy he felt at seeing me. It was because he'd been drinking, and was already nearing his threshold. Soon he'd be past it, and wouldn't I know it! An official appeared and guided us into position like a theatre director shepherding actors around his stage. John and I – the lead roles in this tragedy – were brought forward, whilst the over-dressed extras were herded into a dog leg around us. They looked on, all Brute aftershave and Airfix smiles, as the blank-eyed official muttered something about commitment and fidelity. I felt the skin around my finger pinched slightly as a ring was shoved onto it, then all eyes were on me and it was my line. I swallowed hard. Was this really happening?

"I do," I said, after a not-long-enough eternity.

"Awwww," everyone cooed, their make-up cracking.

Lips, dry and coarse and browned by ale and fags, then smashed into mine. Lips I didn't have any memory of ever kissing before, but presumably I must have when, two months earlier, I'd allowed myself to set in motion this whole cataclysmic chain of events. If I'd known then what I was about to enter into, how much my world was about to change, and with what violence, I'd have run towards the window and jumped out. I wouldn't have cared if I'd landed in front of a bus, because there's not much more damage a bus could've done to me than what awaited me in the two-and-a-half years that lay ahead.

Stepping away, John wiped a smudge of lipstick from his mouth, like it was cream and he was the cat who'd got it. And who'd have argued with him if he'd claimed he had? He was 36, and had been through all this before – *twice*; I was 18 and, until a few weeks ago, every inch the virgin from all the Arthurian myths and legends I grew up being obsessed about. The people who made up the dog leg offered their hands when we turned towards them. Stealing all the goodwill they had to offer, John stepped forward and shook them all, one quick jab each, already thinking about his next drink, probably, and which sucker would buy it for him.

And it was about this time too that I felt the first stirrings in my stomach. What was it, I wondered … the first sign of morning sickness or something far more sinister? An ill-omen perhaps, of what was to come, as full of menace as a raven perched on top of a baby's pram, or an owl screeching at midnight?

In just a few hours, I would know.

BLITZKRIEG

I remember a lot of banging when I was growing up. If you'd started your foot tapping at any point during the time I was being dragged, kicking and screaming through my childhood, it would have fit the chaotic rhythm of bangs and thumps that served as the soundtrack to the madhouse I was raised in. The noise was constant, the violence too; doors being slammed, plates being hurled, punches being thrown, at walls, doors and the backs of heads. It seemed my childhood was nothing more than one long, drawn-out slap across the face. The only thing that separated each day from feeling like an episode of *Game of Thrones* was the fact that we didn't have dragons shitting in the back yard, and no babies were ever eaten by dogs. But then, we didn't have a dog.

You'll have heard about Bootle already, but not for any reason it'll make your heart sing to think about. Google it and see what appears. The first image you'll see is a terraced street of fire-ridden houses, with wooden boards for windows. 'HELP ME!' they seem to be pleading, a plaintive cry shared by most of the people still unlucky enough to call the place home. It's not a town known for its poetry, its street theatre, or its art galleries, that's for certain. It's known because of what festers there: burnt-out buildings and burnt-out minds, things that fit the overall attitude of Bootle like a broken leg fits a plaster cast. It was a vibrant place once – if you can believe that – even going so far as to sport a lovely-sounding name, 'Bootle-cum-Linacre', which makes it sound like the kind of place where titled men with country estates went hunting for deer. And maybe they did. The docks were vast once too, a living, breathing, mechanised, river of industry, that just one human life-time ago, were considered such a threat to Germany's war effort that Hitler had to throw everything he had at them to keep his long-cherished dream of a Thousand-Year Reich alive and well. History knows that he failed in his wider aims, but in turning the once grand 'Bootle-cum-Linacre' into a town-sized bowl of porridge, he couldn't have been more successful. 90% of the houses were laid as flat as a chess board in the first week of May, 1941. It was England's Ground Zero. Only Dresden suffered more. Such destruction is a hard thing to bounce back from and, sadly, Bootle was never able to. Its will, as well as its houses, its roads and its infrastructure, had been bombed into insignificance. Within barely a decade, Liverpool, just three miles up the road, had taken down all the signs reading 'Bootle' from the front of its trams, and had started to dismantle, brick-by-sobbing-brick, the 'Docker's Umbrella', the iconic Overhead Railway that had served as the main artery linking the two towns for over half a century. I, along with all five of my older siblings, grew up in what was left: debris-strewn streets populated by people with debris-strewn minds, and rusty tram tracks that ran only as far as our parents' stunted ambition.

My own father had his own version of ambition, I'm sure. It might have been to win a fortune at cards, it might have been to assemble a fine collection of vintage cars. It certainly wasn't to be a good dad. He might also have had an ambition to sleep with every woman in the neighbourhood, and if it was, then that was the one he undoubtedly came closest to pulling off. God knows how many kids ran round the streets with his blood in them – we lost count at six! He was called 'Big' Richie because, during one of his many dalliances, he managed to squirt out a smaller version of himself with some "slut up the road", though we only ever saw *Little* Richie during the school holidays, 'cause mum would have nothing to do with him. He was handsome enough though, my dad, with a full head of hair, a cheeky smile, and a dimple in his chin I used to poke my little finger in – on the rare occasions I wasn't running from him in terror. He certainly put more effort into his appearance than he did to the house, that's for sure, one of many traits he shared with my mother, Olive, herself no stranger to odd habits and questionable proclivities that would make a priest choke on his digestive.

The house that contained the bitter fruits of their frequently toxic union was a fairly modest one. From the front, it was your typical charmless, northern terrace, but it sat on one end of the street, with a vomit of concrete spilled around all three sides to create the impression of a yard big enough for Richie's impressive car (the only impressive thing about him). The main entrance was right at the end, and if you stepped inside (holding your nose to avoid the smell of dead mice, rats, and God knows what else) you'd see the staircase directly ahead. At the top of that, if you dared ascend, you'd find a hall, the never-empty bathroom, and three airless bedrooms – though Olive and Richie added a fourth by stringing up a curtain in one to provide the quaint illusion of privacy for the older children. It could've been nice, it could've been magical, it could've been like the pillow-fight scene in *The Sound of Music*, but the only sound you'd ever hear was the sound of carnage as every single person in that wretched place fought a quiet battle with themselves, and a noisier one with each other – and somehow we all just kept losing.

For the most part, I shared a room with my sisters, Georgina and June, but everyone seemed to rotate through each room at some point or other without any thought being given as to what might or might not be appropriate. Our parents, I suppose, just thought of us all as one big tangled jumble of prepubescent arms and legs, and didn't consider for one second that, at some point in the future, a switch might flick on in the boys' brains, turning a low-lying curiosity about S.E.X. into something … well, far more damaging.

That damage was never more pronounced than when it was Raymond's turn to share with me, and I can say, with all honesty, that even now, well over fifty years later, I still convulse with horror when I remember what a spectacular error of judgement this proved on the part of Olive and Richie. Being much older, nine years in fact, Raymond would slink up to bed much later than me; but until that dreaded hour, I'd lie on the lumpy mattress, unable to sleep, staring at the constellation of insect carcasses pressed into the plaster on the unpainted walls. The word 'abuse' wouldn't have entered his mind back then, or mine, because the term hadn't really entered common usage at that point, but I knew it was not right what he was doing to me under those rags we called blankets. But I knew dread, and that's what I filled with at the sound of him saying "goodnight" to everyone downstairs. I filled with it even more when the bed creaked behind me and he climbed in, his sausagey, nail-bitten fingers seeking my flesh like cockroaches looking for crumbs. One night, after sewing another patch onto the blanket of abuse my childhood was being woven into, I heard this voice inside my head:

"YOU'VE GOT TO TELL MUM."

It wasn't my voice, but I heard it as clearly as anything, a loud whisper, just as vivid as the voice I'm hearing now as I try to coax these difficult memories into words. The idea of telling Olive was almost as repugnant as what Raymond was doing to me, because I knew the unrest it would lead to. She wasn't exactly going to pick me up and give me a cuddle and say, "There, there, sweetheart, it's all right – I'll make the bad man go away," but the sheer delinquency, the grotesqueness, of what he was doing to me under *her* roof, to his *own* sister, made me feel sick to my stomach.

Once I'd committed to telling her, I lay in bed the whole night, wondering if the sound of my hammering heart might wake Raymond. It didn't, thank God. Eventually, the darkness dripped away, and the sun announced itself, by degrees, through the thin, gauzy curtains. I heard Raymond climb out behind me, get dressed, and clomp down the stairs. After he'd left, I threw back the blankets and made my way, on my skinny, six-year-old legs, to the top of the stairs, where I quaked for an age, willing myself to go down. It wasn't that I knew Mum would go berserk, it was just a case of *how* berserk she'd go. Raymond was her Golden Boy, the sun shone, bright and wondrous, from out of his backside, and nothing he could ever do was wrong.

The slap across the face, therefore, I'd expected – as well as the string of profanities she belched out when I told her what he'd been doing to me every night – but the flat-out denial I hadn't. I can't recall how many times she called me a liar, but by the thousandth I was starting to realise she wasn't going to do anything about it. I began to tremble, thinking about the possibility that this might go on for years, until either Raymond left home, or I did. But that night, I slept alone. By some strange and unexpected miracle, her Golden Boy was moved immediately out of my room and into one of the others. I can't describe how beautiful the insect constellations looked that night, fossilised in their own blood. Orion appeared proud and mighty on the wall, and his belt stayed well and truly on. Until the day they both died, not a single word – not in shout, or whisper, from my mum, Raymond or myself – was *ever* muttered on the subject again.

Until just now.

I'd always assumed Olive and Richie had loved each other once, but you had to look very closely to see any trace of it, past all the mayhem, the arguments and the constant infidelities. The only time I ever saw evidence of anything even approaching affection pass between them was in the evenings, before they'd head off together to go ballroom dancing – though they'd come back later that same night as hostile to each other as the two Koreas, full of accusations and seething with the same old hatreds. "I saw the way you looked at her," you'd hear downstairs, moments before all the banging would start.

Sometimes, when they were out, I'd sneak into their bedroom, tiptoe over to the wardrobe, and pull out one of my mum's ballgowns. I'd hold it up against myself in the mirror, turning this way and that, playfully admiring myself. But then I'd hear the door slam downstairs, so I'd throw the gown, all crumpled and bunched, back into the wardrobe and scurry straight back to my room, just in time to hear the cannons loaded for that night's battle.

There was one escape: the cupboard in my bedroom. It was only really the size of a couple of pillowcases laid flat, but with the door closed, and a little imagination, it could be anything I wanted it to be: a bank by the side of the Thames where little girls in hair-bands could be found chasing rabbits down holes, or a castle with a circular table around which King Arthur and Lancelot would speak with my dollies and I about the important matters of the day, and everyone would listen to what I had to say. "Ooh, that's interesting Christina," Arthur would muse, or "Never mind Christina," Guinevere might offer, if I told her I was upset about something. To them I could divulge the secrets of my heart, and share with them, in mouse-like whispers, the feeling that I didn't actually belong in that awful place, that I was somehow different. It was like a physical sensation. I didn't feel a connection to any of the people around me, not my mum or my dad, and certainly not any of my siblings. Something was missing, and the only people who understood that were my dollies and my teddies, and those semi-mythical people from the past who I was able to conjure out of my pain.

By the time I made it to my teens, I could see that there were two ways out, and two ways only: school or work. I chose school, but school didn't choose me back, because school can never work as an escape, if what you're escaping from – your home-life – leaves physical marks on you that everyone around can see. Children just aren't that kind. Not in this town. This was a place, after all, where just twenty years later, two 10-year-old boys would lure a toddler away from his mother and into the headlines. Because there was no money, the clothes I was sent to school in were hand-me-down-hand-me-downs, meaning they'd already been recycled through my brothers and sisters half-a-dozen times before they found themselves, all threadbare and tatty, onto my skinny-as-a-goalpost frame. My shoes, for example, had no soles in them, so Olive, not wanting to fork out for new ones, would shove pieces of cardboard into them, which she would replace every time it wore through. Bullies love that sort of thing, though, don't they, and those at my school weren't shy in letting me know that. They also liked to draw attention to how much older my mum and dad were, compared to everyone else's, and found all sorts of ways to address the fact that I must've been an accident of some kind, or a freak, or whatever other pernicious term took their fancy at the time; none of which made my time at school any easier, but it was still a thousand times better than being at home.

So, I had to give work a go, and see if I could force an escape that way. As a plan, it was partly successful. I went asking around and very quickly landed a job in the General Store just up the road, which was run by David and Wendy, a lovely couple that everyone knew. The job was nothing earth-shattering, just running things through the till, a bit of shelf-stacking, and cleaning the floors at the end of each day, but it served a dual-purpose: it put money in my pocket (not much, 'cause Olive and Richie took most of it off me), and also served to keep me away from the house for two oh-so-precious, precious, precious evenings each week. I'd go straight from school, always finding the extra energy for three hours of being nice to people, and have them be nice to me back; a huge contrast to all the bullying I'd have to put up with at school. It was odd to discover that people could be civil to each other, and have conversations that didn't turn into fists flying into walls at the drop of a hat. I liked talking to people, and building up relationships with them, even if it was only for the length of time it took me to count out the change from a one-pound-note into their hands. And because I was always polite, people were always polite back. I basked in their smiles, and took them home with me, bringing them out again to look at when things turned sour at home. One lady I remember, a striking dark-haired lady with a touch of the Elizabeth Taylors about her, would always ask me how I was.

She'd only ever come in to buy the odd item here and there, a loaf of bread, or some butter – sometimes it was like she didn't even know what she wanted – but she was always polite and had such a warm and kind face. Her eyes would dance about my features and she'd focus on me like I was the most important person in the world, which made me feel like I was. One day, when I was a little bit older, as I was wrapping some cheese for her, she leaned over the counter and said to me, "You're better than all this, Christina," and she moved her hand a little, as if to indicate the shop. "If you want, I could see about getting you a job in the hospital?" I was flattered, but thought nothing of it at the time, other than that she was just a very nice lady who seemed genuinely interested in me. It turns out she was interested in me, although I wasn't to find out the reasons why until I was eighteen years old, and had just fled the nest for the very last time.

VOICES IN THE WIND

Just what is it about graveyards? Ever since I was little – when most of the headstones would be taller than me – I've always found myself drawn to graveyards, and the community of silent souls that congregate within them. When I'd go past one on a bus, or in Big Richie's car, my head would twist towards the graves like the petals of a flower tracking the course of the sun, compelled as if by some mystical force. What I knew already, even then, was that if evil existed in the world, *real* evil, it wasn't to be found in a place where the dead go to rest for eternity. They don't judge, those who have passed on, and they don't condemn either; they just invite everyone who chooses to spend some time with them a perfect slice of the quiet that they themselves are now enjoying. If you want to cry, go ahead. If you want to shout at the world, and all the injustice in it, feel free. All those now-resting souls around you did that too once. They've been there. They know.

Perhaps it's the awareness of what's to come that draws the eye; a sub-conscious reminder of everyone's ultimate destiny, 'precognition', is that the word? And the thing about is, it doesn't matter who you are, you're not going to escape it. One of the most comforting things about being alive, I read once, is that every single person who has ever lived has already, or will, pass over at some point. Kings, queens, billionaires, paupers, and everyone in-be-tween; there isn't all that much anyone can do about it really, and all that will remain, beyond a couple of generations, is a person's name, carved – if that person was thought of fondly enough – onto a headstone. But that wasn't what drew my gaze. For me, there was something else, and although I might not have been able to pin down precisely what it was just then, I was able to recognise that my senses were attuned to *something* out of range of what the eye could see. In later life, I'd come to understand what this was, but in the years when my age could be counted on my fingers, and I had a better relationship with my dollies and teddies than I did with real flesh and blood people, this sensation was just like the white noise between radio stations – I could *hear* it, but I couldn't tune into anything specific, couldn't hear the words in the songs; but I could feel the faint melodies being transmitted, as if through the vibrations of the air around me. Some people need a recognisable faith to attach these feelings to, but it doesn't really work like that for me. I don't need a special building to pray in, or to give thanks for what I've been able to come through in my life. Prayers are prayers, and you can do them anywhere. Surely you don't have to traipse your way up to a big church three miles away to tell God you're thinking about Him. If He's all-seeing, as he's supposed to be, then he'll hear you, whether you're kneeling on top of Paddy's Wigwam waving a giant crucifix around, or cowering in fear in the dark cupboard under your mum and dad's stairs.

Once, when I was about nine or ten, I found myself wandering around a graveyard during an all too rare day out we had together as a family. You might even call it a day trip, if you can remove the illusion of joy that ordinarily comes with the term. I think we'd stopped off for something, possibly to have some sandwiches on a picnic bench we'd spotted and, as was usual for me, I wandered off to be around people who weren't constantly at each other's throats and, let's be honest, had far more time for me. The church I saw from the bench on the other side of the wall was beautiful, old and gothic and full of gargoyles, whose menacing expressions probably hadn't changed since Guy Fawkes's day. Even so, they still seemed more approachable than any member of my family. The sea of headstones I waded into, all riddled with ivy and cracked with age, towered above me, and as I wandered amongst the fixed expressions of the Holy Mothers and the imposing granite crosses, I began to hear a gentle wind blowing. It was odd because none of the leaves were moving on the tress, and the tall daffodils that fringed some of the graves were as still as they would've been inside a greenhouse. Then this gentle breeze found lips, and a tongue, and turned into a whisper, all ghostly and measured, and began to make a sound that I soon recognised as ... well, if I wasn't mistaken, wasn't that my name?

"Chriiiiiisssstiiiiiinaaaaa," it breathed, " Chriiiiiiiiiiissss-tiiiiiiiiinaaaaaaaaaa ... "

I wasn't scared. At least, I don't think I was, but I was confused, and I remember trying to work out what was going on. Where was this whispering coming from? Was someone trying to reach me from what I'd heard Olive called "the other side"? – someone that considered this place, away from my family and the cloying distractions of my home, more attuned to the message that it needed me to hear? Anything was possible, I suppose, except the idea that it was one of my siblings playing a trick on me, as that would require them to be interested enough to devise this level of craftiness. I kept wandering around, trying to trace the source of this unearthly sound, creeping through the headstones and the statues and amongst the trees, but couldn't pinpoint it at all. The voice – if I can call it that – was everywhere and nowhere, but was as distinct as the screech of an owl, and it seemed like it went on for an age, with me tripping over rocks and stones, desperate to find the source of this aural apparition, until—

WHUU-UUMP!!!

I collapsed on the path as if a tree had just fallen on me. I don't know why, I have no recollection of feeling dizzy beforehand. The intensity of feeling perhaps, or the incomprehensibility of the situation. Maybe my young mind hadn't evolved enough, in the alternate realms of which it would be one day be so familiar, to absorb the full meaning of what was trying to navigate its way into my mind, and when it did, it reacted the only way it was equipped to: it brought the curtain down and called a halt to proceedings. "Woah!" I can imagine it saying. "She's not ready yet."

My family, when they found me on the path after I hadn't returned, didn't put any thought into what might have happened, other than to assume I'd fainted in the heat. They just dragged me back to the car, took me home, and put me straight to bed, more inconvenienced about having to cut short their day out than they were about my health.

But the strangeness of that day didn't end with me being put to bed, nor with the fitful sleep that came shortly afterwards, because when I woke up, the strangeness had only intensified. At the foot of my bed, barely discernible in the dark, moonless room, stood a lady in a long, black dress. Not old, not young, not threatening, just exuding the same air of civility and politeness that I've come, in the years since, to associate with those who have crossed over.

"Hello, Christina," she said softly, as if she'd just returned from the shops.

I froze. Did I know this lady? Had we met before? She seemed so familiar in how she addressed me, but if we had, why wasn't I able to recognise her voice, or any aspect of her? Yes, it was dark, but even so …

If I was to experience this again, with all I've come to understand about the world since this day, and about people, and the journeys they make – physical and otherwise – I know I'd react differently; but fifty-odd years ago, my own instinct – driven by terror more than anything – was simply to pull the blanket up over my head and pray that the mysterious figure would go away.

But she didn't.

For an age I lay there, my heart pounding so forcefully I thought it might actually make the blankets go up and down. I still remember shaking, wondering if I'd ever leave that bed. I could sense the lady there, just a few feet away, watching my form, through the blankets. But eventually, as the goose-pimples faded from my skin, I started to sense that I was no longer in her presence, and before I dared lift the blanket to confirm this was the case, I just had time to consider one thing: either I was dead or I'd gone stark, raving mad.

No prizes for guessing which one my family thought, and they weren't shy about telling me, when I came down and babbled to them, as clearly as I could, what I'd experienced. The fierce slap I was given to silence me, however, was just one of the many reasons I stopped opening my mouth to tell anyone in my family about all the other strange things that started happening to me after that. There's only so many times a girl can hear: "There's something wrong with you," before she starts to believe it, and it may take a long time before she gains enough insight towards understanding that, sometimes, it might not be *her* that there's something wrong with, but the family telling her there is.

What I didn't know at this time (sorry, one of the millions of things) was that I'd actually been born a twin. An identical sister had been brought out of my mother moments after me, but hadn't been able to grab some of the same life-supporting air that was able to sustain me. She was fully formed, but whether she'd died during the delivery itself or at some point in the hours beforehand, I never found out. She'll have sensed my presence though, in the months prior to our separation, as I would hers, and that's comforting to know. But the death itself wasn't the most tragic thing about that particular episode. What I find much sadder is that the woman I went on to start calling "Mamma" a few months after this wasn't even aware there had been two of us, let alone that one had died. It wasn't because she'd been knocked out by a load of drugs to minimise the agony she was feeling, or to facilitate an easier delivery, but for a reason far more simpler than that: when I was born, my mother hadn't been in the room. In fact, she hadn't even been in the same town.

Another step towards the realisation of these abilities came during an episode that is one of the most tragic I'll be recalling in these pages, and I do so now, more than fifty years later, with no lessening of the grief that resulted, but a greater sense of frustration that none of the so-called grown-ups involved were able to change the outcome.

He'd have been just over fifty now, Billy, but because of the basic lack of common sense that God had shared out between the members of my family, he wasn't able to go to his Maker with even fifty weeks of memories tucked under his lovely black hair. He was, I remember, a beautiful baby, with bright blue eyes and a cheeky chipmunk smile, one that would've melted the heart of a statue. At five months' old he was very much the centre of our lives, especially Gina's, who doted him like you wouldn't believe. In time, he'd be followed by a little sister, Debbie Anne, and then Jason, his little brother, but between Billy and Debbie Anne there would be five miscarriages that would send Gina on a bit of a downward spiral. Some people said that the miscarriages were brought on by the shock of what happened to Little Billy, and that's possible, because what happened to Little Billy, the whole unexpectedness of it, would destroy any mother.

There were no storms on this particular night; no thunder, no lightning, just the flickering of the little black and white tele that Richie had bought, and that we'd tucked into the corner of the room. Billy – who we called "the baby" – was lying in my mum's arms, cooing away as babies do, with his granny, and I was stroking his foot, keeping him relaxed with the odd nursery rhyme, "Rock-A-Bye Baby", and all that. All babies cough, so nobody worried when Billy started to. It was actually quite a cute noise at first, making him sound like a kitten sneezing. "Aaaah," you'd probably say if you heard it. "God bless him." What started alarm bells ringing and changed the mood of the room was my reaction, because it was totally out of proportion with what seemed to be happening. Within just a few seconds of hearing him catch his breath, I jumped up onto my knees and, without being able to stop myself, started screaming out: "He's dying, he's dying, the baby's dying!"

I can recall the panic now, as strongly as I felt it back then, and it upsets me no less. I'm still at a loss to fully explain what put the thought into my head, but I can make a guess that it came from the same place as many of the other messages that have come to me in the years and decades since. With Little Billy, as with the voice in the graveyard months before, I was only able to recognise that there was *something* coming through, but untutored as I was

14

then in the language of these mysterious somethings, I was only able to translate it into a babbling panic that spread like a disease into everyone around me. The coughing did get worse though, and fast, so much so that you didn't need Dr Kildare to tell you that the baby was choking. Olive, who'd dragged up more than a handful of her own kids by this point, knew roughly what to do, and went about it with the kind of practiced efficiency that made you wander how many times she'd been through something like this before. She span the baby round, flipping him onto his tummy, so that he was face-down on her lap, then started hitting him between the shoulder blades with the flat of her hand. But whatever she was expecting to happen, didn't, and you could tell by the worry-lines on her face that things were going very wrong. She was scared.

SMACK!

The coughing continued.

SMACK!

More coughing, but weaker now, and more urgent.

SMACK!

Hardly any coughing now – because Billy had barely any breath left in his lungs to cough with. The sound was like the last few drops of water going down the plughole after a bath had been emptied. Everyone crowded around Olive as the panic started to write itself across everyone's face in big letters. Feeling utterly useless, Gina threw her hands up in the air, trying to pull down some divine help down from above, but God didn't seem all that interested.

SMACK!

Olive hit him so hard that time that you thought she might actually break his spine, but if it got him breathing again, so what? You could feel the whole world shrinking into this one tiny point as all eyes burnt themselves into this single horrifying scene. And then it wasn't just me screaming; everyone was at it, shouting, calling, yelling, all at various levels of hysteria

SMACK!

With the terror a bone-crunching reality now, it felt like the ceiling had been lowered to just an inch above our heads and was pressing down on us, squeezing out all the oxygen in the room, and as it sank lower and lower, Little Billy started to change colour – red first, like a healthy tomato – then beetroot – then, slowly – as if his face was some special effect in a film, it turned an unnatural shade of blue, like a piece of fruit that just been found down the back of the sofa. As the sounds from my nephew dwindled away to nothing, Raymond, my brother, fled out the door to the one place he knew our dad, Big Richie, would be – the pub. It was the same one June, my sister worked in, and was just up the road, but as if in a dream, as he started to run, it seemed to stretch on forever. This is what he told us later. Maybe if he'd gone to fetch him earlier, or he'd taken him seriously sooner (Richie thought he was winding him up at first), or if the call for the ambulance had happened the moment Little Billy had first started coughing, or when I'd started screaming, the outcome might've been different. But the outcome, much as it fills me with tears now, was the one I knew it was going to be the second I started screaming.

By the time Richie arrived back at the house, with a shaking June in tow, the ambulance was pulling up on the kerb outside, its blue light luring in those that hadn't already been aroused by the commotion beforehand. Everyone parted to let Big Richie and the ambulance crew enter to see what kind of final chapter they could end this night with. They didn't wipe their feet. I remember them now, coming in, their bright yellow coats filling the doorframe as they entered, and looked down to see the little blue ball that was being cradled in his mum's arms. He wasn't choking now. He wasn't doing anything now, except lying there with his eyes closed.

One of the ambulance crew took him from her arms and laid him down, but my view was obstructed by the wall of bodies that filled the space between us. I tried to listen, but everyone was speaking. I could hear a pump going, and a few words of encouragement, but that was it. Eventually the pump stopped, and everyone sighed, but not with relief. And then I saw, through a gap, one of the ambulance crew shake his head, and I knew, from that action alone, that there was no more life in Little Billy now, no more life than there was in any of his teddies watching, with button eyes, from the mantelpiece.

Denial landed on us like a meteorite. It didn't just strike me, but every single member of the family. Little Billy was meant to have been the answer to all Gina's prayers. He was her angel. She'd been desperate for a baby for ages, which is what made the years ahead so much more difficult to endure. The more she wished, the more she suffered, and we all had to share in that. Billy had been the embodiment of all our prayers, and we'd stormed Heaven with them to bring here.

Maybe the Devil had intercepted them on the way.

They did an investigation, but what was found wasn't for my ears, so I wasn't to know what had taken my nephew away from us for some time. And I daren't ask either because I didn't want my insensitivity (how they would've seen it) to earn me another slap around the face. I might never have known what had happened if a few strange things hadn't occurred after the funeral, the most significant of which featured everyone's favourite marionette: Andy Pandy.

He and Teddy were playing on a swing, and I was lying on the floor watching them. This was a while after Billy had died. But as they went about their kiddish shenanigans, I could hear another character in the background. I thought it might've been Looby Loo at first, maybe she'd hurt her knee or something; but Looby Loo doesn't sound like a baby coughing. Then the crying got louder and turned into what I now recognised as choking. Also, it wasn't coming from the tele, but upstairs, and we didn't have a tele upstairs. Confused, I stood up and ran into the kitchen and told my mum that I thought I could hear the baby choking up in his room. She looked down at me like I was mental. I tugged at her hand, urging her to go and help him, because I could hear him getting worse, I really could, but all this did was infuriate her and she smacked me across the face.

"The baby's dead," she spat. "Do you understand me? *Dead!* Now go off and play, I don't want to hear another word about it again."

So I didn't utter another word about it again. Ever. But that didn't mean it went away. I kept hearing it for ages, that same haunting cry, at various points throughout the day, and in every room, but never the one I was in. It was as if Billy had left an impression of himself inside the house, but because he wasn't able to speak, he was trying to make himself understood the only way he knew how.

But then even that changed too. Frustrated at never being able to make himself heard, perhaps, not properly, his method for reaching out to the family took on another, more terrifying aspect, and once again it was me who he reached out to. I was in my usual position, on my tummy, lying in-front of the tele. I wasn't eating anything, and I hadn't drunk anything for ages, but just like that, out of the blue, I lost my breath. There was no reason for it. Panicked, I jumped up and grabbed my chest, then my throat, trying to bite a fistful of air from the room, but my body was having none of it. I couldn't get any air into my lungs, and just like Billy had done before me, I started turning blue. I could feel the colour draining from my face. As the fear rose up inside me like sick, I managed to gasp out to my mum, "I CAN'T BREATHE, I CAN'T BREATHE", and she ran out of the kitchen to see what the hell was going on. To her credit, she didn't slap me around the face for bothering her, but dragged me out the back door to our neighbour, Maureen, to see if she could help.

More than a month had had passed now since Little Billy had died, but no one had considered me grown-up enough to tell me how he'd come by his death. As Olive dragged me through our back yard and into Maureen's, however, I became struck by the terrifying thought that I was reliving *exactly* what Billy had in the seconds before God took him. I became utterly convinced that this was about to happen to me, and to stop it, I tugged desperately at my collar, tearing it open as if it might help. I knew I was just seconds away from blacking out, and I remember my mum holding my arm and looking helpless, like she had with Billy when she nearly broke his back to make him breathe again. Maureen – the only one now thinking straight – rushed off to ring another ambulance, but before she'd dialled, something changed inside me, and my windpipe opened up just as suddenly as it had closed itself. I bent double at once, in a strange kind of ecstasy, and gulped down lungful after lungful of delicious Bootle air. I swear to God, nothing before or since has ever tasted as nice.

It was a build-up of mucus that had put Billy in the ground. It had accumulated in his windpipe until, after weeks, it had shrunk the passage through which the air was to pass, and prevented any more from entering. Maybe wiping his nose once in a while might've helped, instead of just letting him lie there on his back all day, allowing the steady stream of snot to fall back into his throat where it built up. What made it all the more tragic was that a simple procedure could have saved him. All he'd needed, the doctor told Gina after the investigation, was for a tube to have been put down his throat. They could've done this in the ambulance in seconds, and if they'd arrived in time the whole character of this book might be different. Even though my biological relationship with him would have changed with the revelations I would go on to learn years later, there would still be one more fifty-odd-year-old man in the world – and *his* children, and *their* children – who would've gone on to help shape the small universe around them, writing their own life stories with their actions and friendships. And who knows how that might've gone on to change the structure of my own tiny little universe?

HONEYTRAP

People talk of red-letter days in their lives, don't they, but the day I finally did move out of Olive and Richie's could be described as a red alphabet day. It was *that* important to me. Like a moon landing. My mum, of course, didn't care. When the much longed-for day came, she saw me with my holdall, fastening up my coat, and said barely a thing. There was no hug, no pat on the back, no anything, mostly because my leaving meant she'd be getting less money coming in. Dad, for all his faults, put on a much better front. I'd gone to see him at the pub to say goodbye, and he staggered out to me, clutching the walking stick that had been holding him upright these past couple of years. He took my arm with one hand, the same hand he used to knock me about with, but this time there was no violence in it, and no stern lessons to tattoo into my cheek. I saw his chin crinkle, possibly with sorrow, and noticed the dimple I used to poke my finger in when I was little. "I'm sorry, Christina," he said. I was only hours away from knowing what was really behind the words he was about to say, but I didn't know that yet, and just let him say them. "You've had a really horrendous life with us, and we've treated you appallingly." My eyes filled with tears and I did my best to hold myself together, but I failed miserably when I saw his own eyes fill up. There was real sorrow there, I could tell.

"It's alright, Dad," I said to him. "You don't need to say it."

I landed in Tranmere later that day to begin my new life. I was apprehensive, certainly, but any anxiety I felt was outweighed by the fact that I was finally away from that stinking hellhole, even if I hadn't yet fully escaped the gravitational pull of my family. The new place I was moving into was Georgina's, which might not have been ideal, but the room she was offering me would do as a stop-gap until I could get myself sorted out more. I didn't know Tranmere at all, and had no idea what I was going to do with myself there, or even how to get money in, but Gina, thinking only of the rent probably, explained to me about Housing Benefit, and from her front door pointed me to the bus stop just up the road. "The dole office is *that* way," she said.

As I was waiting there, I got speaking to a girl my own age. She was very forward, a bit too forward, and when I told her I was going to the Jobcentre her face lit up as if she'd just found out we were long-lost cousins. "Oh, that's where I'm going right now," she beamed, offering to take me there herself. And that is how I got to know Pauline Gader.

My new friend waited with me during the small-eternity it took the Dole people to process my application, and when we emerged, hours later, I said I had to give my sister a quick ring, to tell her I was running late. As we approached the nearest telephone box, down by the market, we saw the figure of a man inside, just wrapping up his call. Or so it seemed. Pauline and I waited outside for him to finish, carrying on the conversation we'd started at the bus stop, and continued during the hours' long wait at the Jobcentre. It seemed we had loads in common: musical and cultural interests, a love of this, a passion for that, and I was starting to sense that Pauline – despite seeming a corkscrew short of a Swiss Army knife – had a roughly similar background to me. Eventually, the man in the phone box hung up the receiver and turned to exit, putting his full weight on the door to open it. It was one of those old red phone boxes, so the door was heavy, like a submarine door. I thanked him and ducked under his arm, assuming he would step out once I was inside. It would, after all, have been the gentlemanly thing to do.

But this man was no gentleman.

"I just thought it was a friend of yours," Pauline said later, as I sat in a chair in Gina's house, with a cup and saucer on my lap, wating for the police. Even then, at 18, I'd still never been with a man, or even ever had a boyfriend, so when this vile creature, who smelled worse than the coal hole in my parents' house, pulled the door closed on the both of us, and told me he was going to "get his penis out and make love to me", I seized up. What the hell? It was Raymond all over again; except it wasn't Raymond, it was a complete stranger, twice Raymond's age, and twenty times as fucking grotesque. What the hell did he think he was playing at? Is this how people got raped? Got murdered? Got … ? I don't know. He told me that with my blonde hair and big blue eyes I was "every man's idea of perfection", but I didn't want to be anyone's idea of perfection, certainly not his, and wanted to get the fuck out of there as soon as possible.

I saw Pauline walking away from the phone box as if unsure of how to react. Was she smiling? I wanted to scream out to her, but was too petrified, and couldn't find my voice. I tried to wriggle past the man, fending off the hands that came snapping at me like cobras. After what felt like hours, but was probably just seconds, some kind of survival instinct kicked in, and I found myself engaging with him. *Talking* to him. Very calmly. Very matter of fact. I told him I needed to get back, but said I was free to meet him there the next day, and, if he liked, I could wear something nice for him. I don't know where this came from within me, but his eyes were eating me alive, and I thought the promise of showing him more, but in a prepared way, might be something that would appeal to him.

We all have ideas of about our own self-worth, don't we? and maybe this peculiar man, in his full-length 'flasher mac' regalia, thought there actually was some quality in him that an 18-year-old virgin, who he'd just assaulted in a phone box, might find attractive. All I knew was that it couldn't hurt me right now to let him think there was. We agreed a time – three o'clock the following afternoon – and I was out of there quicker than you could say "statutory rape", a term the man would become very familiar with over the next five years.

When three o-clock finally rolled around the next day I was probably more surprised than he was to find myself retracing my footsteps of the previous afternoon. My being there, however, wasn't to honour my part in the 'agreement' I'd made with the wannabe rapist, but to honour my part in the one I'd made with the police, who'd asked me to go along as planned. 'Honey trapping' I think they call it now. That was the solution they'd come up with after they'd sent two officers round to Gina's house following the call she made when I'd finally made it back there with my new friend. Under the watchful eye of my sister and her next-door neighbour, Chris, I'd blurted out the whole story, the how's, the why's, the smells, the flesh-creeping fear. Looking very earnest, they nodded and took notes and then, after a quick conflab, decided to cast me as the lead role in an episode of *The Sweeney*.

"There's no way she's doing *that* on her own," Chris said, sitting forward, once it became clear what was expected of me. I was to be the bait in a very dangerous fishing expedition. I knew things like this happened on the tele, but I didn't think for one second that they actually happened in real life.

"I'll go with her," Chris said, "Just in case." The officers swapped a look with each other and told him there'd be no need to, as they would be looking on, waiting for the moment that the suspect revealed his true intentions. At this point, professionals that they were, they would swoop. But Chris didn't seem convinced. Maybe he'd watched too many episodes of *The Sweeney* and knew how these things could go. If that was the case, then thank God he had.

I remember thinking, as I approached the phone box at five-to-three the next day, that the police were amazingly good at their jobs, because I couldn't see them at all, and there were so few places to hide. Maybe the team they'd called in were ex-special forces, possibly even SAS, and knew exactly how to merge into the landscape like chewing gum on a pavement. My heart was pounding when the dreaded hour came, and I approached. I could still smell the man in my nostrils, the stale odour of his 'flasher mac', and the even worse stench of his cruel intent. I couldn't stop thinking what might have happened if I hadn't been able to convince him I'd meet him the next day.

The telephone box was just a few feet ahead now, a blood red shard sticking out of the cobbles, but I couldn't see the man yet. Or smell him. Maybe this was just all nonsense and he had no intention at all of appearing, and yesterday … well, maybe that was just a bit of fun, something he did all the time, whenever the opportunity arose; or maybe he was just waiting for me to —

— THERE HE WAS! Suddenly, bang, out of nowhere, I could see him. He was approaching me without a trace of suspicion. My heart slammed full force into the roof of my mouth, but I knew the police, out of sight but "watching closely", would have clocked my reaction and would be swooping in any second now.

Any … second … now.

I tried to sense them in my peripheral vision. Where were they? The man's footsteps were getting louder.

Where the hell were they?

His blurred face was turning into features now. Two eyes, a nose, a knife-blade of a smile between his gaunt white cheeks. *Oh Jesus!*

Suddenly panicked that they weren't appearing – *WHERE THE FUCK WHERE THEY?* – I twisted my head to where I knew Chris was lurking. Was he still there? The man, just yards away now and approaching fast, saw the glance, acknowledged it, and followed its course, guessing something was amiss when it landed on Chris, who was staring right back at him. Desperately trying to decipher the situation playing out before him, Chris was provided with a full and immediate translation when the man, realising the game was up, turned suddenly and fled the way he'd come. The street was suddenly filled with the sound of one set of pounding feet, then two, as Chris gave chase, leaving me totally alone, wondering what on earth had happened to the fucking police.

"Something came up," they told us later on the phone. "Something, uh ... more important."

"More *important?*" Chris thundered. He'd rung them from the phone box, after he'd pursued the man back right to his house, where he'd he spent an age banging on the window. "If I hadn't been there," he yelled down the phone to them, "what do you think would've happened to the poor girl?" They had no answer, only a feeble apology.

The man's eventual arrest came, not because of his egregious behaviour and assault in the phone box, but because of all the "strange items" the police had unearthed in his flat later that day, when they'd gone round to question him; items that clearly pointed towards what his *real* intentions had been. To this day, I don't know what exactly they found there, but it seems clear that if I'd gone back with him, and given him a chance to act out any of these so-called "intentions", it's likely he'd have gone down for a lot longer than the five years they threw at him.

But then ... I might not be here to tell the story.

The day wasn't over though, not by a long chalk. I still had to make the single biggest discovery about myself that I was ever likely to make; one that brought all the pain and horror of the past eighteen years into a focus so sharp it could've severed an artery. Still shaky from the assault, Chris had suggested we go for a drink. Not really a drinker, I agreed, thinking I could grab an orange juice at the local just up the road, while he had the pint he so clearly craved. He'd done so much for me, the least I could do was have a quick drink with him.

When I left a short time later, I was not the same girl I was when I went in. During the hour or so I sat with Chris the whole world, or at least, the whole world as I knew it, was turned upside down, and literally every single thing in my life that I thought was secure, became detached from its moorings and went flying around me like a hurricane in an origami shop.

"What a day," Chris said, taking the first sip of his pint.

"Yeah." I said back, not really knowing what else to add, other than to repeat it.

I think he sensed I was a bit detached, and so asked what was on my mind, *if* it wasn't what we'd just been through together.

"'Dodo' Black," I said, sipping my juice. A woman going by this name had been asking around about me. Chris didn't even blink. Had Georgina already told him? I'd overheard my Auntie May telling my mum that she'd got into a discussion about me with Dodo. No big thing, you might thing, but the argument was over what age I was at my next birthday, which I found extremely odd. Chris sat there, nursing his pint with a bemused look on his face. I couldn't even begin to understand what this had to do with anyone else, I told him, especially not a stranger called 'Dodo', so I'd started asking around. But every time I mentioned it, to my mum, my auntie, or any of my siblings, they went all sheepish and tried to avoid the subject. "Can of worms, Christina," Georgina had said when I'd raised it with her. "Just leave it alone." The others had said the same.

"You really don't know?" Chris asked, wiping away his foam moustache.

"No. Every time I ask my mum about her, she just lays into me." Which was true, the last time I asked she belted me across the face and told me to shut up.

"Probably wants to hide the fact that she's your mother."

He said the words so matter-of-factly that I didn't really process what he'd just said and so I just bumbled on. "Why would Olive need to hide that from her?" I asked him. "What business is it of hers?"

Chris frowned, realising it hadn't registered.

"No, not Olive. Dodo Black. *She's* your mum. Dodo Black is your real mum."

And it was on hearing those words that I felt myself enter zero gravity. Try to imagine it: eighteen years of knowing one thing, of thinking of yourself as one particular thing – even though it's hurt like hell to have to accept that thing – and then to find out that that thing is wrong. All the catalogue of hurt and pain and rape and abuse that I'd had to put up with over that time ... The only reason I'd been able to accept it was because I knew I had no choice. This was my family, my blood, so I'd had no choice but to accept the shit they'd put me through, no choice but to accept the abuse from Raymond, no choice but to accept the slaps, the punches, the hair-pulling, and all the fucking put-downs from everyone I was cursed to share that awful, shithole of a house with.

As for 'Dodo', it was short for Dorothy. My mum's real name was Dorothy Black. Apparently, she looked a lot like Elizabeth Taylor.

"You all right?" Chris asked.

Before I felt myself crushed by the sheer magnitude of this discovery, I managed to get to my feet and walked on rubber legs to the toilet. From the corner of my eye I saw someone else in there with me, another girl about my own age, hunched over, looking like she was going to be sick. It was only when I reached the sink for support that I saw that the girl had my eyes, my mouth, my hair, and was wearing the same clothes as me. But who was she? What was her name? Where had she come from? The second I made it over to the cubicle the tears exploded out of me and I started howling. I hadn't even closed the door when I felt myself slumping down, down, down, like I used to in the cupboard in my bedroom, with my dollies and my teddies, to escape the noise. Here I was, ten years later, and I was still hiding from the chaos that strange and unknowable family had made my life into, the catastrophe they had made all our lives into. I was Alice down the rabbit hole, lost to the world and a stranger even to myself. I cried so much I thought I might actually flood the toilet and drown in my own tears.

Oh, if only I had.

WOMB SCRAPE

All girls get periods but not many have blackouts because of them.

I blacked out.

It was my body's way of getting blood to where it was needed – my brain – by laying me flat on the ground as soon as possible. I'd drop like a stone. This condition, starting about the same time I began working in the shop, was a big part of me by the time I made it to eighteen. They were so heavy, these periods, that they prevented me from joining the army – another dream I'd started to kick around, not because I wanted to fight for Queen and country, but because it offered a more immediate escape from my 'family'. But it wasn't to be.

To combat these blackouts my doctor encouraged me to have a D&C (dilation and curettage) more commonly known as a womb scrape, a procedure every bit as eye-watering as it sounds. Following his instructions, I went to hospital and was subjected to all the delightful agonies the procedure could provide, contracting a rather severe bout of Red Flu in the process. They called it Red Flu because it was believed to have migrated over from north-eastern China recently, passing through Russia on the way. For some reason it didn't just affect Communists but all children and young adults under the age of 23. Whatever it was, and however it arrived, it totally wiped me out and, after my discharge from the hospital, left me pretty much in a near vegetative state for weeks. This was no joke, I couldn't feel my knees or my legs and I started to lose all sense of myself. I didn't even want to get out of bed, but the doctor told my sister that she had to keep getting me up to walk around or the loss of feeling in my legs would be permanent. For Gina, who had very little time for me already, this was simply too much, so she called up one of her friend's, John (who she knew had a bit of a thing for me), and asked him to step in.

John was Gina's next-door neighbour. He'd fallen hard on his face after the car crash that had been his two previous marriages, but was just finding his feet again and trying to get by as best he could. Like a good Samaritan, he'd pop round each night after work and coax me out of bed, walking me up and down the road, just a tiny bit at first, but getting further and further each evening, until he deemed me fit enough to walk to the pub with him. It was then that I noticed his Good Samaritan act was just that, an act. He wasn't doing this out of the goodness of his heart, he wanted something from me, something I really didn't want to give, especially not to a twice-divorced bloke who was twice my age.

"Why won't you let him take you out?" Gina would ask, "What harm could it do?"

He started writing letters to me, slipping them under the door, or giving them to Gina to pass on. That might've been cute, if he'd been my own age, or even near it, but he wasn't. John was on his way to being 40 and really should've known better. Bowing to the pressure, I eventually agreed to go to a house party with him being thrown by one of his mates. My thinking was, if I just went to this one thing with him, this one little event, and got it out of the way, he'd see I wasn't really 'girlfriend material' and stop hounding me. But how little I knew men, especially sad, little ones with the emotional maturity of a fucking scorpion.

I remember getting ready to go to the party; I remember arriving at the house with a bottle of wine and John knocking, turning to me with his wonky grin; I remember the door opening and hearing the music, and all the people in there, standing about in doorways; I remember all the talking, the dim lighting, all the bottles of booze on the kitchen units and tables, and everyone hunched in hallways or slumped on sofas, all the smoking and flirting and laughing and everyone trying to talk over the funky disco music. And I remember waking up in a bed and seeing John lying next to me, face-down and snoring, his clothes in a pile on the floor next to mine, our pants tossed with them like discarded tissues. What I have no memory of, and I've tried so hard to recall it over the years, is the moment I gave up my dreams and said goodbye to all the hopes and aspirations I'd been quietly nurturing in my heart. But that's exactly what I did that night. Somehow, during those insignificant hours, in that small, innocuous house in Birkenhead, I gave up all my dreams and swapped them for a suitcase full of nightmares.

When you read behind the scenes of Lancelot and Guinevere's relationship, it becomes far trickier than it appears on the surface. As a child, poring through my big chunky book of myths and legends with its ornate gold and silver lettering, I didn't think I'd processed the fact that Guinevere was having an affair with Lancelot, and that Arthur was her husband. When she, in her flowing blue gown and her shiny, ruby-encrusted crown, batted her eyelids at the tall and dashing Lancelot, and spoke of her undying ardour for him, she was actually betraying her husband, an act that would lead to a Civil War and see her spending the rest of her life holed up in a convent. So as I got dressed that morning, mortified at what I'd allowed myself to do – even though I had no recollection of doing it – I should have more been accepting of the fact that the myths we put so much stock in and hold ourselves up against, are just as messy and chaotic as our real lives.

A month later there had been no blackouts, but this wasn't because I'd been cured. Two weeks after this, my initial concerns had turned to fear, which in turn gave way to terror. Gina told me not to panic, but I could barely hear her through the white noise buzzing in my head. I didn't even know about home pregnancy kits, but she advised me to get one, and when, after a panicked race to Boots, I stumbled out of the toilet holding one in my hands like a bloodied dagger over a fresh corpse, I could barely speak. No amount of blinking my eyes in disbelief, or shaking with apprehension, would change what had revealed itself on that tiny little strip.

Oh, fuckin' hell.

"Well …?" Gina said, wondering why I wasn't delighted. "What have you got to say?"

I thought about a million thoughts very quickly, but they all coalesced into one short but screamingly simple question. "Shall I slit my throat now?"

I didn't know the full extent of John's alcoholism until the night he became my husband. I didn't find out a lot of things about John until the night he became my husband. Like how short-tempered he was, how violent, feckless or medieval in his attitudes. The violence wasn't entirely unconnected to the drinking, I suppose, and one of the things I learnt very quickly after I'd been branded with the name 'Mrs Suckley' was that my new husband liked eight cans of Colt 45 malt liquor every night, irrespective of how much he'd already had to drink in the hours before.

At his insistence we'd all gone to the pub straight after the wedding – hastily arranged for two weeks after I'd revealed to him that I was pregnant. John wasn't shy about not holding back on his drinking, just as he wasn't shy about blackmailing me into marrying him, which is pretty much what he did. "Either put up the bands," was how he'd worded it after I'd summoned the courage to tell him, "or get the fuck out."

After the pub, a few people drifted back to the house, but no one could ever claim that what followed was much of a celebration. The bar had been set particularly low by the non-arrival of John's two daughters, Emma and Nina, who he'd been counting on coming for emotional support. Their no-show he took as a personal insult, and set the tone for a very sombre evening. But as low as it was, it didn't mean, once he'd chucked a few drinks down his neck, that my new husband couldn't drag it down a few levels. As the night wore on the people drifted away, leaving behind their tired smiles and exhausted best wishes, until it was just my brother Raymond and his girlfriend Carol, who hung about the place like a virus. Whilst they were still downstairs, finishing off the dregs from the leftover bottles of booze, John had followed me upstairs when I'd gone to the toilet, and after bundling me in to the bedroom, finally took off the mask he must've been aching to all day.

"It's your fucking fault!" he hissed, the words hitting me like he'd fired them from the shotgun that best described this ridiculous wedding.

"How is it my fault?" I asked, not yet understanding which buttons I could push and which never to go anywhere near. He was looking for someone to lash out at, but I didn't know this yet, because I didn't know *him* yet, so I just spoke as if I was having a normal conversation with a normal human being. But when his finger started jabbing me forcefully in the chest, pushing me back towards the bed, alarm bells started going off. This was a little too close to how Big Richie used to speak to Olive after he'd been out on the piss, and staggered back at stupid o'clock in the morning. Trying to break the tension I said it was understandable that Michelle, his ex, didn't want her children to watch their father marry another woman, and that he'd be able to see them next week. But John's way of breaking the tension was to break me, or at least try to. He slapped me across the face, and before I'd even had time to respond, I found myself crumpled up on the bed with his hand gripped tightly around my neck. I'd been hit so many times by Richie growing up that the smack didn't even bother me, but being strangled was a totally new sensation. My instinct was to scream, because I knew my brother was downstairs, but I just couldn't get enough air into my lungs, and every attempt barely made it to my lips. Not that it mattered to John who seemed to know how to interpret the choking rasps coming from my throat: "If you make a sound, or scream for your brother," he spat into my face, "I will fucking well kill you."

We didn't have sex that night. John was just too paralytic and no more able to get it up than he would've been able to a wire a plug with one hand tied behind his back. He fell asleep next to me with his clothes on, his face buried in the blanket, snoring like a machine gun on Normandy beach. This man who, just a few weeks ago, when I told him I didn't love him and probably never would, had replied: "That's a'right, I've got enough for the both of us."

Next day there was very little in the way of an apology, just a list of instructions I was to obey in order to keep life between us as frictionless as possible. Follow these, they seemed to imply, and everything would be hunky dory.

Firstly, as John's new wife, I was to submit to his demands for sex whenever he wanted, morning, noon and night. That was my first duty. That's what wives did.

Secondly, he was to have meat on his plate every night after he got home from work. Men ate meat, had done since we'd lived in caves, and John was no different. If there was no meat on his plate each night. there would be "Consequences".

Thirdly, and as already mentioned, he had to have his eight cans of Colt 45 every evening. If ever he was short and couldn't stretch to cover the purchase himself, he'd take it out of the housekeeping. If that didn't cover it, he'd take it out of my face. The housekeeping amounted to £20.00 a week, which he would give me from his job as an electrician. From this, he had to be fed and so did I, and any children we subsequently had, they had to be fed too. As long as he got meat on his plate every night nothing else mattered, except for the cans, of course. And the sex. One evening, unable to scrape together enough pennies to buy in some beef or chicken which I knew he liked, I improvised an omelette, thankful that I'd been able to dig out some ham from the back of the fridge.

"What the fuck is *this* shite?" John barked, prodding the offending item with his fork as he sat down to gorge.

"Uh … a ham omelette," I replied nervously, seeing the colour running out of his face.

It took me over half an hour to wipe up the resulting mess from the floor once John had finished communicating his dislike of my improvisation skills. Who knew a dinner plate could be smashed into so many pieces? Needless to say, I never made that mistake again. It was chicken or beef the whole way after that.

A few weeks into the 'marriage' John took to following me around everywhere, convinced that, sooner or later, I would repeat the habits of his previous wives who had both left him for other men. As is common knowledge to all grown adults (but not me then), this kind of obsessive behaviour only ever points towards one thing: people who don't trust their spouses know they can't be trusted themselves, and in this John demonstrated no originality whatsoever. Within months, maybe even weeks, he was off screwing other women behind my back, something you're probably not surprised to hear I didn't care about in the slightest. If he was getting it from other women he'd be less likely to want it from me, which was fine, as it meant I might be in with a chance of getting a few hours' sleep. But you couldn't always guarantee it. If he was home though, the usual pattern of an evening would see a sort of grim replay of how things used to be with Raymond all those years before: I'd drift up to bed and lie there like a zombie, praying he would drink himself into unconsciousness. Every fifteen minutes or so I'd hear the hard, metallic *pssht* of the Colt 45s being opened, followed by the gentle clanking sound of the scrunched-up cans being tossed into the bin. After the magic number of eight was reached I'd hear some staggering around, followed by the TV being turned off, then the lights, then his heavy footsteps clomping up the stairs. There'd be more staggering around in the bathroom as his nightly ablutions were tended to, and then, finally, the walk along the landing towards the bedroom and the much feared inevitable. I'd pretend to be asleep, but John would barely ever register whether I was awake or not. He didn't give a shit. All he wanted was a body, a young body preferably, to control and manipulate, to sate himself with; and as he did his business, noisily, sounding like a bear tucking into the remains of a dead deer, I would dream, just as I used to, of a time and a place beyond this one, of a distant tomorrow where my future was my own and I could sketch out a destiny that didn't fill me with dread.

Amidst a good deal of kicking and screaming, Sabrina was eventually pulled out of me in St Cat's Hospital. As I knew already the devastating impact this was going to have on my life, you might understand why it wasn't the baby doing the kicking and screaming. When they'd first wheeled me into the delivery room a few hours before, I was about as scared as I'd ever been. I never thought I could feel any lonelier than when I used to hide in the coal cupboard under Olive and Richie's stairs, with all the rats and cockroaches, but as the double doors banged open before me, and I saw all those people in scrubs staring at me, I knew I'd been wrong.

31

"Everything's gonna be okay love," I heard, but I don't know from behind whose masked face the words fell. Certainly, it wasn't from someone who knew me very well, because just my being there was a sign of how un-okay my life was. I wonder what they thought of me, these doctors: this baby-faced 18-year-old lying on her back, spreading her legs, about to say *sayonara* to her freedom. Did the wedding ring confuse them? I reached out my hand, as if on instinct, to grab someone who might be able to offer a sign of reassurance, but it just remained there, un-held, five fingers stretched out expectantly, waiting for something that would never come.

As my breathing quickened and my anxiety-levels rose, I tried to convince myself that whatever got pulled out of me at the end of all this might at least bring about a change of mood in the person who'd put it up there in the first place; a man I knew better for the fear he instilled in me than any tenderness he'd ever shown. I didn't expect a miracle, but not treating me like a mat to walk on every day would be a start.

The contractions … well, what can I say about those that not every mother already knows? If I'd known that each one would feel like a bull gorging me in the stomach, then at least I could've prepared myself, but because Olive had never sat me down and told me what was what in that department, I thought it was all going wrong. It's not possible to experience this much pain, surely? Not without meeting your Maker. Saying that, no matter how loud I screamed, I was drowned out by the howling of the woman on the other side of the curtain, who sounded like she was being eaten alive by rats. Between lungfuls of gas and air, I begged the masked figures around me to stick some tape over her mouth so I could at least endure my own agonies in peace.

When Sabrina finally did come out, the overriding feeling wasn't joy, it was relief. But even that faded within thirty-seconds of holding her in my arms, when the burden of what I'd been lumbered with for the rest of my life instantly made her feel twice as heavy. I looked down at her face, surprised to see how small it was – like an orange that had just been peeled. She hadn't even opened her eyes yet, and already her face was riddled with questions. But eighteen-year-old me, as I lay there on those crumpled sheets, tired and ruined, waiting for the wave of maternal love I'd been promised to take effect, I knew I didn't have an answer for any of them. I wanted to tell her what that doctor had told me earlier, that everything was going to be okay, but that would've been a lie. Still, I said it anyway, and I gave her a kiss.

John was nowhere in sight, of course – not then, or at any time throughout that first night. He only showed up when he brought his mum and stepdad along the next day, unable to disguise the "quick-half" he'd chucked down him on the way in.

"Aaaah," his mother cooed, pacing over to the plastic cot they'd put her in. "Isn't she lovely?"

"You've done well there, mate," his stepdad said, nodding towards me as if the real congratulations lay in the fact that he'd been to get his end away with a pretty girl half his age without the police getting involved.

They stayed for half-an-hour, but it was half-an-hour too long, and my face, by the time they'd left, was aching due to the smile I'd had to plaster on it. No one wanted to hear about the agony I'd been through, or how lonely I'd felt the whole time, so I just swallowed that down and let them go on with their fussing. When they'd gone, I looked down at the baby, Little Sabrina – a rolled-up bath towel with a doll's head on one end – and started to cry, because her very existence meant I was now pinned to something I didn't want anything to do with. She really did look like a doll, and in many ways I wish she had been, because I could have just thrown back those covers and walked out of there without looking back once. I could've stopped off at my sisters, chucked some food into a bag, a few sandwiches, some clothes, then hopped onto a bus, any bus – it wouldn't have mattered where it was going, London, Timbuktu, anywhere would've done – because all destinations met at the same point anyway, didn't they? My future. And for a time that future could've been anywhere, any town, any city, with me doing anything I wanted. But I'd not known that until I was lying there in that hospital, with my hours-old baby resting just a few feet away from me, and it came to me with the violent force of a stoning.

The baby's eyelid's moved. What on earth could she possibly be dreaming about?

When I was discharged the next day, the first thing I needed to do was to re-establish my routines. I knew all there was to know about raising teddies and dollies, but not very much about dollies that actually cried and shat everywhere. No one in the hospital had shown me what to do, so I was feeling my way in the dark. I didn't know how to change a nappy or even prepare milk, or what clothes to buy. Did babies wear vests? Shoes? There was no internet to log onto, no apps to open, and no smart phone to open them on even if they did exist. So just like every other teenager in history who'd fallen into this trap, I had to guess, and hoped that in the nerve-jangling period of trial-and-error that lay ahead, none of my guesses would end up making Sabrina join Little Billy in God's eternal nursery.

Things weren't helped by the fact that Sabrina was a terrible sleeper. And because she was, we had to be too, something John didn't adjust well to at all. He liked his sleep, did my 'husband', and because he wasn't getting much, he decided that was a good enough reason to slide back into caveman mode and make me pay the full price for our baby's restlessness with my body. When he wasn't blaming me with his fists, he was humiliating me with his words, and between the two he'd find time out of his busy schedule to force me into sex, something I submitted to with the enthusiasm of a robot whose batteries had run down. To call these bodily exchanges anything other than rape is to flatter everything that psychological abuse stands for. To limit the damage I would just lie there and endure it like a tree endures the pecks of a woodpecker. When it was over, I'd go and tend to the baby, who would most likely have been crying throughout, as her daddy dragged the blankets over his head and screamed at me to "shut that fucking thing up."

"There, there," I'd say to her, before repeating the words I'd heard in the hospital just before she was born: "Everything's gonna be okay." She didn't have to know I had my fingers crossed when I said it.

When she did finally drop off I'd watch her for ages, wanting to delay my return to the *rape room*, whilst, with a tissue, I'd soak up the drops of self-pity that built-up on my chin. All this baby would know, I thought, is anger, and all she would see, when she finally started to take in everything around her, were two people finding new ways to hate each other. What an introduction to the world.

Georgina and I had only been speaking again for a short time when she noticed all wasn't well in the oubliette she'd pushed me into. I'd started to find her company quite toxic in the days before Brina was born, and she, in turn, grew weary of my complaints about her friend. Much of that, I suspect, was connected to the guilt she might've felt about pushing me in there in the first place, but maybe I'm giving her too much credit for that. Oh well, she probably thought, she's a grown-up, she can take care of herself. But Brina's arrival meant that we now had more in common than just the terraced jungle we'd both been dragged up in across the water, and I think she responded to that.

Also, because she was family, Georgina was one of only a handful of acquaintances that John would allow me to spend any time with. His own looks fading fast, and with middle-age biting at his heels, John was opposed to the idea of me making any new friends, male ones especially, figuring that if he let me out of his sight for two minutes, I'd probably start shagging the first one I was left alone with. There was very little I could ever talk about anyway, even if I met a bloke, as my life – miniscule to start with – had shrunk down to the barest possible minimum, meaning whenever Gina and I did get together, all we could talk about was the baby, or John (about whom there was nothing nice to say anyway), or what had happened that week on *Coronation Street*. Gina would give it the caring-big-sister act, when I did let slip what was on my mind, but that's all it ever was. Her brain, stewed for so long in a pan of small-minded gossip, split everything she heard into categories of facts that were divisible only by the amount of shock-value they could instil in people. "I won't say a word," she'd say, whenever you needed to get something off your chest about someone, and then she'd go and rattle off a thousand to the very person about whom you needed to get that thing off your chest. Knowing how good she was at stirring things up, I did try to keep my own personal problems under lock and key whenever she was around, but the pressure I was under once Brina had arrived, no one alive could've kept all that in without exploding.

One time I did open up to her was a few months after the baby was born, when I was at my wits' end. I was tired, *bone*-tired, getting little-to-no sleep, and John was treating me like shit. I knew he was having affairs, lots of them, and if I wasn't there when he got home, pissed off his skull most nights, to tend to all his needs, he'd take it out on me. So when Gina came round this one time and asked me what was wrong, I just opened up to her. Both barrels she got. I just touched the trigger and off it went. BANG-BANG! I told her about John, his affairs, how he treated me, undermined me, used me, what he called me, and she could tell, just from watching my hands shake in front of me, that if something didn't change soon, the tether I was at the end of might very well be replaced by a rope. And I wasn't kidding.

"You've got to tell his mum" she said.

"Are you effing serious?"

"Tell her. It might make him change his tune. You know how much he loves her."

I did know that. He lived to please his mum. He was her little golden boy. The idea of him not living up to the high standards she'd set for him was something constantly on his mind, which is why I'd had to put the mask on when he'd brought her along to the hospital. I'd never thought about it before, but after Gina said it, it was *all* I could think about. But the stakes were so high; if he *ever* found out, my life wouldn't be worth living. He'd see it as a betrayal. I'd be crossing a line. He knew it and I knew it, and so did Georgina. Even thinking about it made me scared. What if I accidentally mentioned it in my sleep?

If I was going to do it, I'd need to make sure that the long-term gains would outweigh the short-term fallout, fatal if in any way misjudged. I would need to press my case so forcefully to his mum that her reaction, when she confronted him about it (because she would have to) would be so strong that he would have no choice but to change his ways. "I don't want you treating the poor girl like that anymore," was all she had to say.

"Yes, Mum," he'd say.

It was a gamble, but wasn't every night I spent with him a gamble? One slap round the face at the top of the stairs, one stumble, and that was me done for.

The next day, after a sleepless night, I took the baby round to Gina's, knowing she had a day off. I knocked hard. She answered.

"Can you look after her for a few hours?"

She didn't even ask why.

Maybe he would've changed his tune. Maybe he'd have felt so embarrassed by his behaviour when his mum forced him to take stock of his life that he would've instantly turned himself around. But it wasn't to be. I made the trek over to Rock Ferry, where his mum lived, terrified that somehow he'd find out what I was planning and intercept me on the way. He would appear and drag me back home and the next time people heard of me would be on the news. "Have you seen this woman?"

But it didn't happen. I got there, walked up to the front door, wondering if I'd even have to knock, or would she just hear my heart thumping through my coat and open the door? "Hello, Chrissy, love, what is it?" I went through in my head exactly what I was going to say to her. I'd been rehearsing it all night, polishing my delivery, getting the dramatic pauses right. Then I was there. On her doorstep. And there was my hand in front of me, raised and ready to knock. Should I do it? I did it. There was the echo to prove it. And there were the clouds above me, all grey, looking down with a raised eyebrow, and a neighbour walking past behind, possibly wondering who I was. No going back now.

Thirty seconds passed. Then a minute. I heard nothing inside, no movement; nor did I see any behind the net curtains. No shadow. No outline.

I tried again, louder this time, but like before, nothing happened. "Please-please-please-please-please," I said quietly to no one. I knew I'd never get another chance at this. It was such a rarity that I could get out the house without having to explain myself, and even rarer to find someone who'd look after Sabrina (Gina was hardly ever around), but after five minutes, maybe even ten, I knew my cause was lost. I considered sitting on the front step until she arrived, but that would look ridiculous, me just sitting there, and I knew I had to get back to relieve Gina from her baby-sitting duties. So, tail between my legs, I turned round and traipsed back to Gina's, no less terrified at being caught than before, but at least thankful that her monster of a son couldn't possibly have known what my intentions had been.

"He's been here."

They were the first words out of Gina's mouth when I got back. I hadn't even got my foot inside and already she'd managed to kick my heart up into my throat. "With Raymond," she added for maximum effect.

"What did he want?" I asked nervously, knowing, before she'd even answered, that what he wanted was probably irrelevant to what he went away knowing. I pictured Gina standing over a pot filled with shit, stirring it for all she was worth.

"He wasn't happy that you went round to his mum's. He's gone looking for you."

I know they were the words she *said*, I saw her mouth form them, and the devious smile that accompanied them; but what I actually heard was: "While you were out, a jury passed a death sentence on you and the executioner is out looking for you right now."

I looked down at the floor, hoping I could find a huge black hole in her hallway that I could disappear into for at least a few days. It wouldn't take a degree in relationship counselling to realise that this was the worst of both worlds for me. I'd steeled myself to commit the mortal sin of grassing him up to his mother, painting him as the vile monster I knew him to be, in the faint hope that she'd encourage him to change his ways, but now I had to face the consequences *without* the 'crime' ever being committed.

I didn't find any hole in the ground, but I thought I was definitely going to end up in one within a few minutes of John finally catching up with me later that evening. I'd foolishly thought that, if I arrived back at the house clutching the baby, talking about something nice, it might disarm him a bit and he'd go easy on me.

Not a bit of it. I was on the floor within seconds, trying not to get too much blood on the carpet. I'd got the baby to safety before the really heavy punching started, but as I struggled to pull myself to my feet, ready for round two, I wondered how long it would be before I'd be able to see out of my right eye again.

Raymond, who was there with him, watched all this as if it was a sport and he'd been lucky enough to secure himself a ringside seat. Instead of coming to my defence, like any normal brother would do, he just asked me why the fuck I'd been daft enough to go round to see his mum in the first place. In his warped head, such stupidity warranted being beaten to within an inch of my life, just as years earlier my youth and innocence had warranted the full bruising impact of his sexual deviancy. Clearly the two of them, husband and so-called 'brother' had found common ground in their dehumanisation of me, but then, why wouldn't they? I mean, what's that saying about thieves? And this pair were as thick as any that had ever trampled the soil on God's earth.

WHIP-ROUND

Before the girls came along you could've counted on one hand the number of times John and I had been out socially, and since they'd arrived that number had dwindled down to zero. Even if we'd had the desire to, we had no babysitters to call on, so I didn't even waste time entertaining the fantasy that, even for just one night, I could aspire to a life like most other women. For my twenty-first, however, Olive and Richie made an exception. Putting aside their characteristic lack of charity, they took out a hat and had a quick whip-round for me, padding it out with a pile of notes themselves before waving it under the noses of one or two of my siblings. "It's a special occasion," Olive had said to me on the phone, "We want you to go out and enjoy yourselves. Have a lovely meal, you bloody well deserve it." When I hung up I was close to tears. A meal out. An actual meal out. Like a proper grown-up couple. Like Elizabeth Taylor and Richard Burton.

To make sure we got the money Raymond called round himself, handing the cash, in an envelope, over to John, who slipped it into his inside coat pocket. It wouldn't be right, would it, if when the bill came it was me who pulled out my purse. What, the *woman* paying? This was the 1980s. *Ridiculous!*

I bounded through the day with a spring in my step, and didn't mind at all John leaving for a couple of hours to go and do a job down the road. I could look forward to a night out later on, a candlelit meal, maybe even a couple of glasses of wine, ("I'll have the red, please!") followed by a lovely dessert ("Mmmm, I think I'll try that gorgeous-looking tiramisu.") I was thinking of this when I picked up the ringing phone that afternoon. If we had enough left over, I mused, bringing the receiver to my ear, I might even go for an Irish coffee. How decadent would that be?

"Hello?" I said.

I knew what was coming the second I heard the receiver being fumbled with at the other end, as if the caller hadn't quite got a secure enough grip of the phone and had dropped it. Even so, hearing the slightly slurred words, and the lack of respect they carried within them, hit me like a slap across the face.

"I've spent it."

I could see John in my mind's eye attempting to steady himself against the wall, trying to hide the fact that he was in a pub, but failing miserably due to the raucous chatter of men around him and ELO's *Mr Blue Sky* blurring from the jukebox he was standing next to. I'd already said no to a party because I thought this meal, with just the two of us, was a far wiser investment for the family, and our future.

"I hope you're joking?" I said, hoping there was a punchline to come.

"It's all gone, every penny."

I felt the bile rise in my throat, but I did my best to swallow it down in case I said something I might regret later on. "My mum and dad are coming round tonight, to babysit – the first time they've ever offered – so you are going to take me out for a meal." And as I spoke, I felt a strength building in me I'd rarely felt when speaking to John before. It was as if I could sense I was reaching the end of my tether. "I don't care how you get the money, John, just get it."

He did take me out. He took me to a Chinese down the road, under the promise he'd be able to get us a discount on the final bill because he'd recently done a 'foreigner' for the manager there. One good turn deserved another, after all. The ruse worked, albeit barely, and when the bill was finally placed in a saucer between us on the table, it listed only a starter and a dessert, making no mention of a main meal, or even any drinks – luxuries we'd had to forego because the meagre amount John had been able to scrape together that afternoon wouldn't stretch to cover them. So much for my Irish coffee! What did arrive we ate with barely a word exchanged, not any polite ones anyway, and left after about half an hour without leaving a tip. Such extravagances were, of course, way out of our budget.

Outside in the cold we wandered aimlessly around like characters in a Russian novel, not wanting to return too early in case Olive and Richie realised we'd not been able to take full advantage of the gift they'd kindly provided us with. By the time we got back, shivering and frozen with cold, feet blistered from all the walking, I was starving. It hurt not telling them that we'd not even been able to use the money, but what hurt even more was the fact that it had happened in the first place; that on my twenty-first birthday – one of the most significant days in a person's life – I wasn't even able to sit down in a nice restaurant and eat a proper meal. This wasn't how life was supposed to be, surely? I didn't spend two decades enduring all that shit, absorbing all those shouts and punches, just to end up sitting silently across the table from a faithless husband, who I didn't even love, on my twenty-first birthday. There must be more to life than this. Surely it was within God's means to introduce me to one person, just one, who it wouldn't hurt to treat me with an ounce of respect. But for that to happen, I thought, wandering around those charmless streets with achingly sore feet, listening to the weary ramblings of my middle-aged husband, perhaps I needed to start respecting myself a bit more.

By the time we'd arrived home and I'd gone in to kiss the children good-night, my mind had already been made up.

It normally takes six-weeks to process a decree nisi, but the judge, when he thumbed through the small mountain of paperwork that had accumulated since I first sat down in a solicitor's office months before, just sighed and shook his head in disbelief. "It's horrific what you've been through, Christina," he said, his pen skating over the dotted line to push it through immediately. "Absolutely horrific." Other than the judge and the typist, there was only Olive and Raymond with me in the small courtroom. They'd tagged along thinking we were going on a shopping spree, not realising that the detour I was leading them on was to the local magistrates' court.

Someone who wasn't there was John himself. He'd taken the whole thing like a mouse, and skulked off already, back to his little cave, or whatever other mediaeval dwelling he'd hobbled out of. He'd pleaded with me not to leave him, begged on his knees like a toddler not wanting the stabilisers taken off his bike, but his petulant displays just made me more determined than ever to be shut of him. By the time he finally left, tail dangling limply down between his legs, I felt so little for him you couldn't even describe it as a feeling. There was no pity left in my body, just this fervent desire to breathe again, without feeling that every breath I did take would be my last.

On his way to the exit, John was clear about one thing: he wanted me to have the house. "I think it's better if you have it," he said, seemingly without rancour. "You and the girls." (We'd been joined by a second daughter, Kelly, soon after Brina). At first I thought this generous offer might represent a turning point in my soon-to-be-ex-husband, a recognition of what he owed us during the two-and-a-half years we'd had to put up with his unpardonable behaviour. But I was wrong. I'd noticed the brown envelopes arriving each month through the letterbox, and seen in the little window the bold type-face: 'FAO: MR JOHN SUCKLEY'. Without any thought I'd pick them up and leave them on the table, where they'd sit until John appeared and stuffed them into his pocket. They were bills, obviously, and John took care of those, so there was never any need to question him about them. When he'd gone, those same envelopes continued to arrive and I, as before, continued to pick them up, placing them in a drawer so John could collect them when he visited to see the kids.

After about a year, I noticed that the name in the little window had changed. It went from reading FAO: MR JOHN SUCKLEY to FAO: THE HOUSEHOLDER. Well, I thought, if I wasn't the householder, who the hell was? The thing about that question was: I wasn't the only one asking it. The council too had also started wondering the very same thing, and this is what I realised, with mounting horror, the second I tore open one of the envelopes and discovered that no mortgage had been paid on the property for more than twelve months. John had simply stopped forking out for it. I felt my legs getting weaker the more I read, and all I could pick out from the scary legalese was the fact that I was in a lot of trouble. I still wasn't working at this point, and was only receiving £20.00 a week maintenance from John – something the court had made a condition of our eventual settlement. Even if there were no other outgoings – a laughable suggestion with two small children to raise, and a third on the way – it would still take me well over a year to pay back the £1,000 rent arrears that had built up since John's departure. And that was *only* if the outstanding debt was frozen there and then, and not allowed to increase. So, what I'd thought of as a parting gift from John, one final act of contrition, was nothing more than a last blast of the shotgun, one directed, not just at my head – which I could've accepted – but at the heads of his own daughters. How on earth could any man, any human being, be that callous?

If God received any of the prayers I'd been sending His way since I first tore open that letter, He didn't pass them on to Wirral Council. Blind to any signals from Him, and deaf to any pleas from me, they went ahead and did exactly what they'd threatened to do from day one: they turfed us out – me, my two daughters with John, and a by-now six-week-old baby I'd had with Chris, who I'd met during the previous year in a club. We didn't land in the street, fortunately – the faceless bureaucrats at Birkenhead Council might all have hearts made of stone, but they were still hearts. Where they finally settled us, however, wasn't much of an improvement, in the same way that, to a homeless man, a sleeping bag beneath Waterloo Bridge is better than a cardboard box on top of it. But only just.

We were moved to Dacre Street, a road that couldn't have been more of an advert for dilapidation if Saatchi and Saatchi had used it on a poster to promote the downside of poverty. There was, I suppose, a kind of logic to the council's thinking in all this: the houses on the street were in the process of being pulled down, which meant at some point soon they would be forced to re-house us somewhere nicer. It was like they were thinking: if we house you in the worst place on earth, the Powers That Be will be forced to shift you elsewhere, but until they do, you'll just have to ride it out. So ride it out we did, along with the mice, the rats, the cockroaches, and what seemed like every heroin addict within a ten mile radius. What fun it was pushing Baby Deryn's pram over all the used needles we'd find outside the front door each morning.

Chris, who I was with throughout all this, lasted for about a year. He was on leave from the army when I met him, on a night out with friends in the Hamilton nightclub, the only half-decent club on the Wirral where people could let their hair down at the weekend. I didn't let mine down all that often, but when I did, I did it with Pauline Gader, who'd remained a good friend since our trip to the dole office all those years before. I was usually very guarded about letting strange men buy me drinks, but the odd one would sometimes say something that would sneak around my defences and make me either a) curious to learn more about that particular person, or b) defend my standoffishness, a quality I was very proud of, knowing what men could be like. With Chris, I don't mind admitting, it was a bit of both.

"Jesus Christ," he said, after I'd turned my nose up at his first offer to buy me a drink. "Who the hell pissed in *your* ice-cream?"?" He was charming, that was for sure, and not a little handsome, but he could tell straight away that I'd been hurt and seemed genuinely interested in the how's, the why's and the where's. Even so, my guard remained up way past his first approach, as I clung tightly to the advice that Olive had drilled into me whilst growing up: "Whenever a man wants to buy you a drink, all he's really wanting to do is get into your knickers." But my guard got lower and lower as the weeks wore on and we started to see Chris and his mates more and more. Eventually my guard was laid so low it was down on the floor, along with the very gar- ment Olive had told me to keep pulled up tight, proving her right after all. But I didn't mind because by that point I'd grown quite fond of Chris and more than welcomed his company.

There was only one problem: what I'd taken to be respect wasn't respect at all, or so I was informed by Gary, a mate of his from the army, who told me that whenever Chris was back in Gibraltar, where he was stationed, he made a habit of using his redoubtable charm to loosen a few more lady garments when he was out strutting his stuff. It was a great shame as the girls took to Chris and liked being around him, and didn't at all mind being joined by the little sister that came as a result of our brief time together. But I couldn't possibly allow myself to be treated disrespectfully ever again, not after all I'd been through. If Chris was to play a significant part in my life, then he'd have to start treating me as if I was a significant part in his, and you couldn't do that if you were jumping in and out of bed with every woman who wanted to see your six-pack.

The real injury in all this though wasn't Chris's lack of respect for me, but what I discovered much later, when Chris was all an but forgotten memory and had moved on with his life. The problem was Gary. It seemed he'd developed a bit of a thing for me, and had been very jealous of my relationship with Chris. His tales of Gary's exploits, sordid as they were, all proved to be fiction, and were devised simply as a way of trying to split Chris and I up, so that, presumably, he could get his mitts on me himself. I hope in the decades that followed, Gary was able to discover that lying, particularly about so-called 'friends' is never the surest way into a girl's knickers, and even less so into her heart.

So there it was, an actual shot at happiness with someone I was starting to care quite deeply about, scuppered before it had even had a real chance to take flight. It seemed to be a pattern in my life, I was noticing, and one I couldn't escape. Every smile, every fleeting moment of happiness, had to be fought for, and wrestled for, with blood, with spit and with bile, and when I finally achieved it, or at least any tiny part of it, something had to be sacrificed, something far more meaningful than I was ever likely to gain anyway. All my life this had been the case, it was one nervous step forward, two violent leaps back; how much further, I started to ask myself, would I have to keep leaping back before there was nowhere else to go, before I got trapped up against a wall with no possibility of escape? I had to start moving forwards soon, the laws of nature demanded that I couldn't keep going backwards forever. It just simply wasn't possible … Was it?

It turns out it was. If I thought I knew misery, I was sorely mistaken. I didn't know anything yet.

CAN YOU HEAR ME, LOVE?

The policemen standing in the middle of the junction was doing his best. He didn't have a sign, just his hands, and he'd raise them to stop the traffic when there was a break in one direction, so he could wave it through from the other. Rain was pouring off him, bouncing almost, and he had to give his hands a flick every few seconds to get the water droplets off.

I watched him through my visor, over Tony's shoulder, as we waited for Karen and her fella to catch us up at the front of the queue. We were on our way to North Wales at the time, the four of us desperate to get away from dreary Birkenhead. Our desires raced ahead of us by some distance, zooming off in advance to stake out a lovely pub that served decent food with good music, whilst our bodies lagged hours behind on the wet roads, zipping in and out of cars, lorries and trucks like a piece of cotton on an electric loom. We would've zoomed straight through at the lights, but because we didn't want to put too much distance between us and the others, we decided to wait.

Another 'flick' and up went the policeman's hands. Tony twisted his wrist and the bike let out a Jurassic 'roar'. Red Rum at the starting gate.

When Karen and her fella finally joined us there was some banter through our rain-streaked helmets, wishful-thinking mostly, that the weather would ease off so the boys could show us girls what their bikes – shaped like youthful bulls – could *really* do. Thirty seconds later the policeman raised his arms to halt the traffic crossing towards us, another 'flick', then he waved us through; but all I heard was a rocket taking off beneath me. I hugged Tony tighter to stop myself flying off the back, and the scenery around us blurred like the stars in a sci-fi film when a spaceship goes soaring into hyper-drive.

Also in hyper-drive at that exact same moment was the driver of a red sports car on the *other* road, the one crossing ours. He'd been arguing with his girlfriend, so we learnt later, and hadn't noticed that the lights weren't green, because he hadn't noticed the lights. Nor the man standing in the dark uniform who'd replaced them. And if he hadn't noticed those, he certainly wasn't going to notice the bike flying at speed towards the centre of the same junction at exactly the same time. By the time he had, the bonnet of his car looked like Godzilla had taken a bite out of it, and Tony and I were doing the kind of somersaults you only ever see during the Olympics.

Deryn was about a year old when I started seeing Tony. He lived for his bike and the open road, and was what you might call a free spirit. You meet them often when you're young, but not so much when you're older. Real-life zaps that spirit, chopping it down like it does the long hair that goes with it, and replaces it with bags under the eyes. I'd never met anyone like him before, so for me he really was a breath of fresh air, literally so, when he threw me on the back of his bike and whizzed me off to places I'd only ever seen on maps. We weren't together all that long, just a few months, and it is possible, after we'd separated, that I might have gone through the rest of my life without ever thinking about him again. But because of the single event I'm about to write about, which lasted only a second or two, that's not possible. Even if it faded from my conscious memories, it would go on enduring in my unconscious ones. And you can't ignore those.

We'd met through his sister, a friend of mine who I'd got to know after John, and became more than friends when another friend, Karen, started going out with his best friend, Lee. That qualified us as a 'foursome' – so Karen announced – and before I knew it, she and I were hanging on to the back of these two free spirits, as they tried to break speeding records on these bikes that were so powerful if you hit the slightest bump you'd be in the air longer than the Wright Brothers were during their first ever flight at Kitty Hawk.

"Can you hear me, love?" a voice said, sounding as if through five fathoms of water.

My legs were in a hedgerow next to the road, but my upper body – my chest and arms and head – hadn't made it that far, that was lying on the path that ran alongside it. Fortunately, they were still connected. I could feel raindrops landing on my face, and something was flickering in front of it – fingers; thumb and middle-finger – they were clicking. *Click-click-click.* "Can you hear me?"

It was the rain-soaked policeman. He was kneeling down beside me. "Hello! Anyone home?"

Click-click-click. The fingers again.

He wasn't expecting me to respond, he told me later. Car doors slammed, lots of them, as figures hurried over, putting up their hoods, looking for a story to relay to their friends and family later that night. "Guess what I saw today …?" Convinced my neck wasn't broken, the policeman, helped by some passers-by, slowly peeled off my helmet.

"Ah, she's so pretty," I heard one girl say. "Is she gonna live?" I don't remember hearing him answer.

Another person appeared. A young woman with a blonde fringe. She pulled off a helmet and kneeled down next to me. "Chrissy, it's me." It was Karen. "Can you hear me?" She took my hand and started to stroke it. Then a thought exploded into my mind – *My kids!* – and I vomited a plea, to her, the policeman, and anyone else around: "Don't let my kids be on their own."

I woke up in hospital. I don't know how long after. The roll call of injuries I'd sustained was like a career criminal's rap-sheet and the doctor's eyebrows went up as he read them off to me. The fractured skull was the one that seemed to cause him the most concern, but there was also internal bleeding, an assortment of cracked ribs, damaged kidneys and a foot that looked like a smashed ashtray. I was going to ask if there was a partridge in a pear tree too, but it wasn't Christmas. He called me a "lucky girl", and said he couldn't quite believe I was lying there in-front of him, chatting away, and not lying downstairs in a fridge with a tag over my big toe. Remembering it had been a year to the day since Big Richie had passed away, I joked, "My dad must've saved me."

"Well someone did," he said, "'cause you really shouldn't be here." He was referring to the fact that the car we hit was quite low-sided – a sports car – and no other vehicles were nearby. Often, when people go flying off bikes it's not the impact with the ground that sends them to the mortuary, it's the lorry coming the opposite way whose wheels they vanish under. Also, if we'd hit any other part of the car, or if its front hadn't been so low down to the ground, we'd have been turned into pancakes, and I'd have spent the past thirty-five years up in Heaven stroking Little Billy's foot. Looking back on it all, and knowing what I now know, it's fair to say that there might well have been someone looking after me when I did my triple-front-somersault-with-half-twist into that hedge, but if it *was* anyone on the other side, I'd lay odds it wasn't Big Richie.

Tony was upstairs in a different ward. His injuries hadn't been as extensive and so hadn't required quite as much round-the-clock attention. But they did end up putting a metal plate in his leg to help him get mobile again. "Not a dinner plate," they told me. At the time of the accident we'd only been going out a few months, so we didn't really know each other that well; but I did like him, and wasn't past thinking there might have been a future for us. Going through an experience like that, they say, can really make or break a relationship. By getting through it together it can strengthen what you already have, and allow you to go on to great things. Or it can simply expose the lack of connection you have and cause you both to go your own separate ways, saving you a good deal of heartbreak further down the line. Days must've passed before the staff were comfortable enough with the idea of me leaving my bed, and the first thing I did, once they'd sat me up, was to ask if they'd take me up to see my Tony.

"I don't see why not," the nurse answered.

He was on the top floor, and so the nurse, once she'd gone to fetch my dressing gown, took me to the lift in a wheelchair. When the doors opened I saw other visitors standing at the far end, shoulder to shoulder, some holding chocolates, others flowers, and I wondered if I should've sent the nurse down to get me some from the little stall downstairs. Some *chrysanths* might've been nice. I hoped Tony would forgive me for not thinking of it earlier. Perhaps he'd be happy with a little kiss instead?

We arrived on the top floor and everyone spilled out. The nurse then zig-zagged me along all the brightly lit corridors, past all the wards, until we arrived at Tony's, then she parked me in the waiting room and told me to wait. I wanted to surprise him, but it didn't work like that. She needed to check he was awake and up for receiving visitors.

He was up for it all right, just not from me. His ex-wife, who was in with him, insisted they not be disturbed, and when the nurse came back to tell me I could see how embarrassed she was. She knew all about Tony, I'd told her about our relationship over the past few days, and she knew I couldn't wait to see him.

I didn't say a single thing to her as she turned me around and pushed me back towards the lift, but I let out a tear when the doors opened and out spilled another sea of visitors, all clutching flowers and chocolates to give to their loved ones.

"What were you doing on the back of a motorbike, you stupid cow?" That was how June, one of my own so-called 'loved ones', greeted me when she eventually decided to grace me with her presence. "Are you fuckin' mental?"

Instead of bringing me flowers or chocolates, she just launched into an admission that she was planning to tell Social Services what I'd been up to so they could decide what to do with my kids. "I'm only thinking of *them*, Chrissy" was how she justified it, though probably it was more to do with the fact that I'd started to enjoy my life a bit, a concept that was simply unheard of within the masochistic tenets of my family. Still, jealousy can be a vicious weapon, and when June started to wield hers and come at me with it, I had no choice but to try and defend myself.

"You need to discharge me right now," I said to the doctor when he did his ward round later that afternoon. "I need to get home." He looked down at me, covered almost head-to-toe in bandages, with my right foot still in plaster, and he chuckled aloud.

"That's not going to happen," he said, unpeeling my fingers from his white coat.

"My sister is trying to get my kids taken off me," I cried. "She's getting Social Services to come round, and she wants to get them taken away." He paused. "We can't sign you out," he said eventually "Your foot's still in plaster, you've got a fracture to your skull, pelvis and your kidneys aren't yet fully recovered." In the end, we reached a compromise: he would sign me out as long as I had someone to drive me home, and on the promise that I would contact the hospital the moment I felt the slightest twinge anywhere. I'd agreed even before he'd finished speaking, and had half my clothes in my bag, but in all honesty if it meant having my kids taken away from me, I'd actually have to be standing outside Heaven itself, watching St Peter take the bolt off the Pearly Gates before I'd even think about contacting the hospital again.

"All right," I said, anyway. "You have my word, doctor."

Nobody talked about Post-Traumatic Stress Disorder back then, but that doesn't mean it didn't exist. It's even in Shakespeare if you look hard enough. But if you hit a car and fly thirty feet through the air and land upside down in a hedge, and the doctor who treats you tells you you should, by rights, be dead, then there's a very good chance it's going to leave behind an after effect or two.

I had the full works. My sleep was the first thing to go. Just when the baby was getting into a normal sleeping pattern, I was getting hauled out of mine; and when I did finally manage to drift off, I'd keep relieving the accident, hearing the sound – that awful *THUD!* – then feeling again the sickening lurch forward. It's incredible how long a single second can last when played out again through the filter of a near-death experience. When you're asleep, and dreaming, it can last the whole night. And the night can last forever. The mental struggles weren't at all helped by my sudden lack of mobility either. When I needed to be up and about, looking after the children and staying on top of things in the house, I found myself slithering around like a mermaid with a ripped tail. Most times I would lie on the couch with my feet up and the TV on, but no matter what was playing, it wouldn't let me forget how Tony had dismissed me when I'd tried to see him that day. The sense of betrayal was overwhelming. I might not have had much, but I did have my pride, and even if the events of recent years had shrunk it down to the size of a fig leaf, I was going to keep tight hold of it. He'd ring and I'd answer, but once I knew it was him I'd hang up. "Chrissy, listen — " he would manage to squeak before I slammed the receiver down, wishing the cradle was his skull. You couldn't filter calls then, or block them, just as you couldn't stop people from turning up at your door, unannounced, which is eventually what he did.

"I just want to explain," he belched, as I stood there in the door trying to support myself on my crutches. But by then I'd already found out from Karen that he'd carried on seeing his ex-wife the whole time he was with me. So even as he stood there babbling on, with the plate in his leg, trying to justify his behaviour, I knew that what was coming out of his mouth was nothing but bullshit.

"I just want you to turn around and walk away," I said to him.

"What if I got down on one knee?" he asked, doing that very thing.

"You can get down on all fours if you want, Tony" I said, "but you're not coming in." It was hard to say it, but having been through what I'd been through, I just couldn't put myself in that situation again. I told him it would be best for everyone if we never saw each other again. And we never did. I closed the door in his face, grabbed my crutches and then hobbled back to my couch to watch the end of *Crown Court*. There was a riveting case on, and I wanted to see if the fella was guilty or not.

Turns out he was.

WHO'S A SILLY BILLY?

You wonder how things can get so awful sometimes. Especially if they started off so well. Look at a bunch of roses, how beautiful they seem outside the florist, with the sun shining down, dappling the light beneath them through the lovely red petals. You buy them because they look so perfect, so full of life. You take them home, cut off the stems, add water, and put them in your poshest vase, because you want to take that perfection home with you. "God, aren't those flowers beautiful!" you want people to say.

But a week later they're in the bin. They're in the bin because, when you weren't looking, when you were too busy getting on with your life, they turned ugly and died.

A few years into my relationship with Billy Harris I went to see a doctor. He sat me on a bed, turned my head this way and that, pressed my tummy in, then looked at my shoulders, my knee-joints, and made me say "Aaaah". Based on all this, he then said he had me down for being dead in about six months.

He was very nearly right.

Billy was 23-stone, 6'8", and the head bouncer in a Chester nightclub. He was the only man I knew who could stare a statue out. Knives were scared of him. As bad as John Suckley was (and he was bad, let's be under no illusions about that) he was little more than the warm-up act for the human wrecking-ball that was Billy Harris.

My introduction to this calamity of a man came in layers. There was no love at first sight, no cupid's arrow hitting me between the eyes, just a growing sense of familiarity that I confused for something else. You might have experienced something similar yourself. The first layer came when I was out with Pauline and another friend, Carol, in the Hamilton nightclub, the neon-lit sweat-box situated on Love Street, where Billy Harris, in his long, dark overcoat, stood sentry every night, his double-barrelled-gaze cocked and ready to go off in the face of anyone who even hinted at trouble. The three of us stood in a tight-knit stilettoed triangle around our handbags, bopping to Adam and the Ants, and Soft Cell, trying not to catch the eyes of men who thought a night out was only productive if it involved a trip behind the bins and a hiked-up skirt. Though we were mostly successful, one pair of eyes I couldn't shake off were those of a creepy looking fella with cheeks like machete blades, who'd latched onto me. Friendless (for good reasons, I don't doubt), he'd rub up close to me when I was dancing, follow me to the toilet when I needed to go and then wait for me to return like a Jack Russell outside a betting shop. As for his conversation, I'd had better ones with my alarm clock when it accidentally went off at five o'clock in the morning.

"See that doorman over there," I shouted to Pauline over *Tainted Love.* "Can you get him to come over and pretend he's my boyfriend?" Pauline had already seen the rapist-in-waiting latching onto me and knew the score, so, with just a nod, she was on the case. The doorman (not Billy Harris) was over a couple of minutes later, gliding towards me with his arms spread wide and his grinning teeth made even whiter by the ultraviolet lights.

"Chrissssyyyyyy," he beamed, getting into the role far better than I could ever have hoped. "You didn't see me come in?" His name was Mark, he told me later, and though not as big as Billy Harris (who was?), he was still someone whose shiny black brogues you wouldn't want to spill your pint on.

"Oh, hiya love," I said, spinning into his tree-trunk arms for a cuddle. When he let me go, I said to my wannabe-rapist that I had to go now, "because my boyfriend's here." Getting the message, he slunk off fairly sharpish, back into the dry fog and the Ultravox, in search of his next stalky obsession. Mark, who is still a friend to this day, was a perfect gentleman that night. Pauline had explained the situation to him as she'd led him over, and he knew exactly what was expected of him. It was a role he'd clearly been called on to play before, and it fit him like a pair of *Speedos*. I got to know him very well in the weeks ahead, to the point where he'd call round and have a cup of tea on his way to work. There was nothing romantic there at all. I just felt safe in his presence, especially in the club when I was out with the girls, because I knew I could pop a mini dress on, or a short skirt, and if any so-called 'admirer' thought that was an advert for a trip behind the bins at closing time, I knew Mark, or one of his mates, would be over like a shot.

"Everythin' alright here, Chrissy, love?" they'd ask, and before I'd even answered, my new 'admirer' would've scarpered.

Billy Harris was one of those mates.

"How are you girls getting home tonight?" Billy asked Pauline and I one night, just before the lights came on and turned us Cinderellas back into scullery maids.

"Taxi," Pauline chirped.

"We only live round the corner," I added, wanting him to know it was only a couple of quid so wouldn't exactly bankrupt us. But the man-mountain who was harder than the steel toe-caps in his boots, was having none of it.

"No, no, no," he insisted, shaking the Doric column that was his head. "I'll sort you out a lift, girls." I knew we'd be safe because the owner of the club, Charlie, who I'd gotten to know after seeing him on the beach a couple of times with his dogs, had mentioned Billy to me already, and referred to him as a "good'un." In minutes the 'good'un' had us clambering into his big, swanky car, and was driving us home himself. As he told us about his job in the club, I looked up at him, unable to believe how he was able to fit in the front seat without being folded in half, and I wondered where he was able to buy a coat that went all the way down to his feet. It must've been a special shop whose customers were characters in fairy tales.

The next day that same coat was around the back of my kitchen chair, and the giant was sitting down, blowing into the cuppa I'd made him to make it cooler. "Hot this," he said, but not in a complaining way. Were the next thirteen-and-a-half years all mapped out in his head? Who can say? All I know is that, having dropped me off the night before, the giant had seen where I'd lived, and not sixteen-hours-later, as he was on his way to the club, he called round.

"I hear you make the best cuppa this side of the Mersey?" he said.

"Had no complaints so far," I answered, and opened the door.

As he clomped past me in his size fifteen boots and headed towards the kitchen, I can't say I had a glimpse into the future of what awaited us both. I've seen darkness in people before, men whose insides are coiled up so tightly that you feel they just want to shout and spit at the world, but Billy Harris wasn't like that. He didn't need to put on any tough-man act, because he was, to his core, a tough man, so the act – if there was one – was the 'soft-on-the-inside' one he tried to charm all the ladies with.

He blew on his tea again. His hands were so big, I remember thinking as he blew into the mug, that he could've put them around my waist and the tips would've touched on the other side.

Within a week, we'd proved it was possible. And then the week after that, when he turned up on my doorstep with his bags and a smile as big as a watermelon, we thought anything might be. My only worry was that my wardrobe might not be big enough for his coats.

One of the things about cemeteries that used to make me sad was seeing graves that had no flowers on them. It was never new graves, always old ones, and you'd know that for three or four decades people would've visited that grave and tended to it, put flowers on it and spoken to it, as if the person was still alive and listening to them just a few feet beneath the surface. It might have been their mum in there, or their dad, or a sibling, or even one of their own kids. You'd see those too, with little teddies on, wet from the rain. But then, as the seasons came and went, those faithful family members would've aged and moved on, or passed away, and the number of visitors would have shrunk down until there were no more fresh flowers and the conversation moved elsewhere, to another spot, and another grave. Seeing them bare like that would tug at my heart, so when I was little, I'd take flowers from the new graves – just a few, not all, and I'd *always* ask – and put them on the forgotten ones, in the little rusty pots full of old rainwater. I did this because I wanted to make nice what wasn't nice, pretty what wasn't pretty. Where there was rot and decay, with just a little sprinkling of affection, I could bring life, *new* life. And I think that's why, when everyone told me to get as far away from Billy Harris as I could, I stayed. I wanted to make pretty what was ugly.

During the thirteen-and-a-half-years that Billy and I were together, I'd often try and work out what it was that made him the way he was, what made him 'tick'. Was it the Irish Rangers, whom he'd served with at the height of the Troubles?; or over in Germany during a time when it was struggling to re-establish its own identity?; or the childhood that wasn't a childhood, so punishing was it to get through – dealing with his dad's own fierce brand of discipline? But trying to work that out was like trying to work out where the violence comes from in anyone. For some it's a defence, for others, just an effective way to establish control, and what is control if it's not total power over someone else?

This more loathsome aspect of Billy Harris wasn't revealed to me overnight. Like the affection, it came in layers too, the real aspect of the man appearing in bits, like chinks on a car windscreen, as the familiarity we'd established between us slowly gave way to the contempt it all too often goes on to breed.

But22222

But in the end, it was probably none of these things that made him behave the way he did. Instead it probably just came down to the fact that his own first marriage had just exploded, whilst he was desperately trying to defuse the bomb his vile behaviour had made it into. He hadn't wanted it to fail, and was clearly still infatuated with his ex, but because he'd lost control of it, he'd made a grab for the first thing that floated along that he thought might stop him from drowning. I was that thing, but instead of stopping him from drowning, he just drowned me too.

Slap or punch. I can't remember what it was, but the first time he used his hand on me, I know exactly where we were and what we were doing. There was blood, I remember that. We were in his car, on our way to choose a pram for the baby we were about to have together. My fourth, his third. This is in Bromborough, a small spot on the Wirral Peninsula with just about enough people in it to qualify it as a town. The ex-wife I knew about already. Billy had told me about her, mostly in disparaging terms, but it was left to a mutual friend of ours to plant the seed that those disparaging terms might be a cover for the fact that she was more than just an ex. I held off jumping to any conclusions though, because I'd lost Chris due to doing exactly that, and besides, I knew this 'friend' had more axes to grind than a blacksmith before the Battle of Bannockburn.

So when I raised the issue with Billy in the car that day, I did it as delicately as I could, expecting him to just dismiss it and laugh it off. "She said *what*? Silly cow!" But as I searched around the car for a handkerchief to mop up the mess pouring from my nose, I could only think he was kind of overdoing his defence a little.

"Get out the fucking car," he spat.

I didn't know Bromborough at all then, so wouldn't know where to go if he dumped me there and drove off. I was still reeling too from the shock of what he'd just done. Had that *really* happened? As a storm of dark thoughts cluttered up my mind, I simply spluttered out one word, "No," trying not to think about what kind of father this man would be to the five-month-old foetus growing in my belly.

The blood was gushing out by now and I just couldn't stop it. There was nothing around to help either, no tissues, no towels, no sympathy – *definitely* none of that – and if any was to come, he'd have to calm down first and stop screaming in my face like a nutter. He'd turned the argument around so that it was me in the wrong now, me who'd caused the offence by asking about an affair that, until ten-minutes-ago, I'd not even believed a word of anyway. His hands were clenched and the veins in his neck were bulging and I think the only reason he didn't hit me again was because he didn't want to send the blood splashing all over the upholstery in the car. If he wanted me out he was just going to have to drag me out and dump me there, something I didn't believe he had it in him to do. Fortunately I was right, that level of contempt would come later, so he drove me, shaking and crying, to his parents' house, where all our arguing roused the attention of his dad, who heard it from the front room and came stomping out to see what all the screeching was about.

If Billy was looking for moral support from his dad he didn't get it, because he started laying into him the second he saw him. "You shouldn't be hitting the poor girl," he said, feeling perhaps that my being pregnant meant a line was being crossed. In his world, it was okay to beat your partner into a near-coma only if she wasn't 'in the club'. He invited me in, to clean myself up, but I was too embarrassed to get out the car, so I settled instead for a hanky. The neighbours were looking, and I didn't want to be seen clambering out with my top soaked in blood. What would they think?

During the drive back to the house not a word was said. Even though it was just a short drive, it felt like an eternity, but I could feel the tempest in Billy's mind slowly moving away. By the time we'd reached home, it must've blown itself out, because instead of fire and brimstone in his eyes there were now tears, and he was nothing less than apologetic.

"I am so, so sorry, Chrissy," he said. "I don't know what came over me." The veins had gone down in his neck and his hands were unclenched. I reminded myself what Charlie, the club's owner, had said to me on the beach, when I'd seen him out with his dogs. "Oh, he's a good'un, that Billy Harris. You can rely on him for anything."

Well, I thought, if Charlie says it, then it must be true.

Over the next four months, leading up to Will's birth, I saw less and less of the 'good'un' and more and more of the person who revealed himself in the car that afternoon. The 'teddy-bear' I got to know in my kitchen, who'd blow on his tea to cool it, had only hard blocks inside him and not the soft stuffing I'd convinced myself was there. As the due-date arrived and I got bigger, Billy's distractions became more distracting too, until I barely saw him around the house any more. "Just gonna see a man about a dog," was all

I heard him say, or words to that affect. He certainly never came back with a dog anyway.

I hoped he might soften up a bit after Will's birth, but there was very little indication he might. From the second we arrived at the hospital, until the moment we left, there was nothing but chaos and acrimony. In fact, you could argue it was set-up to be a disaster, not for the reasons you might expect, but because of the three-ring-circus the hospital turned the birth into. The staff had known in advance the baby was going to be born with a veil over its face, so they went about arranging for a horde of medical students to be brought in to witness this medical 'miracle'. It wasn't really a miracle, but veils aren't exactly two a penny, so the supervising consultant thought it would make a nice treat for the students to see what one looked like. Known also as 'cauls', veils are thought to be associated with good luck, but in reality they're just leftovers from the amniotic sac. Either way, they were rare enough for the staff to think that the benefits of treating the whole thing as a spectator sport far outweighed the private agonies of the twenty-something woman who had to suffer through it. Billy didn't quite agree with their final assessment, however, and wasn't shy about telling them. Still, in case there was any confusion, at least all the students, and everyone else within a three-mile radius, got to discover that the delivery room in Arrowe Park Hospital wasn't "a fucking circus!"

Despite that, there was actually a change in Billy. Even though we had five other children between us, Will was the first boy, so it was natural that such a man's man (as Billy liked to think of himself) would find a connection with him. He became besotted. The girls too loved having a little baby to play with, as he was far more responsive than their dollies, and they pushed him round in a pram, fed, clothed and bathed him, and helped change his nappies, something the 6'8" man-mountain couldn't quite stretch to.

Billy had other interests, and other things that kept him far busier than I thought a simple bouncer's job entailed, but I didn't really ever question him about any of it, because I was starting to enjoy the relative peace and tranquillity that had settled over us since Little Will had arrived. As the baby grew though, and the challenges of raising four kids increased (Billy's daughter had wisely chosen to stay with her mum), I started to think that some help might be nice. His response, when I dared ask, caused the veins to start bulging in his neck again. Funny, I only noticed I *hadn't* been walking on eggshells when I heard them crunching beneath my feet again. I didn't want to complain, but I was starting to feel just like an accessory in Billy's life, as I had been in John's – a doormat who made the tea and fed his kids. His deeply-rooted insecurities meant he could only interpret what I said as a criticism, and his only defence for that was to criticise back. And so, all the verbal sparring started up again, until the voices grew louder and the arguments more pathetic. In no time at all I was back in that white-knuckle world once more, the one I'd been raised in, where the site of a man's arm at my throat was as familiar to my children as the faces of Zippy and George on *Rainbow*.

Early on, when I realised what kind of rough ride I might be in for with Billy, I said to him: "I've been through all this before, with John Suckley, and I am not going through it all again with you." And I meant it. But I still went through it, telling myself, *deluding* myself – even when the children would be clinging to my leg in fear, not leaving me alone, even for a second to go to the toilet – that it was *never* really that bad, that it could *always* get a lot worse. But at what point does someone realise, when they're living through something like that, that they've already entered the 'lot worse' phase? How many indignities do you have to suffer? How many slaps, cuts, punches, kicks, bruises?

Looking back, I can see now that I was living inside the 'lot worse' phase for most of the relationship. If it was a cyclone, you could say I was in the eye of it, trapped, raising my kids; and if I stepped outside I'd just get thrown to my death. In the centre, Billy would roar and rage and smash and crash, and then, after he'd exhausted all his anger, he'd be calm, the plates would be picked up, the pieces of glass scraped into the bin, I'd put a plaster on, and then the sheepish look would come, followed by the apology, "Chrissy, I am so, so sorry. I don't know what came over me, etc, etc." The performance would conclude with me thinking of my kids and accepting the apology. What choice did I have? If he genuinely hated me, I'd try to tell myself, then he wouldn't seem so earnest, would he? And if he had genuine feelings for his ex, and all these other slags people kept telling me about ("Let's just keep pretending they're rumours," I'd say to myself) then he'd leave me, wouldn't he?

But he doesn't. So I must be special.

THE BADGER DUCKERS

He sat forward on the couch, his hands held out in front of him, almost like he was holding an invisible football. He had perfectly manicured nails, and gold cufflinks on his crisp white shirtsleeves, and couldn't have been cleaner-cut in his appearance if he'd been carved out of soap with a razor blade. His pin-striped trousers alone probably cost more than the sofa I'd directed him to, but he didn't seem to mind. He could use part of his 'cut' to buy another pair.

"Look Christina," he said. "I want to see you set up with your own house and everything here because *you're* the victim in all this and that's what you're entitled to. Just look at your injuries." He nodded down towards my legs as if to remind me of everything I'd been through since my discharge from the hospital (as if I needed reminding). All those weeks in plaster, the lack of mobility, the falls, the headaches, and the mountain of stress that went with it. There was no way of determining how long any of these injuries would affect me, but the physical ones would most likely resurface later on in my life. That's what he said anyway.

"It might not be the nicest thing in the world to talk about," he added, "but there is a price that can be put on that."

Fifty grand was the figure he had in mind. Obviously the bigger the payout, the bigger his cut would be. "I'm just thinking of you here, Christina," he said for the hundredth time. The problem was, to justify a claim that big, there would have to be evidence that the injuries I'd sustained from the accident would have a "detrimental effect on my future", or something, and that would mean a lot of trips to the doctor. Evidence was the key word, that's what they needed.

"Oh, you'd like that, wouldn't you, eh?" Billy said, when I told him I wondered why he was looking at me like that. "Like what?"

"The doctor putting his hands all over you. You'd fuckin' love that."

Even though the accident had happened long before I'd ever met Billy

Harris, he and I were already raising our own child by the time a judge came anywhere near it. But Billy wasn't joking. He really didn't want me to push ahead with the claim, and was on my case about it every day. Eventually I had no choice but to ring up my solicitor on Hamilton Square and tell him that I didn't want to proceed. I didn't tell him Billy forced me into it.

"Christina, if we get to court without the doctor's reports," he said, all antsy, "all we're going to be looking at is three grand, max. It'll be the bare minimum." I had to weigh it all up: three grand and an easy ride from Billy, against fifty and an atmosphere of hell in the house. As toxic as it was starting to seem now with Billy, I knew it had the potential to get a lot worse, and I didn't want to put my kids through any of that.

In the end, we got three and a half. The driver, a Chinese man, was done for Driving Without Due Care and Attention, and his insurance covered the pay-out, probably with a big sigh of relief. We all went on with our lives: my solicitor back to his comfy leather chair and oak desk, Billy back to being a sod and a bastard, and me back to my life of benefits and handouts. Mind you, three-and-a-half grand was quite an amount back then, certainly for me, who was expected to keep a home and raise three kids on what amounted to little more than Billy spitting in my pocket each week.

Thinking about it, it was the amount that was clearly the problem for Billy. For him, me turning my back on the claim was nothing to do with the money, and everything to do with control. If I'd gotten my hands on fifty thousand quid, he'd have known what a life-changing amount that would've been. What would it have given me? Power, control, and through that, the freedom to tell him to go and "Do one." I wouldn't have needed his support. Even so, the £3,500 that did finally settle into my account was still too much for him, and from the moment it was deposited, he tried to come up with ways of getting it off me, either through loans he never intended to pay back, or the various schemes he liked to embroil himself in. One of the most extreme of these arose when his elder brother got done over by the 'Badger Duckers' and found himself bandaged up like Mr Bump in Arrowe Park Hospital. I'll probably never know what triggered the precise catalogue of events that led to it all, but my involvement started one evening when I heard the phone ringing in the living room. We were watching tele at the time. *Morse* was on.

"Yeah," Bill said into the receiver, a statement more than a question.

His massive brow instantly knotted up like the tread on a wellie boot, and when I asked him what it was, he snapped at me to "Shush." Moments later, his feet nearly punched through the stairs in his rush to bolt up them and I was instantly on edge because Billy Harris is not someone who bolts to or from anything. Upstairs, I could hear him rummaging around, a burglar in a hurry. Cupboards opened and closed, he huffed and he puffed – "Where is it, where is it?" I heard – then, thirty seconds later, he bounded down the stairs clutching something in his hand, something that glinted. Or did I just imagine that? Will was still a couple of months away from coming out at this point, but already it looked like I'd stuffed a washing machine up my top and walking was tricky. Even so, when I saw what Billy was trying to stuff down his coat sleeve I nearly collapsed on the spot.

"What the *hell* is that?" I yelled.

"They got Dave," was all he said, as if that was all the answer I needed.

"Who's got Dave? What are you talking about?"

"The Badger Duckers."

Dave was his brother and worked in another club, also on the door, but before he felt the need to explain any more, or tell to me why he was heading out the door with a 15" machete hidden up his sleeve, he was gone, leaving me to wonder if the next time I saw his face it would be on the next day's news.

An hour later there was a phone call. It was Mark from the club.

"Christina, you've got to get out of the house." I was convinced he was about to tell me that Billy was dead, but it wasn't as clear-cut as that. He asked how quickly I could get a few things together and get out. I told him the kids were still asleep, and that it would take about half-an-hour, but he just growled. "I'm seven months pregnant," I reminded him. Sounding annoyed, he told me he was coming round straight away, "in case anything happens." As soon as I put the receiver down, it rang again. I snatched it up, thinking it was going to be Mark. "What do you mean 'in case anything happens'?" I said. But it wasn't Mark.

"The police are outside." It was Billy this time, sounding almost excited, like he was enjoying this. "Don't be scared, they're just there to protect you." Bloody hell, I thought, how much protection do I need? Without hanging up, I went to the door, just to check, but there was no sign of them (how familiar was *that* scenario?). I went back to the phone.

"What do you mean they're not there?" Billy roared when I told him. "They said they'd be there."

"Well, they're not."

"Fuuuuuuuck's saaaaaaaake!"

He was calling from the hospital where he was still with Dave, but he didn't want to leave him in case the Badger Duckers turned up to "finish him off." He assured me that the police were on their way, but didn't have time to explain anything more. I told him Mark was coming round, and he echoed what Mark had said, that I should get some clothes together and get out.

"And go where?" I asked, but by the time I'd got the first word out, he'd already hung up.

It wasn't even ten o'clock yet, but it already felt like it had been the longest night of my life.

I was nearly packed when I finally heard the machine-gun *rat-a-tat-tat* on the door that only people in authority know how to do. I assumed it to be the police.

"Christina, it's Mark. Let me in."

When I swung back the door, Mark brushed straight past me and went over to the windows, making sure they were all closed, with the curtains pulled. You could see his army training coming through.

"You need to get the kids up," he said.

"What the hell is going on, Mark? I haven't got a clue what's happened."

"It's the Badger Duckers. There was a barney in the club and Dave didn't come out of it too well. He's in the hospital now."

The Badger Duckers I knew by reputation. You won't find out anything about them on Google today, but back then, Badger Ducker and his cronies helped give Birkenhead the less than reputable reputation it's never really been able to shake off. If the name hasn't made it into the annals of crime quite as much as Reggie or Ronnie Kray, that's only because Birkenhead didn't offer the same retail opportunities as London's East End, and there were fewer big-boobed celebrities to hang out with. But the Badger Duckers, just as the Krays were with their 'Firm', appeared to be driven by the same lethal impulses and got off on the fear and intimidation they knew they could instil in others. They were only the smallest of fish, admittedly, but don't forget, the pond they were in was a million times smaller.

"They had a sawn-off shotgun on me, Chrissy," Mark said, making sure the last of the windows was closed. "They said unless I gave them your address they were gonna blow my brains out. "

"So what did you do?"

"Well, I didn't bloody give them it, did I? I knew you'd be here with the kids."

What I didn't know, until later that night, was that the Harrises had been engaged in a blood-feud with the Badger Duckers that had gone on for years, and although there was no way I could've known it, just by involving myself with Billy, I'd risked putting myself, and what's more, my *kids*, right in the crossfire.

"The thing is," he went on, "they know you live in Moreton. I saw them as I was coming over. They were at the roundabout, going round in circles. I think they were trying to work out which road you lived down." Aware that Mark didn't have a gun himself, I'm not sure what help he'd have been if Badger Ducker and his cronies did turn up brandishing a shotgun or two, but still, I'd rather have him there than not.

Desperate for an update I picked up the phone and rang Arrowe Park, wanting to speak to Billy. With my words spewing out of my mouth like hot lava, I couldn't have made much sense to the nurse on duty, and probably scared her half-to-death when I stared prattling on about gangsters and shotguns, but I did eventually get patched through to the ward and left a message with someone who promised to take it to the patient's brother, once I'd convinced her of the urgency.

After a few fretful minutes, during which time Mark and I must've checked the windows a hundred times (in case the Badger Duckers had managed to find out where we lived) Billy eventually rang me back, but by the time I'd finished screaming down the phone at him, he probably wished he hadn't.

Billy arrived at the house the same time the police did, and I let them in together. There was no flashing blue light on the car when it finally arrived, so at least none of the neighbours knew what was going on. The first thing everyone did was find agreement in one thing: that we had to get out of the house as soon as possible. The police wanted me to take the kids over to what they called a 'Safe House' – a term that, up until that point, I'd you only ever heard in films. The whole situation was laughable, but Billy wasn't laughing, and neither were the police. I really felt like I'd somehow ended up in an episode of *The Professionals*.

"Is there anywhere you can go?"

There was nowhere, really, just Gina's, and so I suggested that. The police agreed that would be acceptable, but only for tonight. I'd need somewhere more long-term, they said, as it would only be a matter of time before the Badger Duckers were able to track us down. Really it was Billy they wanted to harm, but the first thing you learn in Gangster School – or wherever the hell it was these people got their educations – is the best way to hurt someone is to destroy what they care about most.

I could've laughed. If only they knew how much Billy Harris *really* cared about me, they might've thought I'd be safer with Badger!

I didn't even get the kids out of their pyjamas for the trek over to Gina's. They remained on the back seat for most of the journey, cuddled up together like coats that had been tossed onto it. By the time we arrived, it had gone 2am, and Gina opened the door in her dressing gown, probably working out even then what price such gossip would have in her circle of friends. Once we were inside, Billy skidded straight back to the hospital. I thanked the police for what they'd done, but they didn't want to leave without reminding me of the seriousness of the situation we were in.

"We know these people," they said, sternly. "We know what they're capable of. As soon as you've had your breakfast tomorrow, get as far away from here as you can, because this lot, they're not going to stop until they give that big fella of yours something to cry about."

Whether Billy would ever have cried for me if anything had happened remains to be seen, but I did. All night. And I didn't stop until, just as dawn was breaking, I heard a van pulling up outside. I froze. A door slid open. Breakfast was going to have be taken in a service station, Billy said, once he'd woken us all up. He wanted us on the road as soon as possible. When I asked what service station he just replied, "The one on the way to London."

"LONDON?!

It wasn't much of a breakfast, but it was certainly expensive for what we had. Dawn was long behind us at that point, as was Birkenhead, but the memory of what we'd just been through, that insufferable night, I didn't think I'd ever get far enough away from. Billy had spoken to Dave's wife, Maureen and she'd agreed to let us stay with her for a while, at least until Billy had been able to resolve everything up here. But what exactly did he mean by 'resolve'? Was it the same kind of 'resolve' that the Krays used to sort out their difficulties with back in the sixties? That worked out well for them, didn't it?

"There's no way we're going down to Maureen's," I told him, wiping the sleep out of my eyes. "This is our home. The kids are at school, we can't just drag them down to London at the drop of a hat." But we could, and we did. The more I came to understand Billy's background, and his family's ongoing feud with the Badger Duckers, the more I came to realise just how limited our range of choices were.

Maureen lived in a hovel above some shops. Technically it was a maisonette, but to call it that would be to make it sound far grander than it actually was. The stench that greeted us, when she pulled backed the rain-warped door to invite us in, nearly made me retch. You could tell straight away that, to Maureen, a home was little more than an extension of the kitchen bin. Nothing was clean. The sink was filled with dishes, there was a centimetre of dust and hair on the carpet, twice that by the walls, and tea stains everywhere. After the long, drive down, all of us packed together like sardines in the van Billy had 'borrowed' from his mate, it was the perfect insult to add to the injuries I'd had to endure over the past 18-hours. With Stephanie just weeks away from being born, this is not the way I wanted to be living. Like any other soon-to-be-mum, I just wanted my own space with a few home luxuries around me, such as a toilet that actually flushed, and a bath that didn't look like it belonged to John George Haigh, the Acid Bath Murderer.

The hovel was in Woking, not in London itself, near to where the Martians arrived in the *War of the Worlds,* and first showed off their heat ray. That's actually quite apt, because the maisonette itself looked like Martians had been living in it for the past hundred or so years. From the moment we arrived there was not a moment's privacy, and no efforts were made to give us any. The kids (she had two of her own) fought like cat and dog, and Maureen and I weren't much better, communicating through snidey comments and asides. She clearly resented us being there, and went out of her way to make things as difficult as possible for all of us, even putting limits on our phone usage – despite this being the only way I could sort anything out. I basically had to live on it in order to deal with even the simplest problem, for example, sorting a school out for the kids. I'd assumed that would've taken me about half an hour to sort out. Where's the nearest school? Here are my kids' names, when can they start? But it escalated into a nightmare.

The nearest primary they were eligible for, I was told, was four miles away. I thought that was quite far, but agreed to put their names down because, well, what choice did I have? Then we got onto the subject of the school bus, and I asked the secretary, "Where's the nearest it stops to here?"

"It doesn't," she said. "You'll have to drive in."

"I can't. I don't have a car."

"Then you'll have to walk."

I told her that I was seven-months' pregnant and she said, "So what." Okay, she didn't, but she might as well have for all the interest she showed. There were no public buses that we could get either, not without taking two or three each way, the expense for which would've been exorbitant. I started to panic. This was supposed to be the easy part. Maureen didn't have a car either, and even if she did, there's no way she'd have let me use it. Besides, I wouldn't even have fit behind the wheel right then. So I tried to weigh up the walking option up in my mind: four miles there and four miles back, once in the morning, and once in the afternoon, a total for me (f I was to consider doing this) of *sixteen miles* each day. That's *two-thirds* of the London Marathon, *every* weekday, with a one-year-old baby in tow and a stomach that was already the size of a washing machine.

"I don't understand," the secretary said once she'd got her head around my situation. "If you've already got a home up north, why do you need to put your children in a school down here?"

"Because there's gangsters after us," I blurted out to her, as if it was the most normal response in the world. "If we go back north, we'll get shot by the Badger Duckers." But even as the words fell from my lips, I realised something horrifying: it was now *me* who sounded like the Martian.

Billy must've told Maureen about the pay-out from the accident because, after a few days she dragged me into a conversation about money. She was doing me "such a big favour", she tried to justify, that she had a right to some of it. "I'm helping *you* out, so how about you helping *me* out, eh?" It was her bills she wanted covering, not just her gas and electricity, but her rent too, which was ridiculous – we'd only just arrived. I had no choice though. To take my mind off how awful the place was, I took it upon myself to start sprucing the place up a bit, just so me and the kids could sit down somewhere without feeling we'd have to burn our clothes immediately after. For the best part of a whole week, it was just me and my old friend, Mr Sheen, getting down and dirty by the skirting boards. Neither Maureen nor her rat-faced kids offered to help, and even though I could barely squeeze myself in under her kitchen sink, when I got down on my back to try and clean the mouse shit that had collected beneath hers, no one even showed the slightest bit of interest, other than to say: "Oh, is that what that is? I always wondered what smell was."

At the end of each day, after I pulled off my Marigolds and put the kids to bed, I'd lie down, exhausted, under a threadbare sleeping bag we were all sharing, and rest my hands on my swollen belly. There was little Will, then no bigger than a pineapple, behaving as if he couldn't wait to get out and meet his family. It was hard not to pity him really. If I was him, and could see out through my tummy right now, at his mum and his siblings, all doing their best not to go mad in a Woking maisonette, hiding from a rag-tag mob of 'Woolyback' gangsters, I'd do everything in my power not to come out.

We lasted barely a week in Woking. From the second Billy woke me up at 6:30am with her crying, till the moment I dropped down, half-dead, later than night, mentally scarred from trying to survive another day of Maureen and her gobshitey kids, I found myself being pushed ever-closer to breaking point. Whatever the situation was back home, I knew it couldn't be any worse than this. Yes, I might have to live on eggshells, but at what point in my life had I ever not been living on those? At least if I was back home I could choose the type of eggs I'd be living on.

"That's it," I said to Billy when he rang on the eighth day. "I've had enough. I'm coming home." I'd never been this direct with Billy before, but I didn't give a monkey's how he reacted. If he wanted to punch me into the next life, that was fine, at least it would be quicker than being dragged there this way.

He drove us back himself the next day. I didn't say a word to Maureen when we left, nor leave a card thanking her for her 'hospitality'. The kids played a game of I-Spy on the way up, but other than that not a word was spoken, except when they asked if they could use the toilet in the service station.

"No, you can't play on the fruit machines," I had to add. "They're for grown-ups."

Billy was a grown-up, but you wouldn't have thought so, given what he was putting us through. This was his stupid game, not mine, and if he wanted to play gangsters with his mates that was up to him, but there was no way I was going to let my kids suffer indignity after indignity in that cramped maisonette because the man they'd just gotten used to calling "Dad" chose to live his life like a Poundland Scarface.

He got us a dog in the end. A German Shepherd that he'd managed to get off the back of a lorry. He was a skittish thing; lovable, but totally unpredictable, with eyes like a scary teddy bear. The main thing about having him was that we knew he'd be a great help if we ever did get that unwelcome knock in the middle of the night that everyone told me was coming. But it never did come. If the letterbox ever did rattle, it was either the kids playing with it, the postman shoving another bill through the door, or a ghost from the future knocking to tell me that if I could just hold on tight, *really, really* tight, and not fall apart, I'd survive all this.

But there was still a long way to go yet.

An incredibly long way.

THE SONG OF THE SHIRT

The poverty of my physical and emotional existence during this time was more than matched by the poverty of my financial one. Money was coming in, so I was told, but I didn't really know how much. If I'd have guessed, based upon what I was seeing with my own eyes, I'd have described it as more of a trickle than a flood, but only because the full amount was being held back by Billy, who structured his life in such a way as to keep me blind to 99.9% of everything he ever got up to. After a few weeks back north, things had returned pretty much to as they were before our little 'adventure' in Woking, and the whole thing soon felt no more real than a weird dream. If it wasn't for the dog, whose presence occasionally served to remind me of what Billy had insisted we kick under the carpet, I might have forgotten it had ever happened. Dave had got better and was discharged from the hospital, Billy had returned to the club, and I went back to worrying about how I was going to keep a house on the pitiful £20 he threw in my face each week. He called it 'maintenance', but God knows what I was supposed to maintain with it. Out of that I was expected to feed and clothe the kids *and* get a decent meal on the table each evening. The household bills, all in his name and never shown to me, he took care of himself out of the £200 he said the club gave him each week. Where the rest went, I have no idea, but It certainly never went towards buying the children clothes for school. If I didn't want them to suffer the same indignities I had to endure when I was their age (wearing hand-me-down hand-me-downs, for example) I'd have to come up with a plan to get more money into my pocket because, as most parents know, school uniforms don't grow on trees.

I still had some money from the car accident, which provided me with a small cushion, and there were also some benefits I was able to access – as an unmarried mother of four – but this was so meagre it wasn't difficult to see why some women in my situation took to walking the streets asking men if they were "looking for a good time." The strategy I eventually arrived at came after a friend planted a seed in my head involving 'factory seconds' – items of clothing that had failed a quality-inspection test prior to being shipped out to a retailer. Not wanting to write them off completely, the manufacturer, usually under a slightly different branding, will flog them to the public at a knock-down price. This is what factory seconds are. The margins would be small, but even if it was only a couple of quid each time, it was still better than a kick in the teeth.

The factory was in Manchester, and so that's where I started heading out to a couple of times a week whilst the kids were at school. I'd take a few bags, fill them up with stuff, jeans mostly, and then come back and start flogging. People would be happy to buy them because you wouldn't even know there was anything wrong with them. It might just be a pulled thread here, or a mis-sewn seam there, but in the high-stakes world of fashion only perfection is good enough. Birkenhead, of course, is not Paris, so a mis-sewn seam could easily be lived with if it meant people still had enough money left to pay the gas bill with at the end of the month. They'd all happily slip me a fiver for a pair of high-quality jeans that I'd picked up for three quid, and the difference of £2.00, built up over the weeks, meant I could send my kids to school in shoes with soles on them, and Christmas presents that didn't come from the local Barnardo's. As each item flew out of my hands, the wolf, whose incessant growling at the door I'd become so used to in recent years, wandered off in order to start pestering some other poor unfortunate soul.

One venture Billy Harris set up on his own, away from the club, was a pawn shop in Birkenhead. Furtive as he was, he never involved me in any part of it, but it was something he started to give a lot of his 'day' time to. I was so caught up with just trying to survive and raise my kids at the time that I put no thought into how 'legit' it might be. I just assumed it was something else for him to do in order to bring some more money in, but I didn't know anything about the historical connection between pawn shops and stolen goods, nor what such businesses could be used as fronts for. But then, I also thought being a bouncer meant just standing at doors making sure no pissheads, druggies or troublemakers got in. I barely knew what drugs even were, let alone understood the culture or lifestyles they fuelled. You probably think I'm tremendously naive, but remember what I was thrown into almost the minute I became a grown-up. I'd been to one adult party in my entire life, just one, and woke up pregnant the next morning as a result. My adult life was hijacked before I'd even had a chance to know who I really was, or what the world was about.

Once the pawn shop started doing well, and the burger vans got up and running (another of Billy's schemes) I do remember wondering why on earth he still insisted on working at the club so many evenings a week. It couldn't have been *that* enjoyable, could it? Things came a little more into focus a short while later when I was tidying up the bedrooms one day. I wasn't one for rummaging around, but I was one for keeping things tidy – one of the only ways I felt I could stay in control of things. I was cleaning around the bed when I saw a pile of papers and envelopes on the bedside table next to where Billy sleeps. They'd been dumped there, it seemed, and were very messy, so I thought I'd just give them a quick skim to see if they were important. If not, I'd chuck them out. One was a bank statement in Billy's name, but reading through it I got all confused. It didn't make sense. All those transactions, dozens of them, line after line, going right down the page. Had Billy been sent someone else's bank statement by mistake?

When I picked up that statement, I thought the financial value of both our lives could be calculated only in terms of two unit sums. Everything we bought and every bill we paid could be covered in units of ten or twenty. Only the mortgage ever went into three figures, but that was out of my hands. The single four figure number in my life was the pay-out for the accident, which still sat in my account, though it was getting smaller by the week. The statement went over onto a second page, but this only doubled my shock. Yeah, it was Billy's name all right, and there was this address. But it made no sense. Each week, going into his account, was over £2,500. I looked for the outgoings to see if what was coming in was going out too, as a way to justify to myself why he was always scrounging for money (he'd expected me to pay for the replacement door recently – at a cost of £300 – from my accident money), but there was nothing. The money was just pouring into his account and staying there.

I broached it with him as gently as I could when he got home later. But instead of giving me an explanation, he just used it as an excuse to attack me for going through his stuff. When I mentioned trust and all those things that are essential for a relationship to work, he just evaded it by saying "it's complicated," and the money wasn't really his. I didn't push it any further, because I knew he was on the point of exploding, but before the last word on the subject was said, he agreed to up my weekly maintenance to a staggeringly generous £30.00. "Wow," I thought, I can really turn our circumstances around on this.

The subject eventually went away, and I never felt comfortable asking about it again, in case he pushed my head through a window. But I did now have some ideas now as to how Billy was able to get his hands on the luxury cars he always liked to surround himself with. The "I just got it off a mate" comment he always tossed out at me whenever I asked suddenly started to sound a lot hollower than it had previously.

One thing he did get off a mate was his interest in burger vans. Kevin had been in the trade for years and wanted to try his hand at something new. The van he sold to Billy for next to nothing, and we got it out on the road straight away, hoping to keep the trade Kev had spent years building up as steady as it had always been. I don't think either of us could believe how steady that stream was, though. At public events or next to busy A-roads where there were no service stations for miles, we'd have people queuing up as far as the eye could see. And because the quality was decent, there'd be no complaints. It might not have been Afternoon Tea at The Ritz, but Afternoon Tea at The Ritz wasn't really what lorry drivers, setting off to lug a load of U-bends down to Dover, were after. On the back of all this, the van quickly turned into two vans, and then three, and because Billy didn't really want to get his hands dirty with sunflower oil or chip fat, it would be me up at the crack of dawn sorting everything out, me driving round getting all the stock together, and me coordinating the venues. And it wasn't just burgers. We expanded into other things too, finding nothing got the kids tugging at their mum's elbows like the smell of donuts at a travelling fair. "Mum, mum, can I have one, can I have one?" As a mum myself, I knew exactly what it was like.

If I didn't exactly love the early mornings, I did love meeting the people that came with it. I'd get into all sorts of conversations at the side of those roads. Sometimes a driver might share with me just a tiny snapshot of his life, but I could see from the tired, bloodshot eyes, the life beyond it: the stress of being away from home, how much he missed his kids, or the shadows he still hid from after the stint he'd done in the army. People are icebergs, I've always thought, showing just the tips of themselves, and this is what I glimpsed every day from these fascinating people as they waited for the cheese slice to melt on their quarter pounder.

"Want some sauce on that, love?"

"Go 'ed, love, yeah – just a splodge."

The money was good, but I saw very little of it. The same thoughtlessness Billy paid to his own family was not a quality that translated into his dealings with cash. Every penny had to be accounted for, and accounted for in *his* bank, not mine – though he did slip me another tenner each week for all my efforts. His share of it went towards funding the life he was living when he wasn't around me, and towards keeping himself surrounded by an endless parade of flash cars, which he'd get bored of soon enough. In that way, they were like girlfriends and children, to be enjoyed for a short time and then discarded. This is how I came to find myself in possession of the white Jag he'd been cruising around in for a year or two. He could've just given it to me as gift, but instead demanded £300 from me. I agreed, not because I wanted to drive round in a fancy car, but for the extra space it offered. Up until that point I'd been pottering around in a noisy Mini, squashing all the kids into that for the school runs. I dipped into the money from the accident to get it, not thinking that upgrading my car would make such a big impression on everyone around me.

"Oooooh, look at you with your swish, new car," my friend, Oppo, said when she saw me climbing out of if one day. So impressed was she that she asked if I wouldn't mind taking her to the registry office in it in a few weeks' time so she could marry her fiancé. "I wouldn't mind climbing out of that in my big posh frock," she said. I laughed when she asked, but she was serious, so I agreed, thinking it would be fun. Anything to help a mate. She wanted me to collect her from home, drive her to Wallasey Town Hall, and then return her, with her new husband, to the reception after. She even hired out a uniform for me, to make it look as official as possible.

I was right, it was fun; but little did I know, as I pulled up at the foot of the Town Hall that day, and helped the blushing bride out of her fairy tale 'carriage', that she wouldn't be the only one I'd be helping out of it. There'd be more once word got round. And in no time, it soon did, to Lenny, the boss of Fleet Autos in Rock Ferry, who was married to Brenda, a friend of mine. Lenny already had a wedding car business, but he often struggled to meet the demands made by some of his customers. Quite often they'd require more cars than he was able to supply, or a bunch of weddings would fall on the same day, and he'd have to turn one down. So, when Brenda told him that I now had a Jag, a stylish white XJ, he asked if I'd help him out from time to time.

It was so lovely to play a part in what was, for most people, the best day of their lives, and I loved seeing how connected people could be together as husband and wife. As I'd drive the happy couple from the church, I'd catch glimpses of them in the back seat, holding hands and cuddling up, whispering excitedly about the kind of life they were planning to have together. It was infectious, and as I watched them kiss, and saw the groom's hand go up to caress the face of his new bride, I'd try to imagine what it must feel like to share your life with someone who, not five minutes after shoving a ring on your finger, isn't telling you to "shut the fuck up" with his hand around your throat

At the end of the first one I did for Lenny, I found myself with an extra £120 in my pocket. Two more of those and I'd have made the price of the car back *and* have enough to feed the kids for a week. That wasn't to be sniffed at, which is why I did no sniffing at all when Billy invested in his flashiest car yet, a Beauford, which he said I'd be able to use to take wedding bookings with. Beaufords are kit cars, usually assembled by the buyer at home, but the one Billy acquired had already been assembled. If you can't picture what a Beauford looks like, just think of any gangster film you've ever seen with Al Capone in. They're stylish with a capital 'S', full of swirls and grace, and when people see one, they find it impossible not to stare. Perfect wedding cars in other words. When it came into our possession, word-of-mouth spread fast, and then even faster once I started turning up with it at wedding fairs, where I could distribute flyers and get talking to people who felt their own special day might be just that little bit more special with a touch of *The Godfather* about it. The producers of *Brookside* must've thought so too, for they rang me up one time and asked if they could feature the car in one of their storylines.

What this extra work did allow me to do was start saving a little bit. I'd never been a spendthrift – largely for the fact that I'd never had an opportunity to become one – so the habit of spending money on non-essential items just wasn't in me. It was nice that I could finally buy a few pretty things for the house, without having to sacrifice something else, but it was a constant battle trying to keep what I did have out of Billy's reach. Each time I did get some money I'd divide it into small amounts for essentials, such as repairwork on the cars, or for tax and insurance, or for birthdays, and I had it worked out to the penny. The rest I saved, and thank God I did, because the cushion I needed it to serve as I had to use on a couple of occasions in the days ahead; times when, if I hadn't had something to fall back on, I would have plunged through the thin gauze that supports us in this life, and come out right in the middle of the next.

I'LL HUFF AND I'LL PUFF

I don't think doctors are allowed to go to the police to report instances of spousal abuse. Nor would it be ethical for them to make any explicit judgements about a patient based on their lifestyle choices, but they can advise against it with a raised eyebrow or two. The one who examined me when I was with Billy, who told me I'd be dead if I carried on living the way I was, knew exactly the dangers I was subjecting myself to. Everything he determined about the plight I was in he was able to read from the map of bruises on my body, the shifting islands of distress that spoke of squalls and hurricanes that continually passed over me, but never seemed to go away. You can only tell a medical professional you walked into a door so many times before they know you're lying through your broken teeth.

But again, what choice did I have? If I'd tried to leave I knew it would've been the end of me. Soldiers on a battlefield must feel something similar when their CO orders them to do something they know to be suicidal. It's far less hassle to give up and die sometimes, isn't it, than to resist the order you know will put you in the ground.

I'd settled into a sort of comfortable numbness with Billy. I knew what triggered him, and what didn't, and so as long as I avoided pushing his buttons, there was no reason why we couldn't go on like this forever. For the children, you understand. One thing I've not been able to put across successfully in this account, and will always struggle to, is just how much the kids doted on him. They knew how monstrous he could be, but also how much of a joker, and this was the part of him they would work towards trying to bring out. Billy was an expert manipulator, the way so many bullies are, and he did everything he could to undermine my relationship with my own kids. When alone with them, he would tell them things about me that were totally untrue, building up the lies layer by layer, so that the children had more reservations about my character than they did about his. He was so good at it that he was able to convince, not just the children we had *together*, but those I had with John and Chris too, that I was the world's worst mum,

After about a decade of this, the comfortable numbness that I'd learn to live with became just a numbness, and the comfort just plain old pain. With the children getting older, and becoming less dependent on the financial and emotional support that can only be provided by two parents, I started to consider a future without him. It was only a distant dream at first, but as time went on, I chose to bring it nearer and nearer until the blurred outline it had in the dream took on sharper features. Eventually, I could make out an image: it was me, happy, relaxed and content, a picture I didn't even recognise at first because no such thing existed in reality.

The 'out' came – as it had so many times in the past – in the guise of another woman. It wasn't his ex (she'd long ago disappeared up some other drainpipe), but someone he'd met locally, possibly at the club. "Let me sort you out a lift," he'd probably said to her. However it had happened, he'd built up a whole other life with her, as distinctive in its own way as the one he'd built up with me. The late nights, or the nights he didn't come home, he'd been with her, in a bungalow he'd bought, using money *I'd* sweated to bring in from the burger vans and the wedding cars. Of all the insults Billy inflicted upon me over the years, this was by far the most hurtful. It sounds twisted, I know, but I was heartbroken. All I'd endured from this rat of a man. All I'd put up with so that our children could feel they had a degree of security, when all I really wanted to do was jump off a bridge. I wanted him gone. I was too bone tired to offer him any kind of ultimatum, I just wanted him out of my life.

And then, just like that, he was.

Sort of.

He left with barely a whimper. It took him almost no time to fill his suitcase. He stood over the bed, his head just a few inches away from the ceiling, stuffing his things into it. It looked like a vanity case when he tucked it under his giant arm and marched down the stairs. I watched him tramp away through the net curtains. He didn't look back, only forward, and I did too – his eyes to the bungalow up the road where his slut was waiting, and me to whatever came next. My hands were shaking, but I knew they'd steady in a while. What was I going to tell the kids?

That night, as I slept alone, it was the first night I'd known for sure that my partner was lying with another woman. Were they laughing as they screwed? I'd love to write here that it didn't hurt, but it did. It was crushing. All failure is, but this was doubly so. In the darkened room, as I tossed and turned, I tried to push out all the negative feelings and swap them with positive ones, but the only one I could settle on was the fact that I'd survived.

But had I really? I didn't even know myself anymore. In 13½ years I'd changed so much that the woman in the mirror, who appeared before me when I stepped in front of it, seemed unable to look at me. If I smiled, she seemed late to follow, as if she didn't want to copy the actions of someone who'd allowed herself to put up with so much from someone so unworthy.

A week later I heard the key going in the door. Wondering who it could be, I stepped into the hall, and noticed a shadow appear, far bigger than any of the children's. It was him. He was back before he'd even had a chance to get through all the socks he'd stuffed into his suitcase. The novelty it seems – as it often does with couples who try to legitimise an illicit affair – had worn off. The children were delighted, of course, and hoovered up their dad's affection like Rice Krispies on a nursery floor, but I felt my heart instantly freeze up again. Why had he come back? The question didn't linger in the air for all that long, because he was gone again in no time. Barely had his got his socks back in the drawer before he was taking them out again. The first night he was back he spoke to her for ages on the phone, pretending he wanted privacy, but making sure I could hear every word. Every day for a week this went on, with him flying to the phone every time it rang in case it was her. "Yes ma'am, no ma'am, three bags fuckin' full ma'am,"

It's hard to describe the reality of that week. There were so many feelings flying around, and so many games being played, that it was difficult to know what was what. I was clearly the put-upon clown in this ridiculous circus, but she was the ringmaster. Whenever she cracked the whip and said "Jump", Billy would spring up like a sea lion and bark: "How high?"

When he left that second time, it didn't hurt as much because by then I'd seen where I fared in the sliding scale of his affections (right at the bottom), but the children howled, not mature enough to register that all of this was just a big game that their dad was playing with all of us. My "lack of compassion" allowed Billy to reframe the slow unravelling of our family as something I was responsible for, and so the children dutifully took up arms against me, and became hostile to *me* for giving their dad no choice but to pack his bags.

I don't like swearing, but it was all so fucked up, and I felt about as in control of the situation then as I did when I came off Chris's bike on the wet A-road all that time ago and went somersaulting through the air. But at least my destination was certain back then. Gravity ensured that. What made my destination more unpredictable this time was that just a few months earlier, when I was really trying my best to give it one last push with Billy, I must've pushed a bit too hard because, as a result, it meant I had no choice but to go into the shed and dig out the pram one last time.

Shame really. I'd been hoping to give it to the charity shop.

It was probably a mistake to ask Georgina's husband to change the locks. But he was the only person I knew who'd do it and not charge the earth for it. 'Mates rates' they call them. It was necessary, no question about that, because if I was to build up any kind of life away from Big Billy then I needed to feel secure in my own home.

Things had disintegrated even further after his last walk out. Taken in by his lies, the children had turned on me so viciously that I was forced to march over to the slut's house and beg him to come back. I was on my knees at one point, literally on them, begging him to come home. He didn't exactly spit on me, but the way told me to "fuck off" whilst I was down there left me in little doubt that we'd reached the end of our road. In the time it took me to climb to my feet to make the undignified trek back home, my heart had turned to stone. He was dead to me from that moment on. And nobody wants a zombie turning up at their door with a key. That's why I rang Georgina.

"How's your fella fixed for Friday?"

She probed, and I answered.

"Billy's stopped giving me money and I can't afford to get anyone out."

Gina has a way of getting you to reveal more than you want to. I didn't want to tell her that because Billy had stopped giving me maintenance I was really struggling again, but it just fell out. Predictably enough, she was unable to keep this to herself and rang Billy up to give him what she called a "piece of her mind" but really it would've been just stir things up.

Billy was easily stirred though. He was like a wasp on that score, and his response when someone started poking around near his nest was to rise up and start stinging the hell out of them. So when I heard the loud banging on the back door the day after I'd poured my heart out to Gina, I knew what was coming. Why didn't I keep my bloody mouth shut?

My friend's daughter, Joanne was in the house at the time. She was looking after the kids because, with just a month to go before little Stephanie was due, I was struggling to get around. Joanne was amazing; she loved the girls and didn't mind helping out at all. When the banging didn't stop, Joanne, looking a bit ashen faced, ran in to tell me, but I nearly knocked her over trying to get to the door to see what the hell was going on. It sounded like it was about to splinter.

"I'm coming, I'm coming," I shouted, hoping I could get to the door before his hand came through it like Jack Nicholson's in that film about the hotel.

Reaching up, I turned the latch, just the tiniest bit, and before I knew what was what, I was lying on my back with the kids screaming over me. The door had exploded open, knocking me backwards, almost into the children. Pain shot through me, from my face – were the door had struck it – to my ankle, which I'd twisted as I landed. But it wasn't any of these I was worried about. It was my stomach. There wasn't much time to think really, but I remember my children – just blurred silhouettes above me – howling hysterically. And over them, something else:

"You are not getting a fuckin' penny out of me."

From the corner of my eye I saw Joanne shaking in the corner, unable to believe what she was witnessing. "You hear me, you daft bitch?" A siren of screeches erupted from the kids, and I was about to tell them that everything was going to be okay, but just as I opened my mouth to speak, the air was sucked out of me in an instant.

"NO, DADDY!" I heard a chorus of this.

Then again. Another explosion, as my spine nearly snapped.

"I said, do ye fuckin' hear me?"

I curled up even more, tighter, tighter, into the smallest ball I could make, so that his kicks – which rained down on me in a fury – could not get through to what I was trying to protect. That innocent life inside me. Beyond that, all I had to help me were the kids' screams and my prayers, but I'm not sure they'd offer much protection from the steel-capped boots that were being pile-driven into my back.

I tried to tell him that I hadn't asked for any money, and I wasn't expecting any money, but I couldn't get any air into my lungs. The kicks just came and came and came, pushing my body further towards the wall and my mind towards blackness. That doctor had been right after all, I thought, I was going to die at the hands of this man. The only thing he'd gotten wrong was the timeframe; he'd said six months, and here I was years later. When I was dead, I'd make sure to come back as a ghost and tell him he was way off.

And then it stopped. The tyrant, puffing heavily and tucking his shirt back in to his shiny black trousers, slunk away, like a fat rat, back through the shattered door frame, to the lair he shared with his slut.

I felt like I was under water, beneath a layer of ice. Figures moved above me.

"Muuuum, are you okay?"

I opened my fingers, just enough to test that I still could. Nothing moved beneath them. I sent out a prayer, one last one, to the Creator. It's all I had really. "Please let the baby be all right."

By the time Sue, Joanne's mum, appeared a few minutes later, the children had gathered around me and were pleading with me to get up. God knows what I looked like at that particular moment, but it was enough to make Sue cover her face. She looked like that painting. The Scream.

"Oh God," she gasped. "What's that bastard done now?" She crouched down next to me and put her hand on my side. "Nice and slow," she said, helping me sit up. I leant against her shoulder and the tears poured out of me. I know she wanted to say, "There-there, everything's gonna be okay," but from the way she looked down at my belly, I could tell she didn't want to commit herself. As my spine let out another little yelp of pain, my tears fell onto Sue's shoulder, forming a stain on her creased yellow shirt. It felt like I was being sawn in half. Is this how it felt to be a magician's assistant when his most famous trick goes wrong?

"There-there," Sue said, patting my back. But that was all she could commit herself to.

GOLIGHTLY INTO THE NIGHT

My twin-sister died at birth. I don't know how many breaths she took, if any at all, so don't know if she got to drink down any of the precious life-giving air that kept me, at just over 2lbs, able to battle through the trauma of entering the world. Nor do I know if we were identical or not, but her premature death meant the delivery team didn't have to put a dab of nail polish on either of our fingers to tell us apart. They had a much better way of doing that: I was the one who was still breathing.

I also never got to know what name she'd been given, but the one they gave me was Angela. That's 'Angel' with an 'a' after it.

Eighteen years later, when I stepped into a road near the Strand, right in front of a car spinning out of control across a roundabout, I like to think it was her that pulled me out of the way. I hadn't seen the car myself, unlike the woman who ran up to me straight after to help me up.

"I could've sworn you were a gonna, then, love," she said, as if she had just seen me rise up from the dead.

I also like to believe it was my sister who whispered into my ear that I should drive immediately to the nearest garage in the car I'd bought off my next-door neighbour the day before. Each wheel, the mechanic told me, had only been held on with a single wingnut, and not even tightly.

"I think the angels were watching over you," he said, when he took a look at it.

I didn't even know what a wingnut was.

Sue didn't see her mother leave. Nor did any of her siblings. But they heard the door close, quietly, as if someone was creeping out. She was gone for about an hour, she recalls, and must've taken the baby with her because she couldn't hear her anymore. That was unusual. She was a teary baby, always crying, and so it was noticeable when she wasn't around. Its cot stood empty too, and the blanket that had been kept in it with her, for comfort, that had also gone.

When her mother returned, she seemed quite upset, but did her best to hide it. She went into the kitchen for a short while and closed the door. Then she came out and gathered the rest of her children around her in the front room, dabbing at her cheek with a tissue. She didn't want to cry, Sue could tell, but sometimes you just can't help yourself. "Better out than in," her nan had told her. Or was that about something else?

"Where's the baby?" one of her sisters asked before Sue herself could. Her mother's eyes reddened, and she turned away, the tissue not much good. She should've got a hankie.

"She's ... she's gone, love ... she's ... gone up to Heaven."

She'd probably rehearsed the line a thousand times, but still couldn't get it out in one go. The children let this sink in, and their mother watched them. No one spoke. Their eyes just fell to the ground, then they started to cry, and their mother did their best to soothe them. But who was soothing her?

Poor thing. The children had known the baby had been ill. "She's tiny," they'd said when they first saw her. Maybe too tiny. "The same weight as a bag of sugar", their mum had said. But they didn't know it had remained so, even after it had made up the weight and been brought home. They hadn't even had a chance to say goodbye.

The story changed over the years.

The baby hadn't died, but as Sue grew, and her siblings grew, their mother trusted them enough to tell them the truth: that she'd been very short of money at the time and had arranged for the baby to become adopted. There weren't as many hoops to jump through then, so it was quite easy to arrange. At first, if didn't matter whether they knew who'd adopted her, but as they grew, and the story changed again, they were trusted enough to be told that little 'Angela' had been given to a couple up the road, a nice couple who had lots of children and were very experienced at looking after kids. But they knew, from listening to all the arguments, that it wasn't really about the money.

When we met many years later, Val told me all this. We were both grown-up at the time, with families of our own, and had by then made our own share of mistakes, some bigger than others. She remembered everything about her childhood in Bootle, and lots about mine too, even remembering the few times they'd overlapped. Once, when I was about seven or eight, and she was a bit older, we'd played together in the road, a skipping game, and she told me that we were sisters. "Real sisters," she said, when I told her that friends are often likened to sisters. "No, not like that," she said, spinning the skipping rope over my head with her friend. "My mum's your mum, but my dad's not."

This was fine. I already had plenty of sisters, even if I didn't like most of them, but they weren't as yucky as my brothers.

"You were called Angela," she said. I liked that. An 'angel' with an 'a' after it. "And you weighed the same as a bag of sugar."

I was six weeks old when Patricia wrapped me in my blanket and snuck me out of the house. By the time she was dabbing at her cheek with a tissue and telling the rest of her children that I'd gone up to heaven, I was lying in my new basket, screaming my head off – the latest headache in the lives of Olive and Richie Guy, who were wondering, not for the last time, how to make me shut up. I wasn't yet a victim of their neglect, wilful or otherwise, but as the crowd of heads appeared over the edge of my basket, as they must've, I found myself coming face-to-face with the characters who would perform alongside me in the sinister shadow play that would make up the first eighteen years of my life. I don't doubt for a second that as Richie told me to shut my cake-hole for the very first time that afternoon, he was already wondering how best to spend the money he'd be getting from the government for adopting me.

Olive and Richie had known the Blacks, although not all that well. They lived close enough to be familiar with one another in passing, but not enough to exchange cake recipes or anything like that. The Blacks hadn't been in the area all that long. Patricia had arrived first, with her kids and a Mediterranean tan, and then their father, Freddie, had trundled along sometime later. He was an engineer in the Navy, and they'd been stationed abroad in Malta for a couple of years, a fact that must've made them stand out, if just a little, in the grim terraced houses of soulless Bootle.

Freddie hadn't wanted me. A man's man, like Billy Harris, he didn't really want to take on the responsibility of raising another man's kid, which is exactly what I was. It takes a very strong man to rise up to that challenge, and Freddie certainly wasn't that. Physically, yes; emotionally, nowhere near. Whilst he and Patricia had been stationed out in Malta, living on the barracks, she'd met a charming American named Ernest Golightly, who knew an attractive woman when he met one, and a caged heart when it needed setting free.

"Anyone ever tell you you look like Elizabeth Taylor?" he asked her.

He promised her more smiles, many smiles, and threw them at her like confetti, and she did what anyone in her position would do: she held out her hands and caught as many of them as she could. She wore one when he took her for a meal, something Freddy never did; and when he escorted her to the cinema, which Freddy expressed no interest in; and when they held hands, discreetly, she must've felt the kind of thrill that only the switchback rides at Pleasureland in Southport had ever given her. That thrill would've become so overwhelming that when the hand-holding became something else, she would've given herself wholeheartedly, not wanting him to go as lightly as his name suggested he might.

She had no need to fear on that score.

When 'man's-man' Freddie found all this out, as he was always going to (the evidence becoming harder to disguise by the day) he was forced to rethink everything and made the decision to leave Malta. Shame was a big thing back then, and 'fallen' women often had to be covered in a blanket and hidden from sight, else the sin of their appalling 'crimes' be on display for all to see. Freddie didn't want that, and so, to temper the desires of his own wayward wife, he sought out a new posting that would take her as far away from her dashing *inamorato* – and his shame – as possible. He brought them back to the UK and to sunny, shiny Bootle. The Land That Trams Forgot.

Patricia arrived first, pregnant and miserable, with her still-suntanned children in tow. Back in England, she started to go by her proper name again, her middle name, 'Patricia' not sounding as exotic on the streets of Bootle as it did back in Malta. From now on, she would be plain, old Dorothy again, though people would shorten it to 'Dodo'. Freddy followed months later, having wound up his affairs in Malta, and set about building up the new life that would erase all the pain and all the deceit that had led them there. The new house and the new school would be easy to adjust to, as would the new barracks Freddie would be travelling to each day, but there was one part of their past that wouldn't be so easy to escape from, a tiny, inescapable reality that was growing bigger by the day under Dodo's mohair jumpers.

When I balled my eyes out in that grotty pub toilet in Birkenhead, with Chris still sipping at his beer in the saloon outside, eighteen years had passed. The Beatles had met and split up; the moon had been dreamt of and conquered; and Ian Brady had met Myra Hindley, written a million headlines with her, and both were now a decade into their life sentences. And through it all, I'd been living my lie of a life, my fiction, whose rootless narrative began as a result of Freddie Black's inability to show the tiniest bit of respect for his wife.

"Anyone ever tell you you look like Elizabeth Taylor?"

Once I'd finally re-composed myself (fresh lippy and bit of concealer) and exited those toilets to re-join Chris, I'd changed. I was literally not the same person anymore. Even my name was different. By the time I sat down, I'd already determined that what I'd most like in the world was to meet my mum. My *real* mum. I wanted to know her, so I could finally get to know who I was. I didn't care about the adoption, nor about the circumstances that led to it. Who was I to cast judgement on what made people make decisions like that? Everyone had their problems, and I knew that any number of things could've happened to make my mum give me up. For all I knew, she might've been fourteen and raped by her teacher in a classroom; or a Princess who'd been courted by a footman and fallen pregnant during a single moment of passion in the stables. But it didn't matter. I just wanted to see her, because I knew that once I did, as difficult as it is to describe, I knew for sure that my life would come into focus.

For the Guys, my arrival was just the beginning of their headaches, because it prompted an epic battle with the Catholic Church that lasted the best part of a year. But in case you think there was anything righteous in this, particularly on the part of the Guys, let me stop you right there. For Olive and Richie my presence was about money, nothing more.

And for the church? Well, you can be your own judge on that. Born out of wedlock, as I had been, the Catholic Church had expressed a desire to raise me as a Poor Sister of Nazareth, with nuns in charge of raising me in one of their houses. Back then, of course, nothing was known about the child abuse that would, in later years, become almost synonymous with the institution – which had existed since 1861. But let's face it, how much worse could it have been for me if they *had* managed to get their hands on me? I was damned if they did, and damned if they didn't.

After a lengthy battle through the courts, however, it was the Guys who eventually won out, with the priest in charge moodily conceding that – because I appeared so unhealthy – I was soon likely to follow my twin-sister into God's eternal embrace anyway.

The morning after that drink with Chris all those years later, I confronted Olive and Richie about all this, letting them know what Chris had let slip. Their eyes didn't glisten with "I-knew-this-day-would-come" sentimentality, they just rolled them as if to say, "Oh, for fuck's sake, who blabbed?" It was clear they'd had no intention of ever telling me the truth, and I can barely describe the hostility they expressed, especially Olive, who lost her rag completely when I told her I wanted to visit my real mother.

In truth, I wanted to do it right there and then, just turn around and walk away and begin a new life with my own flesh and blood, no matter that that flesh and blood had pushed me away as soon as I was born. But that didn't matter to me, I would've forgiven that in a second. Life had gifted me with an empathetic understanding of the human condition, and that came hand-in-hand with an ability to forgive. I didn't need any church to teach me that, it was already in me. And it's that same, almost debilitating level of understanding that allowed me to see just how much the desire to see my real mum would've hurt Olive. For all her faults, and they were legion, she had raised me, and I owed her something. Didn't I?

"If you go and see that woman," she hissed, "I want nothing to do with you ever again." Her eyes were so cold when she said it. I can still see them now, red with hostility. A dragon's eyes. "Do you understand me, Christina?" If ever there was a time for flipping the table and telling her to go to hell, now was it, but I just couldn't bring myself to do it. I knew the future was an untraveled road, and I still had a long way to go along it yet. There were plenty of things to be found on the way, and one of those things might just be a loosening of the strings that assurances like this were tied up in. People got softer in their old ages, didn't they? Mellower.

With that in mind, I gritted my teeth and pushed out the word.

"Yes," I said.

"Yes *what?*" she demanded

"I promise not to go and see her."

Dorothy died before I was ever able to make contact. She was 48, thirteen years younger than I am now. To her early grave she took all the answers to every question I'd ever had about who I was. Who I am. Who I could be. Admittedly there weren't that many before I'd popped out with Chris for that drink, but they'd built up in the years after that, increasing by the bucket load as I met and married John, had my children, endured the nightmare of

Billy Harris, all in the belief that one day, Olive might climb down from her high horse and allow me to go and give my real mum the cuddle to end all cuddles. And to tell her that I bore her no grudge. But because Olive herself had been raised by vipers, and saw poison in everything, she recognised my desire to reconnect with my real mum only as a direct threat to her. God only knows what she thought was going to happen.

The years passed and I kept travelling along that road, thinking up and filing away relevant questions in a box marked "Things to ask my real mum" if ever the chance presented itself. The box was still there years later, in some forgotten part of my brain, even after I'd found out she'd passed away, and although it was covered in two or three inches of dust, not a single question I'd filed away there had been forgotten when it finally came time to retrieve it, not to show Dorothy (or Patricia), but to show her daughter, Val. My sister.

"She never stopped thinking about you," she told me, the words brushing aside the curtain of tears on my cheeks. "Not for one minute."

The sense of loss I felt at being told this was equal to the pain I'd experienced when I first heard she'd passed. That I could've gone to her, spoken with her, held her hand when she was dying, told her that I forgave her, but *chose* not to because I didn't want to break my promise to Olive, is something I don't think I'll ever forgive myself for. It still hurts now. But what makes it all the more painful is that shortly after Dorothy had died, Olive turned her back on me anyway, and stopped speaking to me. After that, she barely said another word to me whilst she was alive, except to criticise me. She died a broken and bitter woman, with the poison she'd spouted throughout her life still on her lips. So even if I had run straight from her kitchen at eighteen-years old, and raced straight to Dorothy, through the early morning traffic, with my bags packed, and shouted out "Here I am, Mum!", it would have made no difference to her anyway. Once I'd grown up and left home, and stopped being someone she could get money out of, I was always going to be little more to Olive than a burden, and someone she couldn't have despised more. She just needed an excuse to start her campaign of hatred.

And yet, for all the pain this subject causes me now, this heart-rending scenario does have its silver linings; for I discovered from Sue, who I got to know very well in the years after I met her, that I *did* meet my real mother, and more than once. I even spoke to her, many times, if only to tell her how much a packet of butter was, or to tell her on what shelf she could find the bread. That striking lady who used to come into the shop when I was grow-ing up, the elegant dark-haired lady, with the beautiful features, with a touch of Elizabeth Taylor about her; the one who'd wait around at the back of the shop and not approach the counter until I was all alone so that she could engage me in conversation with a big smile on my face? That was my mother.

"She'd watch you," Sue told me. "Every day. She'd watch you going to school, and when you finished school she'd stand by the gates and watch you come out. You probably just assumed it was someone else's mum, but it wasn't. She was always watching you. And she never stopped loving you."

"You're better than all this, Christina," she'd said to me.

Am I, Mum? … Am I really?

Even thinking about this now, finding the words to navigate my thoughts around it, explain it, I find upsetting. All the opportunities we'd had, if only she'd have taken one of them. But she wasn't allowed, that was part of the deal she'd made when arranging for the adoption. She was never allowed to reveal who she was to me. If she had, I can assure you of this, every single page in this book would be different. There might not even be a story, or if there was, it would probably be a good deal more upbeat.

"I'm your mum. Your *real* mum."

If she'd said those words to me, those exact words, I'd have been out from behind that counter and in her arms before Richie could've even slipped his belt off to hit me with it.

"And you're my Angela. That's 'angel' with an 'a' after it."

GOOD SENSE OF HUMOUR

I didn't go to the hospital after Billy's vicious assault because I didn't want to leave my kids alone. Besides, there was now a gaping hole in the back door, and I'd need to get that sorted out. They'd all taken an age to settle back down (understandably, perhaps) but they did eventually, in front of the TV, watching *Dogtanian*. As they sipped on the beakers of milk I'd given them, Sue's husband stepped in and kindly offered to help with the door. He nailed up a piece of plywood he'd had lying around, and whilst he was doing that, I slunk upstairs to ball my eyes out in the bathroom. Sitting on the toilet with my make-up everywhere, I lifted my top and looked down at my stomach, all pink and swollen. I could see the light blue veins spider-webbing out across my pale skin. The pain in my back was getting worse every second as it continued to respond to the series of shocks it had just suffered. Obviously, my spine was sending out signals of distress to my brain, but were those signals drowning out those coming from somewhere else inside me? God, I hoped not.

Downstairs, I heard nails being hammered into the doorframe; then, beneath my fingers...

Movement.

Under my hand.

Just the slightest. Was it a trapped nerve? *Oh, please, please, please.*

Then more, a little shift in the skin. Something was definitely stirring. Was it another sign of distress, or was the baby just turning itself around to make itself more comfortable? *Come on, come on, come on!* There was no blood in my pee, that was a good sign surely? – so I had reason to hold on to at least a shred of hope. And that's all I had until I went to see my doctor the next day.

"I fell down some stairs" I told him as I lifted my top and turned towards the wall. He looked at me in the mirror over the top of his glasses like I was mad. "What stairs?" I could see him thinking, "The Spanish fucking Steps?"

In the end, Stephanie came out beyond perfect. Just the sight of her beautiful little face made me forget how horrible everything else was, of what I'd been reduced to by that monster of a man who my kids called Dad. Any thoughts I'd recently had of driving to the top of a high car park and throwing myself off were immediately pushed away as I fell back into the routine of raising my gorgeous daughter. Babies have a way of bringing you back to yourself, I've always found. Maybe it's all the hormones flying around, that desire to protect and nurture. Whatever it was, I started to feel better about myself and noticed, after a while, that my heart started asking questions again, questions that, over the years, my body had forgotten the answers to – if it ever knew them at all. Then one day, brimming with love for Stephanie and all my other wonderful kids, I noticed I had a little left over for myself, just a cup full, but it was enough. And so, when I was flicking through the local paper one day and came upon an ad for something called Two's Company, I reached for a pen and circled it. It described itself as an Introduction Agency, which sounded interesting, as it matched people with similar interests together. If I found myself with a couple of spare minutes over the next week or so I might think about ringing them, just to see what happens. It would probably lead to nothing, but it would be fun to find out.

Before the internet arrived and made dating websites as common as Costa coffee shops, people used to meet through the classified section of their local newspaper. Young people didn't, they still met in pubs and clubs and the like, but when you were past all that, or couldn't be doing with all that palaver, this is what you'd do. People (men mostly, but not always) would scribble down a few words about themselves and pay for them to appear in the next day's paper. It didn't cost much, and you didn't have to be Charles Dickens, but if you could avoid sounding like a serial killer that would probably stand you in good stead. Some people went for something witty, whilst others would aim for something romantic – not always successfully it must be said. The trick was to come across as genuine, which was quite hard when you only had three or four sentences to sell yourself with. For that reason, most would toss in a bunch of terms like GSOH, WAA, LTR, so they'd have more space in which to show off their dazzling wit. Anyone interested would then use the box number at the foot of each ad to leave a message, along with their phone number so they could be contacted. It was a bit like *Blind Date* really, only less cheesy, but if you could get through it without feeling too jaded, there was a chance that Cupid's arrow might hit you eventually – hopefully not in the eye!

As it turned out, I did find myself with a couple of minutes to spare that week, and when I did, I dug out the paper from the rack, flicked straight to the ad (which I'd circled), and then picked up the phone. "Hello, my name's Christina, but friends call me Chrissy ..." I got quite into it actually. Over the next few months, I rang about thirty and they all rang me back. Those I clicked with over the phone, and looked smart and sensible, and didn't stammer too badly, or tell off-colour jokes, I decided to meet up with for a drink. Some were overly forward, some were very shy, but on the whole, most were very nice. None of them struck me as potential Peter Sutcliffes or Ted Bundys, which was a relief, but behind the words I did notice a pattern that many of them were unable to disguise: they'd all been let down in relationships and were still nursing their wounds. But who was I to judge?

All except for Mike. He was different from the get-go and, strangely for a man of his age, didn't appear to have any baggage at all; or if he did, he hid it well. He didn't even have any children, which surprised me, as that was the biggest thing the rest of us had in common; our kids. He was also extremely polite; for example, when he pulled my seat out for me in the restaurant during our first meal together, I nearly fell over in shock. I'd only ever seen that done in films. Normally, if a man was reaching for a chair it was to throw at my head. *Nice touch*, I thought. He remained polite throughout the entire meal too, wiping his mouth with a napkin after every bite, and *sipping* at his wine rather than throwing it down his neck. And he wasn't unattractive either.

I didn't want sex. I just wanted company, *male* company – pheromones, aftershave, the toothbrush in the bathroom, and all the rest of it. If you go deeper, you might view that as me wanting to learn to trust men; to know that when they looked into my eyes it was *me* they were seeing, Christina Black, not just a springboard to a bouncy bed and an open pair of legs. Mike recognised that straight away, and though all the physical bruises had faded by the time we sat down together and made our first toast, "To new beginnings", he saw the ones that might never fade, the ones deep down inside. But if they made him wince, he didn't show it.

We saw each other regularly after that first date, for drinks and meals, and the friendship that was building between us grew stronger by the day. I didn't want to pressure myself into exploring any deeper feelings I may or may not have for him, because what we had right then felt right for that time. If Mike had stirred up greater passions inside me, would I have still kept the other side of my bed empty? I don't know. I was still healing and, for the first time ever, enjoyed being me, discovering who I was. But it was a process, I suppose, that had to result in *something* being created at the end, that's just the way relationships work. When people brush up against each other they create friction, friction creates sparks, and sparks lead to fires. The first indication I had from Mike that he might be wanting to warm himself by the heat of what we were creating together came in the form of a question, which he asked when we were out enjoying another meal. We sipped at our wine, dabbed our lips with our napkins (yes, I was doing it too by now) and then out it popped:

"How would you like to go to America with me?"

I nearly spat my wine out.

"America?"

"The big landmass between Canada and Mexico. You can't miss it!"

Unless you count Wales, I'd never been abroad before. People like me didn't get to go on planes and hop across the Atlantic. That was for people who went on *3-2-1* with Ted Rogers and won the jackpot, or whose husbands were solicitors, or in finance – not exactly the kind of circles I moved in then. There was no obvious pressure placed on me by Mike to accept, but he was able to convince me that there was no hidden agenda involved. He just wanted to take me away somewhere nice so we could have some time alone. To his credit, he'd been nothing but gallant the whole time I'd known him, so there was no reason to expect this would change simply because the scenery did. And with that in mind, I accepted. As the date crept nearer, I arranged for a babysitter to come round and look after the kids. She would live-in for the time I was away, take care of all their meals, and make sure the smaller ones didn't run out in front of any lorries. And as she was doing that, I would do my best to give Mike and I some time to explore what exactly it was we had together – if anything. Who knew what would happen away from all the stress of our usual lives?

Then Phil rang, and everything changed.

There was something about Phil's voice. When I listened to him talk, I was hearing so much more than what he was saying. He didn't sound in any way needy, which made me realise that Mike did. Nor did it sound desperate, and it was only when I compared it to Mike's that I could tell the difference. And something else. Phil made me laugh. No one else had done that. Not ever. Mike made me think, he made me smile, but he didn't make me laugh.

I'd contacted Phil ages ago, through the same classifieds, but he hadn't got back to me straight away. I never asked why. I told him immediately that I'd met someone, but I was quick to point out that I wasn't in a relationship with this person. Maybe that was bad of me, but I had such a good feeling about him I didn't want to close the door before I'd seen what he was selling. Still, I felt it would be wrong to pull out of the holiday with Mike because every-thing had been arranged and paid for by this point. Besides, we were only going as friends, weren't we? I wasn't his wife, or his fiancé – we'd never even slept together – and he was under no illusions that I would ever become so.

Being a successful businessman, (just how much of one we'll get to shortly), Phil was good at talking people into things. By the time I was hanging up the phone after our first chat, I found myself wanting to speak to him again. He must've felt the same because he rang back the next day and we spoke for even longer. I picked up the phone and we dived straight back in from where we'd left off. At the end of that conversation it felt inevitable that we were going to meet up, and so when he asked, I felt no guilt at all when I agreed. I felt like I'd known him for years. This was just a few days before Mike and I were due to go away, but there I was, sitting down for a drink with Phil in the swankiest wine bar in town.

Phil was twenty years older than me, but didn't look it. His smile kept him young, and it was a look that never seemed to leave him, even when he was being serious. He didn't want to 'fix' me, as Mike seemed keen to, he just wanted to allow me to be me, and before we'd even got to our second glass of wine I could see the huge difference between the two. Mike thought of me as broken, but Phil didn't. He just thought I needed a bit of oil.

It was his laugh that did it. As soon as I heard it bubble out of him, and saw the effect it had on a room, I knew that he was someone I could make more time for in my life. And wanted to. What I didn't do though was two-time people, and I told him this. I was committed to going away with Mike, and wasn't going to let him down at the eleventh hour. I think he respected me all the more for being so honest, but just from how I approached the subject he could see how conflicted I was about the whole thing. He thought for a moment and then reached into his jacket pocket and pulled out a small silver holder.

"You're going away to a foreign country," he said, placing the holder down on the table in front of him, "with a man you barely know." He opened the holder and from it withdrew a business card which he placed down on the tablecloth and slid towards me. "I don't think you understand what can go wrong." The card had his name on it and a swish logo and looked very expensive to produce, but it was the address that struck me most. "That's my office in Charlotte," he said. "I'll be there for much of next week. If anything goes wrong while you're away, you just call that number and I'll come and get you." I had to hold my jaw in place to stop it from dropping open. I couldn't believe he was serious. I picked up the card to study it. You'd do *that* for *me?* I thought.

When he dropped me off later that night, there was a real sense of anti-climax. I didn't want the evening to end. I wanted to keep sitting there all night, looking at that smile, and listening to the stories that lay behind it. If we were teenagers, or if the context had been in any way different, perhaps the moment would've had a totally different dynamic to it, but neither of us dared test the strength of what it was we were subconsciously building between us. "I've had a lovely night, Christina," he said, knowing one of us had to draw the evening to a close. "You've been such a breath of fresh air." I told him I felt the same. Then, just as I was reaching for the door he reached inside his jacket once again and brought out an envelope.

"I want you to take this with you," he said, passing it over. I took it and peered inside. It looked like Monopoly money but in fact it was US dollars, three-hundred-dollars' worth, made up of ten- and twenty-dollar bills. I didn't know how to respond, so I said the first thing that came into my head:

"You're not trying to pay me for sex, are you?"

He smiled. "You don't have to spend it if you don't want to," he said. "And if you don't, you can return it to me whenever you get back. But I'd feel a hell of a lot better knowing you had enough to cover yourself with if something went wrong." I knew I would never spend it, but I slipped it into my bag anyway, simply in order to take him up on his offer when I got back.

"It's a deal," I said. We shook hands and I left.

Train couplers. That was Phil's business. He didn't set the company up, that was a Swedish chap during the Second World War, but Phil was one of the bigwigs who ran it now. Couplers, in case you don't know, are the things that allow train carriages to connect together, the safety mechanisms that ensure they stay linked at all times and don't come apart when travelling along. It was kind of symbolic really. Phil wanted me to travel safely whilst moving through the swamplands of Florida and not come undone because of a dodgy connection.

The morning after that first 'date', he rang me up and asked if I was home at lunchtime. Already feeling happier that he'd rung I told him I was, and then at exactly twelve o'clock, there was a knock on the door. I opened it and found a man trying to pop his head from behind the biggest bunch of flowers I'd ever seen.

"Christina Black?" he asked.

"Yes?"

"These are for you." Using all my strength I took them from him and laid them down on the coffee table so I could read the note that came with them. *'Thanks for a great evening,'* it read, *'Hope there'll be many more. Phil.'*

It took us a while to decide whereabouts in America to visit, but Mike and I decided on Florida in the end because, to me at least, Florida was the most American part of America, the most 'Stars and Stripesy' part. If you walked past any travel agents at that time all you'd see was Mickey Mouse waving to you from outside Cinderella's castle in Disney World, next to a picture of a killer whale splashing the crowds in Sea World just up the road. To that end, Florida served to represent the dreams of every scullery maid who's ever been beaten down by her ugly step-sisters or raped by her brother. Just to be there, and see it all with my own eyes was to prove that I'd escaped those horrible people, and the coal cupboard they made me escape to, even if it was only for a week or so. I'd always have the memories.

We were in Florida for about ten days in total, but didn't spend all our time in the same hotel. Because there was so much to see, we chose instead to move about, taking in various hot-spots around the state and ticking them off a list we'd made up. To give him his due, Mike remained a gentleman throughout. He didn't pressure me in any way to take our relationship to the next level, but that doesn't mean he was always successful at hiding his frustration that we weren't making attempts to. The first time I saw his mask slip was when we were standing outside a zoo, up in North Orlando. We were waiting in a long line to get in, but we were moving fast, and there was plenty to entertain us as we shuffled along. Some of the street acts we saw were very talented – as good as professionals really – but one that stood out for me was a group of Caribbean singers who had with them a little girl. She was only about six or seven, with a flower in her hair, and as the band performed behind her – a kind of infectious reggae music – she charmed the crowds with her dancing.

"Aaaah, isn't she gorgeous?" I said to Mike, expecting his heart to have melted just as much as everyone else's, but the piggish grunt he offered in return suggested he must've left his back at the hotel. "Oh, aye, what's the matter with you" I asked, assuming I must've caught him at a bad moment. "Don't you like children?" He barely looked up at me as he answered.

"Not really, no."

The little girl carried on dancing, as money started to fill up the hat being passed around, but as that was happening, I was still reeling, not just from what Mike had said, but *how* he'd said it. *Didn't like children?* "Well, for your information mister", I thought, I have five of my own back home, and they are the most important thing in my life. They weren't just the cheap free toy that came with the box of cereal, you know. Later on, as we sat having a drink, I brought the subject up again, but Mike started to back-pedal furiously when he noticed me steering the conversation towards the obvious.

"I didn't mean *your* kids," he said, feebly. "I meant kids in general. Yours aren't like that."

"Like what?" I asked.

"You know what I mean, Chrissy. Yours are very well-behaved, they're not demented like everyone else's." But that was the thing. My children *were* like everyone else's. I took great pride in knowing that, despite everything I'd been through, I'd been able to raise my kids to be perfectly normal. They weren't freaks. What they liked was what other kids liked. But no matter how much he back-pedalled, it wasn't enough, the chain had already come off. If he didn't like children, then he couldn't like *my* children, and if he didn't like *my* children, then he didn't like *me*. Thank God I'd insisted on separate rooms.

About half-way through the holiday I started to get a strange feeling in the pit of my stomach. I didn't know what it was, but I knew it was nothing to do with anything I'd eaten. It wasn't that kind of feeling anyway, it was the 'other' type, the one that also made the hairs stand up on the back of my neck.

"Something's happened at home," I said to Mike once I knew the feeling wasn't going to go away. We were downstairs at the time, in the bar, trying to continue on as if there might still be a future between us. The feeling was like a kind of psychic tinnitus by this stage.

"How do you know?"

"I just do," I snapped back. Poor Mike didn't know anything about my twin-sister, or anything at all about my spiritual gifts. I hadn't ever brought the subject up with him because he was such a practical man, and I was afraid he would just dismiss it as nonsense, which I know a lot of people do.

"You're just worried about them," he said, "because you've never been away from them before. It's perfectly natural." Then he reached over and patted my knee. "It's probably just indigestion," he laughed.

One thing I hadn't done before we'd come away was make any provision to be contacted in case something happened at home. I knew we'd be travelling around, staying in different places, so it just didn't seem practical. To make matters worse, I hadn't even thought of bringing any of the neighbours' numbers with me. Mike's response didn't help. He rolled his eyes as if I was merely confirming what nuisances children could be.

"Why don't you just relax and unwind?" he said. "Everything will be fine at home, I promise you." But as he was promising me that, something terrible was happening three thousand miles away to my kids. I excused myself and went upstairs to the room. After a bit of a kerfuffle I was able to dial home, but the phone just rang and rang. I could see it in my mind's eye just sitting there, attracting the attention of nobody as its ringing echoed off the walls in the empty house. Giving up, I reached into my purse and pulled out the card Phil had given me before we'd left. Crossing my fingers, I dialled the number, hoping Mike didn't walk in.

"Good afternoon, Dellner," came the male voice at the other end. It wasn't deep enough to be Phil's, plus it was American. My heart sank. Tom, an associate of Phil's, sensed the urgency in my voice, but told me that Phil had left Charlotte that morning. As we spoke, he was probably 40,000 feet above the ocean, just preparing to make his descent. I was distraught. I wanted to fly back straight away but just didn't have the funds. Phil's $300 wouldn't even get me to New York, let alone Manchester, and I could never have asked Mike. We'd probably have passed our tipping point, needlessly argued ourselves blue, and what if I'd been wrong?

I spent the rest of the holiday on edge, walking along as if on a fault line above two bickering tectonic plates. I knew an earthquake was coming – I could feel the earth rumbling beneath my feet – but what I didn't know yet was just what magnitude it was going to be.

The hotels all blurred into one after this, as did the scenery. There would be the usual drive-up, the check-in, the testing of beds, the glimpse at the pool, the comments about the weather, and so on, and that continued for the rest of the holiday. My body was there for all of this, going through the motions of it, but I couldn't make the same claim for my brain which remained trapped in a cloud three thousand miles away. After a few days of going through this same ritual – me always making sure it was two rooms, not one – the final drive we did was to the airport. But as we boarded our flight and the tension that had built up throughout the last few days of the holiday began to ease, the anxiety about what I'd find when I got home increased. It would've been nice if Mike could've shared some of that tension with me, but instead he remained indifferent to it, as if all matters relating to my children were to remain separate from him. Although the subject had remained off the table for the rest of the holiday, it became an inevitable part of the last conversation we were ever to have together, and we had it in the back of the taxi as we approached my house.

"It's not going to work between us, is it?" he asked. I'm glad it was him who'd said the words, and not me, because I don't know how I'd have found the strength. Mike had got me out of a bad place, but had I simply confused the destination with the bridge that led me there?

"I don't think it is."

There was much silence after that. I stared at the trees outside, watching them blur into a green and brown streak through the window, and my streaming tears. Perhaps sensing the tension behind him, the taxi driver didn't say a thing, letting the music of Chris de Burgh fill the empty space between us. Eventually we turned into my road and slowly approached the house.

He touched my hand. "I'd like to see you again, Chrissy," I heard in my ear, "but I just don't think you feel the same." Here was my chance to save this. All I had to say was two words and I could've changed the future direction of both our lives. But I remembered the last time I said the words "I do" under pressure.

"I don't want to lie to you, Mike ..."

I didn't need to say another word. The rest he knew. We were a package, me and my kids. There was no me without them, it was as simple as that. He'd had lots of chances to take back what he'd said outside the zoo, but he didn't, and I'm glad he didn't, because If that was the real him, then I needed to see that. As an architect, he might be the best in the world at designing buildings that stay up in all weathers, but he couldn't design a shield to hide who he really was. It just took a little girl with a pretty smile and a flower in her hair to put a crack in it.

GUNS AND ROSES

The house sounded hollow. Nothing moved, nothing creaked, and no one was holding their breath. It smelt musty too, that strange odour you'll notice when dust has settled on something and the air around it hasn't been disturbed for a while. Humans override this scent just by existing – their 'aliveness' disturbs the air, through their breathing, their moving, even their thoughts. But nothing had moved in the house for days: not in the lounge, the bedrooms, or even the bathroom. Indeed, both the bath and the sink were bone dry. As for the food, well that was all out-of-date, in the fridge and in the cupboards. The butter was hard in the dish too. What the hell had happened? Had the house been visited by aliens while I was away?

"Thank God you're back!" Phil exclaimed when I managed to reach him on the phone. For the first time, he didn't sound like he was smiling. "I had half a mind to fly back and get you, but I wouldn't have known where to start looking." This was not the hello I was expecting. However, it turns out I was right to have had concerns that day in Florida. I shouldn't have doubted myself really, but I wasn't as in-tune then as I am now with the full spectrum of feelings I have swirling within me. Call them 'psychic' if you will, but to me they were just the maturing of an ability I'd had since I was little. Phil didn't judge when I explained the unease I'd been feeling, nor mock, he just dived in with what he knew: A few days earlier he'd received a panic-stricken phone call from Pam, my sister's sister-in-law who'd been desperate to get hold of me. She'd spoken to the mother of my babysitter who'd filled her in about what had happened whilst she'd been looking after the kids. Pam knew about Phil because I'd told her all about him just before I'd left with Mike.

"He sounds amazing," she'd said.

Using her common-sense, she'd dug out the number for Dellner, the company he worked for, and started ringing round until she eventually reached him. She thought he might have had a way of getting hold of me in America.

Phil wasn't able to offer me all the details, but he gave a good enough summary of the situation as he'd heard it. The rest I got from the babysitter herself when I saw her. From what she said, the entire incident had played out like an episode of *EastEnders*. It started off quite normal: Billy had turned up looking quite happy, carrying with him a cake and a ring. His plan – if you can believe this – had been to ask me to marry him, having realised that there was no future for him with the slut. *Quelle fucking surprise!*

"Then he just walked in, as if he owned the place," she said, still shaking from the memory. "I couldn't stop him. He said it was his house. Then he went through into the living room and he saw the flowers." I'd forgotten about those. I'd left them there when I went away because they brightened up the room and the kids liked them. "And then he picked up the card that went with them …" My heart sank at this because I remembered what it had said. How it could be interpreted. "He went ballistic when he read it." Of course he did. How could he not? Then he started grilling her about this 'Phil' guy, who she'd never even heard of. "Then he turned on the kids and started asking them, and he was getting more and more uptight in the process, and started scaring everyone." The final straw came when he asked where I was, and the kids told him I was away in America with a bloke called Mike. "It just pushed him right over the edge," she said. I pitied her because I knew what that looked like.

He gave her the third degree, everything but pliers on the fingernails. Fearing that he was going to hurt her, she told him everything she knew. Then she watched in disbelief as he rounded up the kids and marched them out the door. She was shaking with fear as he took them, wondering how she was going to explain it to me.

But that was just the beginning. Billy had also made her tell Social Services that she wasn't babysitting for me at all. He dragged her there himself, taking Phil's flowers along with him, and got her to fabricate an account of my life. "Tell them what she's like," he'd barked at her. And she did, testifying to the 'debauched' life I was now living, and that when I'd gone away to America, I'd made no provision whatsoever for the children.

I used to think Billy Harris thought only with his fists, but I was wrong. Such vindictiveness requires cunning; it requires someone who is driven only by the worst aspects of human nature. You hear of male lions, don't you, who kill cubs because the grief felt by their mother is so profound it makes them become fertile again. That way they can pounce and have their wicked way with her. Billy was of the same stock, the same base, animal nature. He would hurt, maybe even kill, not to experience any pleasure from the act himself, but to stop other people from experiencing the pleasure he was being denied. If *he* couldn't have it, then it would have to be destroyed.

Olive was his first target. He dragged the kids to hers first, turning up outside her house in his big fancy car. Behind him, as he pounded on her door, the kids were balling their eyes out, looking as scared as they would've been in a burning building. They had no idea what his plans were.

"They're not staying here," Olive said, laughing in his face. If she had no time for me, she had even less time for anything that came from between my legs. But Billy wasn't going to give up. His reputation as a monster depended on how monstrous he could be. His goal was to tangle everything up so tightly that it would take me forever to untangle it. Will, Stephanie and Deryn he was eventually able to dump at his sister's. They were his own, so were therefore easier to farm out somewhere. With Brina and Kelly, though, he had to be more resourceful. Although he stopped short of burying them in a coffin under a farmer's field, what he finally came up with wasn't a whole lot more pleasant for them.

As he was putting my kids through all this, laying down the foundations for an experience that would lead more than one of them to years of therapy, I was still thousands of miles away, inwardly climbing the walls. What I could sense in Florida wasn't indigestion, as Mike had joked, it was my kids screaming out in distress.

Getting nowhere with Billy, whose insults when I finally managed to contact him drowned out all the questions I had, I eventually turned up at my sister's, hoping she might have heard something.

"I'm sorry Chrissy," she said, standing at the door, "I haven't got a clue." Seeing the state of me, anyone else would've invited me in for a cup of tea. My eyes were raw from crying and I could barely hold myself up in her doorway. She did look distracted though, as if she couldn't wait to get rid of me. Maybe she had a visitor coming. That she didn't let me in is only because two floors above me at that very moment, in a locked attic, were Brina and Kelly. They'd seen me arrive in my car through the tiny window they had in the attic, and were screaming to be let out. But I'd not looked up. If I had, I'd have seen them banging on the glass, their red faces fighting to be seen through the little porthole window.

"If I hear anything though," she said, closing the door on me, "I'll let you know."

The other three he'd dragged over to Marie-Anne's, the slut's mother, and bundled them into a room together upstairs. There were no beds, just mattresses and a few sheets which had been found in an ottoman somewhere. They might not have been tied to any radiators like hostages in the Middle East, but their treatment wasn't much better. When Billy wasn't around, all three would frequently find themselves at the palm-end of a slap whenever their moans became too much to bear.

"Count yourselves fuckin' lucky you've got me to look after yez," Marie-Anne would shout at them. It was all too much for Sabrina to bear. Being older than the others, and far more independent, she managed to escape when Marie-Anne was busy with something. The others were too scared to leave with her. She flew straight back home as soon as she could and pulled no punches when she described how they'd been treated.

"Mum, it was just awful," she sobbed. The conditions they were in were horrendous. That was when I found out about everything. Until that moment I'd been totally in the dark.

I thought Sabrina's return might mark the beginning of the end of this awful situation, but it wasn't at all. Because of how he'd fixed things with Social Services, it was just the end of the beginning. Three months would pass before I'd get my kids back, and even then it wouldn't be all of them. During this period, I took solace in the comfort of my friends. Talking helped, if only just to get things off my chest. "What are you gonna do?" they'd ask, but I'd just shake my head in response. I had no answer. The law didn't seem to be on my side. Karen, who lived a roads away, became a frequent companion. She was never slow to get the kettle on when I turned up at her door with that 'I-haven't-slept-a-wink-of-sleep' look I wore quite often at that time. "My door's always open," she'd said, and thank God, because I was always walking through it. How had he pulled this off? I couldn't get my head around it at all. Despite him not giving two shiny shites about any of the kids – only two of which were even his – it was me who, in the eyes of everyone, ended up being seen as the more unfit parent.

There can never be a silver lining to a mother having her kids taken away from her, but if there was one, it's that it allowed Phil into my life more. Without him, I'm not really sure how I'd have survived. He made sure my car was always filled up with petrol for all the driving I had to do, and a million-and-one other things. This support, coupled with what we both understood immediately to be a mutual attraction, set the stage for us to take our relationship much deeper, and neither of us shied away from seeing how far we could dive down together.

But as I was getting closer to Phil, I was getting further away from my kids. As each day gave way to the next, the warmth of the love they felt for me dropped by a degree or two, not because they thought my love for them was lessening, but because they were being told it wasn't what they thought it was. What makes a person truly nasty isn't just how quickly they can descend to violence, but how they can manipulate others to align with their own despicable views. Lies are their main weapon. They're dropped into the conversation, small at first, and then bigger, until, over time, the more outrageous ones don't seem as ridiculous as they once did. It's not a million miles away from how a cult-leader builds his followers – nothing outrageous is said first, there's a sort of charm-seduction thing going on. And that's how Billy got into the minds of the kids. The small lies he was spreading were just a distortion of my real behaviours. He'd taken the morsel of information he knew about Mike and Phil, and blown them up into huge things, telling them that I was sleeping with all sorts of fellas, even taking money for it sometimes. And they started to believe it.

Karen sympathised when I told her I suspected this was happening. She didn't offer any advice, she just listened. When I mentioned Phil, she seemed keen to know about him, and wanted to know all the juicy details.

"Sounds like you've found your knight in shining armour," she said with a wink.

"I'd rather find my kids," I answered.

Not long after telling her about Phil, I was upstairs in the house, when I heard a loud screech outside. I popped over to the window to have a look and my heart jumped up into my throat. Two black tyre marks had appeared on the tarmac and they lead up to what I recognised as one of Billy's vehicles. When I looked down from the bedroom, I saw fat cumulonimbus clouds reflected on the roof of his car . A storm was coming. And then the door opened and out he stepped. He'd brought the storm with him. It was in his hand.

Oh Mary, Mother of Christ!

He'd never looked bigger. I saw curtains twitching on the other side of the road. "Here we go again," the neighbours must've thought. "Pull up a chair and let's watch the fireworks." Billy stretched his neck, cricked his fingers and then turned his attention towards the house.

BANG-BANG-BANG!

It was all too familiar now, this sensation. My spine howled in distress at how this might end. At least I wasn't pregnant this time.

BANG-BANG-BANG!

"OPEN THE FUCKIN' DOOR!"

Looking down, I couldn't see him, but then he stepped backwards into view. That massive head. I moved back out of sight.

"COME OUTSIDE YOU FUCKING BITCH, I WANT TO SHOW YOU SOMETHING!"

He held up his hand. There was a brick in it. Another man climbed out of the car. It was Paul, from the club. I used to get on quite well with him.

"I KNOW YOU'RE IN THERE, I CAN SEE YOU."

I knew he couldn't. The net curtains were too good for that, but by imagining me to be there it gave him an excuse to start 'performing'. This was street-theatre of the most brutal kind, and the star performer wanted to make sure he had a big audience.

Through the back windscreen of the car, I saw a little face appear. I hadn't seen that face for weeks, but I knew it well. I'd brought it into the world. I remembered it with the caul over its face, but where was the good luck it was meant to have heralded?

"There she is," Billy announced when I flung open the door. On seeing me, Will went hysterical in the car and started trying to get out. He was like a caged bird inside, knocking himself against the bars. I wanted to go towards him but found myself being stopped by Billy. A noise came from his mouth, something about pestering my sister. He pushed me back, and I stumbled, and by the time I'd managed to recover, I saw him moving away from me. I'd forgotten all about the brick, but I was reminded about it a split second later when he raised his hand and brought it down against the windscreen of my Jag before I could get anywhere near him.

The sound was sickening, a dull explosion that echoed off every house. I was so shocked I couldn't even scream. I needed that car to get around in, and the smile on Billy's face suggested he knew just how much I did. The neighbours were no doubt elbowing each other, "Did you see that? Did you see what he just did?". Doing my best to forget about it, I tried to make my way over to Will, somersaulting in distress on the back seat like a hamster in a wheel, but Billy was between us again, pushing me away. I tried to fight him off, but my arms were like matchsticks fighting off tree trunks.

"Go 'ed, Billy lad, let the little fella see his ma," Paul said, but the words fell on deaf ears. This was just part of the fun for him. When his threshold for boredom was passed, he just pushed me away with both arms and I went tumbling onto the tarmac. By the time I was able to get my bearings back, Billy was closing the door of his car. He gave me a little wink and then he was gone.

I saw shadows behind all the net curtains, but no one came out to help. Feeling heart-sore about not being able to see Will, I climbed to my feet and looked at the car. The whole front window had gone. It looked like someone had emptied twenty bags of sugar into the front seats. I would never be able to get it all out. I turned to look at Karen's house, wondering if she'd heard any of what had happened, and if she had, why didn't she come out to help? Was that movement there behind one of her net curtains? No, there couldn't have been. How strange it was though, that only a couple of days after sitting on the other side of those net curtains and pouring my heart out to her about how necessary my car was to me, Billy had turned up to put it out of action. It must be a coincidence, I thought, nothing more than that. Just a strange coincidence.

WRECKING CREW

All tethers have an end. I reached the end of mine after about three months, but instead of putting my head in the oven, I dug out my address book. I'd known Pat for a long time, and she knew all about Billy, though she was certainly no fan. She was intelligent, which he wouldn't have liked, especially not in a woman. Whenever we'd meet up and I told her of everything I was going through, she listened, as a *friend,* and not as the solicitor she also just happened to be. But now I needed her to be more than just a friend. I needed her to put her other hat on.

I don't know what she did, or how she did it, but twenty-four hours later my kids were back with me. The relief I felt when I saw them climbing out of the police car was indescribable. I started shaking. They looked shell-shocked, as if they'd been hurriedly yanked out of a war zone and hadn't yet adjusted to the reality that no bullets could hit them now. I thanked the police, and Pat, who'd made it happen, then clapped my hands together, trying to remember how to be a mum again to a large family. What was I supposed to say in this situation?

"What do you want for your tea?" It was the best I could come up with.

Kelly didn't want anything. No dinner, no tele, and no company.

"What's the matter with you?" I asked, trying not to notice the look of despondency she'd dragged back with her. She shook her head, she had nothing to say to me. "Kelly, are you all right?" But she wasn't. She didn't want to be there at all, and looked at me like I was something she'd brought in on her shoe. I didn't understand. She sat, coiled, like a snake, looking towards the door, and didn't touch a thing.

Two hours later, she'd gone. The bag she'd brought back with her, that had gone too. I've read of hostages who develop attachments to their captors. Even the most awful ones. It doesn't happen overnight, it takes ages. The awfulness of their situation becomes normalised over time, until eventually the person forgets what their old life was like. In extreme situations they've even spoken up in their captors' defence at their trials. And yet, as bizarre as it seems, I think there might've been an element of this going on with Kelly. Stockholm Syndrome is the medical term for it. All those lies Billy had spread about me, for some reason they seemed to resonate with Kelly in a way they didn't with the others. Perhaps it was because of her age. She was entering her mid-teens and was looking for ways to establish her own identity. Billy, evidently, had encouraged this independent way of thinking, and as he did so, marked *me* out as some sort of deplorable harlot and himself as a saint. He gave her money to get clothes with, and promised her holidays to places she was desperate to visit. It didn't matter that he never followed through with them, it was just enough to be promised them. She got nothing like that from me. But there was something deeper going on with Kelly at this time, something that I just couldn't see in the heat of the moment. Kelly was John's daughter, but she'd never had any kind of relationship with her real dad, who'd been gone from her life since she was a toddler. She wasn't even three when Billy had first turned up at my door the morning after I'd been saved by his crew at the club.

"I hear you make the best cuppa this side of the Mersey?"

Desperate for a father figure, Kelly had latched onto the first man that provided a regular presence in her life. Stability, of a kind. Sabrina was too old, and Deryn too young, but Kelly fell right into the Goldilocks Zone, seeing him as the right man in the right place at the right time. He, in turn, told her that she was his favourite, which she always seemed to like. "But don't tell the others," he'd say with a wink.

She didn't.

It took the intervention of a judge to get her back. I hated making the whole thing into a tug- of-war, but Billy gave me no choice. Kelly deserved better than that, but just wasn't mature enough to see beyond the immediate situation he'd dragged her into. Not being her biological father, his claim that he had a legal right to guardianship over her held about as much water as a paper fish tank; therefore, the expression on the judge's face when he found us all gathered before him to hear his ruling on the case seemed to say just one thing: "Why in God's name are you wasting my time with this nonsense?" He threw it out like a snotty tissue.

But even after that, it still wasn't resolved. Billy's reach into Kelly's mind had penetrated much deeper than anyone would've guessed, and though we got her body back, her head seemed to stay with him. I was determined to make everything okay with her, to get us back to where we were before I'd gone off to America, but within minutes of returning home after the court ruling, she became surly, not letting me anywhere near her. Calming words from Phil, who was there when we got back, just seemed to do the exact opposite. It was like throwing petrol on a fire, and within just a couple of days Kelly had disappeared yet again, ignoring the court's ruling, the comfort of her own bed, and all the maternal love I had it in me to give.

"You're fuckin' dead!"

I'd heard far nicer things said to me over the phone, but the violence with which these three words had been spat at me caught me off guard. It was a couple of days after Kelly had run back to Billy, and I'd been pulling my hair out wondering what to do. It didn't seem right to go back to the courts again, because it just would've made things worse. It was a hot day, and the kids were playing outside, in the gardens of various neighbours. When the phone rang I thought it might be one of them asking if it was okay for Will or Deryn to stay for tea or something. But instead it was the Devil himself, and when I heard his voice it was like being kicked again in my spine. What had I done now?

"D'ye hear me, slag? I'm comin' for ye."

I had no time to respond before he slammed the receiver down. Could I not escape this insufferable man? He'd already put my car out of action for a few weeks, and turned my daughter against me, what more did he want? Not knowing what else to do, I rang Pat to get her take on things.

"Get out of the house," she instructed. "You don't want to take any chances." Pat, knowing Billy's type very well from her work, had long suspected he wasn't done with me. The type of personality he was meant that he couldn't accept defeat, which is how he'd interpreted the court's ruling – both times. But more significantly, he now knew about Phil, and there was no way of knowing how he'd deal with that.

I was starting to panic now. There was something else in Billy's voice this time, a dark edge that I'd never heard before. Get out of the house? Where the hell could I go at such short notice? Weeks ago I'd have rounded up the kids and gone straight round to Karen's but I'd recently found out that she'd been one of the many drainpipes up which Billy the Rat had been scurrying frequently. All those heartfelt conversations I'd had with her, all those times I'd poured my heart out to her. Guess what she'd done with that? She'd gone straight to Billy, and as they'd had a quick knee-trembler up against the wardrobe in her boudoir, she'd told him everything – about Mike, about Phil, all my plans to get the kids back, and about how dependent I'd been on my Jag to keep myself afloat. That was how he'd known to come round and smash it up. It was all part of his plan to destroy me, and it was about to get a hell of a lot worse.

He definitely wasn't screwing Jenny though. She was far too wise to be taken in by a prick like him. Her house was on the end of the street, and I knew he barely knew her. My plan then, as quickly as I could stitch it together, was to run round to hers, ring Phil from there, and then come up with a plan of action. So I grabbed Stephanie, who was playing next door in Pauline's garden, then, with Brina and Deryn in tow, we raced round to Lynne's to scoop up Will, who was playing there. Then, en masse, we marched over to Jenny's. I'd barely been able to fill in the blanks for her when we heard the army arrive outside.

"Oh. My. God, " I heard one of the kids say. Jenny and I stood up and walked over to the window, and we saw it too – a whole fleet of cars and trucks crawling down the road. It was like a scene from *Mad Max*. They were all being driven by Billy and his boys, his mates from the club – other bouncers and their girlfriends, who'd come to gawp. Billy led the carnival behind the wheel of a low-loading truck, on top of which sat a forklift. It seemed utterly incongruous in the middle of our terraced street.

"Mummy, what's daddy doing?" Will asked, looking scared. I had to hide my own fear because I didn't want to terrify him.

"I really have no idea, love," was all I could answer. I then turned to jenny. "Whatever happens," I said to her. "Don't open the door."

"Don't you worry," she answered, "I won't go anywhere near it."

"I KNOW YOU'RE WATCHING, BITCH," we all heard then. It was like a firework going off. He was putting on his performer's hat again, and that was never good. He looked up at the house, unaware that we'd all relocated further down the road. I turned to the kids and put my finger over my lips to make sure they understood: *Not. A. Single. Sound.* It felt like our very lives depended on it. Any of the neighbours might've seen us fleeing over to Jenny's, and if they did, they could very easily slip out and tell Billy where we were, but I think they were probably too scared to involve themselves.

Once he was out of the truck, Billy climbed down and guided the forklift onto a ramp which led down to the road. The noise it made was terrific, meaning the curtains in the windows of every house in the street would've been twitching. Indeed, I saw a hundred figures lurking behind the net curtains.

The crowd accompanying Billy gathered around the forklift as it lined itself up side-on to my jag. They all appeared to be smiling, like a crowd at a netball match. Jenny looked at me. My mouth was open. *No, no, no,* I thought. This can't be happening. Not in broad daylight like this. Billy looked to the driver, then raised his arms. It was a signal. A moment later the two long metal forks came up off the ground until they were level with the side windows of the Jag. Then, with a nod from Billy, it drove forward, its two forks piercing both side windows in a smooth, fluid motion. The glass turned to sugar and dropped away, first on the passenger side, then the driver's, as they came out the other end. I wanted to faint. Why was no one stopping him?

"Oh my fuckin' word," Jenny said, putting her hand over her mouth. The kids screamed in horror at the sheer barbarity of it. Phil had stepped in to help me fix up the Jag, because he'd known how necessary it had been to my business. He hadn't wanted me to fall apart because of the petulant actions of my ex. It hadn't broken the bank to fix up, and most of the mess had been scooped up five minutes after bringing out the Henry Hoover. But this was something else entirely, as Billy's next signal proved.

"Best get onto the police," Jenny whispered.

Smiling from ear to ear, Billy lifted his chin and the forks went up further, crumpling the roof, and taking the entire vehicle with them. My heart sunk even lower when I saw the wheels come off the ground, at first by a couple of inches and then by a few feet, because I suddenly realised that the truck he'd brought along with him wasn't only to be used as a bed for the forklift. It was to have another, far more crushing purpose.

As if stealing my Jag wasn't bad enough, Billy had plans for my other car too. The old BMW that had been sitting outside the house for years. He'd picked it up cheap from a mate (so he claimed) but had grown bored of it, and so he'd given me the keys in case I ever needed it for the business. We'd sorted out the paperwork so it was all legit and that was that. I thought he'd forgotten all about it, but I was forgetting who I was dealing with. Billy doesn't forget favours. After he'd secured the ruined Jag to the back of the truck, he'd whistled over to Bobby Reynolds, one of his mates from the club, and then pulled from his pocket a set of keys.

"There you go lad," he said, tossing them over. "All yours." I wasn't that panicked to see this because, back at the house, I knew I had all the legal documents I'd need to get it back in no time. "Don't get too comfy in it, mate," I said to Bobby under my breath.

There were so many people standing around gawping that I'd not paid any attention to the young girl slunk off to one side looking on. It was Deryn who drew my attention to her.

"There's Kelly," she said.

"What? Where?" I couldn't believe it. But I followed Deryn's arm, and there she was, standing by all the WAGs.

"Why isn't she stopping them?"

I had no answer, other than to think that in a war you choose which side you're going to be on, and deal with the consequences later. Kelly, for whatever reasons, had chosen hers. Her presence there was part of Billy's plan though, and this whole circus was, to some extent, all brought about by what Kelly had been telling Billy since she'd scurried back to him. It all related to what Pam had said. Bullies like Billy Harris put so much effort into making their partners feel worthless that when someone else comes along and tells them they're not worthless at all, but actually start loving them, and giving them confidence again, the bully feels as if he's failed. And when they realise that, hold tight, because that forces them to confront a truth that they're not equipped to deal with, that they've lost some of their power, and the only way to get it back is to start smashing things.

"We'll be there as soon as we can," the policeman said on the phone. "Just sit tight, and we'll get a car over to you." The voice at the other end didn't exactly sound like it was responding to an emergency. More like I'd interrupted a game of dominoes he was keen to get back to with some of the other sergeants.

"Well, he's still here so if you want to get a move on," I panted, "that might be good."

Fifteen minutes later a car turned into the road, but there was no siren or flashing blue light. They might as well have been an old couple returning from a day out to Southport. Billy and his wrecking crew had left just a few minutes earlier, leaving only piles of glass and cracked bits of tarmac where they'd carried out their brutal piece of performance art. I saw the police car turn in towards us (I was already in the road by then), and raced towards them, pointing in the direction from which they'd come, and jabbering away like a lunatic before they were anywhere near me.

"You've just missed him," I shouted, wanting them instantly turn around and chase the bastard. I needed that car back, and I needed my Jag repaired.

"Well, we've just actually had a chat to him, love," one of them said. But he didn't look like he'd just been in a violent confrontation.

"So where is he?" I asked. "Did you arrest him?" They must've brought another car, and Billy must be on his way to the station now, ready to be booked in. I wonder if he'd resisted. That would explain the delay. But this is where the dark evil genius of Billy Harris comes into play. The policeman ran his tongue around the inside of his mouth as if he was waiting impatiently for me to finish my rant.

"He's just shown us a document, love, that told us a chap called Bobby Reynolds is the
owner of the BMW." The other policeman then chipped in too: "And we've just seen Bobby. He was there too," he said.

"But that's not possible."

"Well, it is, love, 'cause I've just seen it with my own eyes."

"Then it must be forged, 'cause I've got all the documents in the house. The *real* ones." The policemen both rolled their eyes. I could tell they thought I was little more than one of those nuisance women. "Look, wait here," I said, "I've got the log-book in the house, as well as all the MOT forms. I can prove I own it." I started to leave, but they called after me.

"If you haven't got a receipt-of-purchase then the log-book means nothing." I blinked my eyes, incredulous. What the hell was he talking about?

"Sorry, love," the other one said. "That's just the way it is."

SORRY? I thought. The man had just turned up in broad daylight and stolen both my cars right in fucking front of me. He'd destroyed one and he'd taken – *stolen* – the other. Right in front of the entire street. And he'd laughed when he'd done it, as if he was putting on a show for everyone. But, of course, that's exactly what he was doing, because he'd planned all this. Every single dented roof and smashed window, right down to the last piece of broken glass on the cracked tarmac, it was all just part of a show, a magic show, in which my vicious ex, The Amazing Billy Harris would make both my cars disappear, right before everyone's eyes. It was incredible. It was David Copperfield and the Statue of fucking Liberty! But that wasn't even the most impressive trick he performed that day, that was just some close-up magic, a little sleight-of-hand set to deceive everyone watching. What no one knew then, and I wouldn't for a good while yet, is that behind the scenes, he was performing an even bigger trick, one that would make him as hard to put away in a cage as a puff of smoke.

RANSACK AND PILLAGE

I felt the sun on my eyelids before I opened them. There was the smell of bacon in the air too. Why could I smell bacon? And was that coffee I could hear percolating downstairs? It didn't smell like my house at all. We didn't even have a coffee percolator. Then I remembered, I wasn't in my house.

It took a few seconds for my brain to catch up, but in those seconds, I remembered all that had happened the previous day. The wretchedness hadn't ended after the police had limped uselessly away, there was more still to come, far more. But before it announced itself, with a screeching of tyres, and a scream from Little Will, I'd gone back to the house and rung Phil.

"Get a bag packed," he said, "One for you, and one for each of the children. I'm coming to collect you." Once he'd digested what Billy had done, Phil's opinion was that this was just the beginning. He hadn't got to the position he had in his life without knowing one or two shady characters himself, and from that he'd deduced it was best to limit Billy's options. "The cars won't be enough for him," he said. It was supposed to be me who was the psychic one, but in this instance it was Phil whose words proved to be the most prophetic. In response, I threw open a few bags on my bed and started tossing clothes into each of them, just the essentials and one or two outfits, assuming we'd only be gone for a few days. Then, a little bit calmer, but still in shock, I went downstairs and rang Pat Parkinson, my solicitor, to tell her about the cars, hoping she'd be able to get on the case and sort something out. The screeching tyres I heard outside could be anyone's, but the screaming that followed definitely wasn't. It was Will's. I might've dropped the phone, and as I started to race to the kitchen window to see what had happened, Sabrina ran in, looking like she was having a heart attack.

"Mum, he's got Will."

I nearly trampled over her to get to the door. I ran outside, cursing myself for leaving Will unattended, even for a moment, and arrived just in time to see Will, who'd been scrunched up under his dad's arm, thrown into the back of his car. I screamed out to Billy, an entertaining encore for the neighbours, no doubt, but he was in no mood to mutter anything more than a "Fuck you to hell" which he communicated with his two raised fingers. Not for the first time that day, I found myself running after his car, but like in a nightmare, I couldn't seem to get any closer. As I hurled myself forward, my feet slapping against the road, trying to catch up, I watched Little Will – a puppet in our never-ending Punch and Judy show – being battered around by the movement of the car, as he fought to stay upright on his knees in the back seat. And then he was gone, out of the shadows of the houses, and then out of the crescent itself.

"How you feeling today?" Phil asked, sitting on the bed. He handed me a cup of coffee. Sunbeams shone through the rising steam.

"Much better now," I said. The coffee was delicious, as was the smell of bacon from downstairs. It felt like I was in a five-star hotel.

"Come down whenever you want," he said. "Breakfast will be ready in five minutes." He squeezed my hand, then stood up and moved to the door. "Oh, do you like fried bread?" My smile told him how much I did.

"Delicious."

After Will had been taken, I didn't slump down in the middle of the road this time, shaking my head at God. Instead, I raced straight back into the house and got back onto Pat. I'd rung her so many times in recent weeks that her number was on speed-dial on the inside of my eyelids.

"He's just come and snatched Will."

"Right," she said, and got straight to work. Again, I've no idea what she did, or how she did it, but she certainly shook some trees, because within only a couple of hours Will was back in my arms, choosing which toys he wanted to take with him to Phil's. Because his actions had been so spontaneous this time, I don't think Billy had thought through what he was going to do with Little Will once he had him. At a loss then, he'd just dragged him to the pawn shop in Birkenhead and dumped him in the back. Pat, by selling it to the police as what it was – a *kidnapping* – had managed to rouse them into action, and they jumped up and put themselves into first gear immediately. Somehow, they were able to track Billy down in minutes and get Will back, but when they were dropping him off later at the house there was no indication that they'd given his kidnapper anything more than a slapped wrist.

Twenty minutes later, with no other unseen traumas to deal with, we were fleeing Witley Close like refugees. We waited at Lynne's, with our bags packed to bursting in her hallway, and counted the minutes until Phil arrived in his large people carrier. It was early evening now, but it was dark, and we sat in our coats drinking tea with the telly on. When Phil finally arrived, like the white knight he was more and more starting to seem like, we loaded up his boot and climbed into the vehicle, not even caring who was watching from behind the curtains this time. "To hell with the lot of you," I thought. The kids, though, didn't seem to be as relieved as I was. They seemed very upset. This was, after all, their home.

"Don't worry," I said to them as we turned out of the close. "We'll go back and get anything else you need in the next couple of days. It's not as if we're going to be gone forever, is it?"

Phil's breakfast tasted every bit as good as his house felt to be in. I couldn't even remember the last time anyone had made me a cooked breakfast, or cared enough to want to. The fried bread was perfectly done, light golden on both sides, and tasted sublime in the runny yolks of the fried eggs he'd cooked to perfection. But there was a note of anxiety I just couldn't escape. Soon the breakfast would be over, I knew that, and the coffee would be drunk, but then what? Yes, we were safe for now, in a house that was like a castle compared to what we'd just escaped, and the dragon who yearned to devour us, *me* anyway, didn't know where we were, but for how long would we be welcome this side of the drawbridge?

Phil already had two daughters. They didn't live with him, they were at boarding school, and stayed with Phil when they were home, but during the holidays they'd come and spend a week or two with him. They were his princesses and he doted on them, as any half-decent father would. His marriage had gone wrong, not because he was a tyrant or a bully, but because he was never home. Phil had sacrificed a lot to make himself successful and the toll it took was a personal one. It took away his family. Not that he was bitter about it, he could still provide for his daughters, and that's what mattered to him most. It was being separated from them, however, that made him more welcoming towards my children, almost as if they served as surrogates for his own. And that's why I don't feel as if we were ever invading his space, which was always my biggest fear. I didn't want this wonderful man, who'd already helped me so much, to feel as if he was being imposed upon. To his credit he never gave any indication towards seeming as if he was, and by the end of that first week, not only had he convinced me that if we ever found ourselves treading on his toes, that's exactly where he wanted us.

It's a good job too, because during that same week, the dragon in whose clutches I'd spent nearly a decade and a half, turned his fiery breath towards the house we'd shared for so much of it, and he'd done so for one reason and one reason only: he wanted to scorch it from the earth.

"We're going to need to board it up." That's what Phil told the police after he'd calmed me down. It was the only sensible option. There really was no other choice. The police said they'd send someone down to have a look at it, which they did, and Phil told them he'd cover any costs.

It was Lynne who'd called me that morning. I'd given her Phil's number in case something came up and I had to be contacted, but neither she nor I thought she'd be digging it out of her bag just a few days later.

"He's been going into your house, Chrissy," she said down the phone, close to tears. "And taking stuff." I didn't need to ask who. I borrowed Phil's car while he was at work, his Volvo Estate, and drove over to the house with Deryn, who wanted to tag along. What Lynne had said had filled me with a sense of dread, but not nearly enough to deal with what was about to confront us when we got there. I could see the damage well before we even got anywhere near it. If a house can resemble a human face, this one looked like it had been dead for weeks. beaten out of it. It was a corpse. A fleshless skull, with gaping holes where the windows had been. But they'd all been smashed now, every single one of them. And the front door … well, that looked like it had been bazookered. The glass was everywhere. Holding my breath and steeling myself for the worst, I stepped up to the entrance, forgetting for a second that I had Deryn with me, until she started tugging at my arm.

"Muuuuum, look," she said in a pestering kind of way. But I was in no mood to be pestered. I was too busy trying to hold down the vomit due to the stench that was escaping from the downstairs toilet. No kidding, it was a visceral feeling, like being punched in the gut. Even sewers didn't smell that bad. Deryn kept tugging on my arm, but I just couldn't deal with her right then, because what I was seeing, as I stepped into the house, was just too much to get my head around. Beneath my feet, things crunched, as if was treading on the spines of beetles. Only they weren't beetles. It was the glass of picture frames that had, until recently, contained photographs of me and the children in happier times, of vases and ornaments, and plates and cups and so many other things that had, for over a decade, made up our eggshell existence.

There's no nice way to describe what Billy had done. I don't know whether he'd done it alone or invited others round to share in the carnage, but everything inside he'd destroyed. Anything breakable he'd broken. And that was just the beginning. The kids' toys he'd taken, all the things they'd loved, or had a special attachment to. Clothes, both mine and the kids', had all vanished. Some you could see on the stairs, in a trail, as if they'd fallen out of a bag as they'd been carried down them. I glanced at Deryn to see how she was holding up, but she wasn't at all. She seemed paralysed. Like I was. She'd stopped tugging my arm though. I wanted to tell her that everything was going to be okay, but I didn't want my daughter to hear me tell a blatant lie. Nor did I want her to be exposed to that godawful smell for one second longer than we needed to, but there was no way to avoid it. It seemed to be coming from everywhere, but mostly from the downstairs toilet to our left. I struggled with this. There was no way it could be what I thought it was, I said to myself, because Billy, whatever else he was, was still a civilised human being, and even he wouldn't stop that low.

But he could, and he did. In fact, he'd stooped even lower, by making sure the toilet was blocked up with toilet paper when he'd done so. He did the same thing upstairs, in the main bathroom, unravelling a couple of rolls each time, and then, once he knew the toilet was completely blocked, he shat in it – perhaps more than once – then flushed the chain. Then he flushed it again. Then again. Then again. Until the filthy, brown, shit-flecked water crept over the rim and spilled out onto the floor. It spread out then, along the hall, until it reached the foot of the stairs, then the kitchen, then the lounge. As if destroying the carpets wasn't bad enough, some of this filthy water he then used to daub messages onto the walls, using our clothes as rags. Predictably enough, when it came to choosing words to memorialise with his own faeces, he hadn't sought the influence of William Wordsworth, but instead opted for something closer to the contents of his impoverished mind: 'BITCH', 'SLAG', 'WHORE', the same words he'd been using on a nearly daily basis to describe me during the last few years we'd remained together.

Five minutes of this was enough. I'd seen all I needed to see, and so had Deryn. I didn't want to subject her to any more horror than I needed to. But as we collected ourselves back on the doorstep, trying to flush the foul stench from our nostrils, Deryn touched my arm again and nodded towards the houses across the street. I followed her gaze and saw for myself what it was she'd been trying to draw my attention to earlier. Twenty years later it's *this* that still triggers her the most, and what she's discussed with her therapist more than anything else. It was our stuff. In the windows of all the houses. Vases. Picture frames. Candle holders. And toys. All the kids' toys. What he hadn't destroyed, Billy had given away to the neighbours. And there wasn't a single thing I could do to get them back.

A couple of weeks later, I was there again, watching a young man in a smart, grey suit climb out of his company car, with a clipboard in his hand. A policeman had been sent out too, to meet us, and him and I watched as the man, who had slicked-back hair, approached along the pavement, his eyes taking in the house behind us. He gave us a gentle smile and extended his hand.

"Christina?"

"Thanks for coming," I said.

He reached for his pen and popped the nib out with a click. "Let's take a look inside then, shall we?"

Billy didn't know I'd been paying insurance on the house. It had added hugely to the financial strain on things, but I'd long had a sense – call it an 'intuition' if you will – that at some point in the future I might need it. The insurance people had been surprisingly understanding when I rang them, but said before they could consider any kind of claim, they'd need to personally assess the damage. That's why we were here now, and why I was so nervous. What the man with the slicked-back hair scribbled onto that clipboard would affect my whole future.

I wasn't able to get into the house myself, because the only key I had was for the front door, and that was lying in bits in the hallway. It was the policeman who had the key for the padlock that kept the replacement one (little more than a wooden board) in place, and so he stepped forward now to open it for us. I hung back and waited for the insurance man to step inside, so I could follow him in, but he didn't make much progress. He stopped after one step.

"Christ," I heard him mutter, but I don't think he was referring to the picture of Jesus lying on the floor – just one of many lying at his feet that had been cracked or smashed completely. The others were photos, mostly of the kids. I could remember when each one was taken; Deryn in her first school uniform, Will's first steps. I had to fight hard to keep myself together. Those had been tough times, and the smiles the children offered up for every click of the camera had been hard won. Each one was a victory over hardship. The man with the slicked-back hair pulled out his own camera and took a few pictures from the hall – you could see quite a way into the house from there – but he didn't venture any further inside. The stench from the toilet put paid to that idea.

"I've never seen anything like this," he said, and the policeman concurred. I'm sure the neighbours did too, who I could see sneaking peaks from behind their twitchy curtains. They'd miss all this when we were gone.

"I don't need to go any further," the insurance man said, slipping his camera back into its little purse.

"I don't blame you," the policeman agreed.

The maximum amount I could've claimed for the damage was £26,000. That means if a jumbo jet had crash-landed on the house and squashed everything flat, the most money I could possibly have been given was £26,000. That this is the amount I finally ended up receiving goes some way to explaining just how extensive the damage had been. The money, I was told, was to be used to decorate and fix the structural parts that Billy had destroyed – basically "to make it habitable again" – but as there was no way I was ever going to live there after all this, my focus was directed towards making it presentable enough to sell on. All the insurance asked was that I get quotes for everything, and they would pay out up to the maximum value. This, of course, is where karma paid me back: because I'd done so many favours for people over the years, people who were in the painting and decorating business, when it came to them furnishing me with quotes, they all pitched them at the lower end of the scale, essentially just to cover materials, with very little thrown in for labour. To be honest, I was overwhelmed by the generosity, as that meant I could put some money aside and use it for buying new clothes and toys to replace the ones that had been destroyed or given away.

Back at Castle Phil, there was no sign of us being asked to retreat back over the drawbridge – not yet, anyway – so, at Phil's invitation, we allowed ourselves to get comfy. Not too much, just enough to ensure we could re-model our old routines to fit within the contours of our new situation. I was still able to get the kids to school on time, and helped them out with their homework, and Phil, when he had a spare evening, would join us. The children adapted to their new surroundings far quicker than me, and once I knew they were happy, I started to feel more content myself. Only occasionally would a dark shadow from the past block out the light from our sunnier present; for example, if one of the girls accidentally dropped a glass and it smashed, I might scream in a way that was totally out of proportion to the accident. Phil, in response, would drop whatever he was doing and run in, expecting to see me cornered by a mad axman or something. After wiping up the glass he'd take my arms and hold me for a few seconds, as has my heart returned to its normal, steady rhythm.

"What the hell did that man do to you?" he'd ask.

During this period, there was still a presence that felt conspicuous by its absence, and that was Kelly. As fantastic as it was to have my other kids around me, I never felt complete when she wasn't there. I just had to keep sending positive energy out into the cosmos in the hope that it would find her and keep her safe. One day she would see where all this love and positive energy was coming from and follow it back to its source. As I lived in hope of this, work continued on at the house on Witley Close. Every now and then I'd pop in to check on progress and have a cup of tea with the lads – sat on paint-flecked sheets – thanking God (and Phil) that we didn't have to keep on living there. Not long after, and not wanting to feel we were imposing too much on Phil, I suggested that I should probably start looking for a place of my own. Even though we were growing stronger by the day, I knew – even if Phil didn't say so himself – that he'd appreciate some space from time to time, especially during the holidays when his two daughters, Nadia and Natasha, would come to stay. Seeing where I was coming from, he didn't disagree, and said he'd sort out the finances himself if I wanted to do the looking around. It was a very kind gesture, and one I didn't expect him to make.

"It's as much for my peace of mind as it is for you," he said, taking my hand and stroking it. "I just want to know that you and the children are going to be safe when I'm not around." That's exactly how I felt too, and I appreciated the sentiment. But deep down, I knew that no matter what calming words he used to reassure me, there was only one way I was ever going to feel safe again: I needed to get Billy Harris off the streets so that he could never bother me again. But how in God's name was I going to do that?

Christina as a baby, L to R Georgina, Christina, Raymond and Phillip

Richard Guy my Stepfather

21 Whitley Close where I lived
with 'Big' Billy and the children

Olive Guy my Stepmother
in her 80's

Christina playing with Stephanie
(aged 1 ½) at New Brighton

Christina dressed as a Bride promoting our Wedding Car

Will (Little Billy) aged 5 on the beach at Llandullas

Barbara and Dave (like my second parents) as a young married couple

Will (Little Billy) aged 5 with
his Dad Big Billy

Christina with Deryn aged 11 at Howells
Boarding School, Denbigh, North Wales

Christina and Elizabeth, my next-door neighbor, in Irby Road, Heswall, Wirral.

Christina aged 43 at Party in Elizabeth's house in Tassel Dress to show off her legs!

Christina aged 43 at same Party.

Sabrina aged 15 and Stephanie aged 5 in Broughton, Chester

Sabrina aged 15 and Will (Little Billy) aged 6 in Broughton, Chester.

Christina and Sabrina aged 18

Christina Night out in London
with Wayne at the
Hilton Park Lane 2016

Christina and Wayne at James Bond
themed party in their Garden
at home in Tarporley 2017

THE SNAKE AND THE GRASS

To anyone sitting nearby we might have just looked like two friends meeting for coffee. Nothing strange about that, you might think, two ex-college buddies catching up over a cup of weak Nescafé and a caramel square. Except we weren't friends, as a closer inspection of our body language would've revealed. The man was a detective who chased criminals and solved crimes, and the woman was the ex-partner of a thug, the type of man the detective liked to chase. The café we were meeting in was in Parkgate, on the other side of the Wirral, i.e. not the side that looks like it was recently the loser in an angry exchange of nuclear weapons. It was his choice, the detective's, as he wanted the meeting to be in a public place, but not so public that every Tom, Dick and Harriet would remember us in a line-up.

"You look nervous," the detective said when he saw me fidgeting with the sugar sachets a few minutes after I'd sat down. "There's no need to be." I wasn't so sure. I knew Billy Harris had spies everywhere – even in sugar bowls if the need required it. I'll call the man 'Lewis' because he dressed like Lewis Collins in *The Professionals*. He certainly took care of himself, and my guess was that he'd once served in the army, because he had that way about him – like he'd found too many of his mates with hoods over their heads up sideroads in Crossmaglen. For years I'd dreamt of having this conversation with some high-ranking member of the police force. I'd imagined them writing down everything and then telling me they'd get "straight on the case," and days later Billy would be in handcuffs getting bundled into the back of a Black Mariah. Once they'd shone even the dimmest spotlight onto Billy, all his crooked shenanigans would be exposed, and off he'd go to pleasure Her Majesty for a few years in one of her finest high-windowed establishments. But experience had told me that this was never going to happen. The police had already proved themselves deaf to any concerns I'd raised about Billy, as if they simply weren't interested in what I had to tell them. Lewis, who worked for the CID, didn't jump to the their defence when I told him what had driven me to get in touch, but understood why they might not have fallen over themselves to react. He knew the limitations placed upon the police; they didn't have the funds or the resources to '"sweat the small stuff" as he put it, so could only focus on the bigger picture. I hoped he didn't think what I had to tell him about Billy was "small stuff". He didn't take notes, which surprised me, but it's possible he had some kind of recording device in his jacket. He knew what he needed to know though, and had a unique way of getting to it, picking at the threads of a subject, even the ones I was uncomfortable discussing, and gently sewing them together until he'd made a kind of tapestry that showed the whole picture in all its ugly detail. Smiling at the waitress as she passed, he asked me, in the most surreptitious way he could, what I knew about Billy's relationship with narcotics.

"With what?" I asked. I knew the word from films, but I was shocked to hear it mentioned now. It sounded pure gangster.

"Drugs."

"He doesn't use, if that's what you mean." And he didn't. I'd never seen him smoke even a cigarette, let alone a spliff. Using was for morons. "He's very much against all that," I told him. But that wasn't what he meant.

"Rarely will you ever find a dealer who uses," he explained. "It's not about getting high, unless we're talking about getting high on power, money or control."

"Oh, he likes those things," I said.

"Most people do."

In many ways, I told him, despite Billy being the central figure in my life for well over a decade, I didn't really know him at all. That didn't surprise him. "How well did Sonia Sutcliffe know her husband, Peter?" he said. As for Billy being a drug-dealer, which seemed to be the angle he was taking, I could offer him nothing concrete at all – except for the bank statements from ages ago which had sounded all kinds of alarms when I'd first come upon them. Obviously, I didn't have any to show him, but he was interested none-theless. He set his jaw a bit firmer, though, when I pushed the conversation towards the robberies I'd suspected he was behind. He shifted position on his seat and leaned forward, putting his elbows on the table. "What do you know about those?" he asked. I had no hard evidence but I'd overheard a lot of Billy's conversations over the years, secret 'chats' he'd gone out of the room to have with this and that mate, and so many things didn't add up. Given the amount of random objects that had 'magically' appeared in the pawn shop, from photocopiers to pianos, if I'd taken Billy at his word I might well have thought I'd been shacked up with Paul Daniels all these years.

As sensational as some of these claims were, nothing I said seemed too much of a surprise to Lewis. He nodded along throughout, as if I was just dotting the i's and crossing the t's on a document he'd long held in his possession, but hadn't been able to make sense of. As I talked, his coffee turned cold and developed a bruise colour on the top, but that didn't put him off. He knocked it back without even wincing, as if it was the sweetness of my words that gave him the real kick he was looking for, not the powdery Nescafé.

After an hour, he stood up and we shook hands and he told me he'd start looking into things. "I know how difficult this would've been for you", he said, staring into my eyes, red from all the emotion I'd been holding back.

"It's more of a relief, if anything," I responded. "You can't imagine how good it is to finally tell someone who can do something about all this."

"I'll certainly do my best," he said. "It's not right that some no-mark like him can get away with giving someone like you such a hard time." We left together and parted at the door, and as I watched him go, I dug out a tissue to dry my eyes.

The place I eventually settled on was a little bungalow in Broughton, just West of Chester. There's a large aircraft factory there now, purchased by De Havilland just after the war, but the shifting sands of the British economy have seen its usefulness whittled down to almost nothing over the decades. Today the factory that once produced just under half the Wellington bombers that dragged the UK back from the jaws of death during the Battle of Britain now just spits out wings for Airbuses. In terms of potential versus efficacy it would be the equivalent of Steve Jobs, after giving the world the iPad, selling plastic phone cases from a little stall in Birkenhead Market. It was hardly glamorous, but then we didn't need it to be glamorous, we just needed it to be safe, and that's exactly how we felt for the year we were there. One year. That was how long we took the lease out on it for; just long enough to stop feeling that every time I opened the front door I was going to find a grinning Billy Harris there gently tapping the blade of a machete into the palm of his hand.

"Well-well, Chrissy," I imagined him saying. "I've been waiting for this moment for a looooong time."

The bungalow, which was picture-postcard perfect (if you squinted your eyes a bit) had a little path leading up to the door with a garage tacked on the side, and thank God, because that's what I ended up using as my bedroom once it was already converted into a bedroom. The two existing bedrooms were hijacked by the kids, the three girls going into one, with Will getting the little box room down the end. It was hardly Camelot, but given what we'd just come through, it was certainly a few steps nearer to a fairy tale castle than I'd ever been before. The lounge was big and had a fireplace, which I always liked to keep lit because it made the house seem alive some-how, like it had a heart. And even if it didn't have a big table around which knights could sit and discuss the business of the day, we could spend our time there together, as a family, reminding each other what we'd come through and how lucky we were to be there.

What I couldn't forget though, was that Kelly wasn't with us. It was like a limb had been removed from me, violently, and I kept wanting to scratch it. I wasn't me without my family around me, my own flesh and blood. You see, having been raised by a 'fake' family I knew the difference blood could make. It has its own way of communicating and the body knows this, even if the mind remains clueless. It's this invisible connection, this psychic 'otherness' that's occupied so much of my time during the second half of my life, and I never get tired of exploring it. What most people don't realise is that these connections don't just affect us here on earth, they reach into the next phase of our lives too, the phase that begins when the blood stops pumping. My twin-sister, for the short time she existed, wouldn't ever have had more than a cupful of blood in her entire body, and yet she's remained connected to me in a more active way than either Olive or Ritchie, or any of my so-called siblings, ever could. So it's more than just blood, and it binds in ways that are next to impossible to describe, way off the spectrum of normal human understanding.

My second meeting with the CID was basically a more concentrated version of the first, only this time 'Lewis' didn't seem quite as relaxed. He'd digested much of what I'd said during our first meeting, and used that as way to ferret out more about Billy and the network he was so clearly hooked-up to. What he'd unearthed he was able to use as a lens through which he could better direct his line of questioning. This, in turn, made *me* ask *him* questions, the answers to which ended up confirming many of the things I'd suspected all along. But there was more to uncover, much more ("We're just scraping the surface here, Christina," he confessed), so it wasn't simply a case of knocking on Billy's door and slapping the cuffs on him. The ripples, as Lewis explained to me, spread far and wide, and it was his job to see which banks on which rivers they bumped up against.

As he talked about the burglary scam I'd signposted him to during our first meeting, I sipped my coffee and fidgeted again with the sugar sachets in the bowl. Trying to keep his tone as relaxed as the first time, he asked question after question, and I did my best to answer them, assuming once again that he was recording the conversation. God knows what Billy would do to me, I thought, if he ever knew I was talking like this about him to a detective. The things I was saying. Lewis would run his tongue around the inside of his lips as he listened, imagining, I suspected, how to turn the information I was giving him into a plan of action. But there was something else going on behind his eyes too, I sensed, something that he didn't feel comfortable sharing with me. Not yet anyway. Instead, he drummed his fingers on the table and told me that people like Billy Harris are very often one step ahead of the curve. "They know what action to take when they sense someone like me creeping up behind them," he said. "So we have to be careful how we play everything from now on." In some ways it seemed like he was preparing me for a fall, setting up his excuses, so if he failed to prosecute whatever plan he and his team were hoping to put into action, I wouldn't be too crestfallen. But if he failed to pull it off, whatever that plan finally was, I'd have no time to feel crestfallen, because as he well knew, I'd be dead in a ditch somewhere.

Our third meeting a few weeks later only ended up confirming my worst fears. Lewis was sheepish from the off and was a little more reluctant to hold my gaze this time. As the waitress brought over our drinks and tray bakes, I sensed he was steeling himself for something. My nerves, I noticed, were all fired up, as if they knew a dentist was about to shove a needle into them without an anaesthetic.

"This is going to have to be the last time we meet, Christina," he said, after a minute or two. His coffee was still swirling around from all the stirring he'd given it with the spoon. He seemed defeated somehow, which isn't a look he wore well.

"Why?" I asked, not really wanting an answer.

"Because you're at risk."

I had to laugh. "What do you mean, 'at risk'?" He was avoiding my eyes, but when he turned to face me, after I'd asked him a second time, I noticed he looked through me or around me, as if he couldn't quite confront the look of disappointment he was about to spit into my face.

"He's out to have you done in."

"Who?"

"Your ex. Billy."

I let my mouth hang open. "Done in?"

"As in … " I watched him struggle for the words. "You know. "

I did know. But it made no sense at all. I already knew I was at risk. That's why I'd gone to the CID in the first place: to remove that risk.

"He's a crafty old sod, isn't he, your ex?" he laughed. I pushed my coffee away, there was no way I could drink it now, not down the pinhole-thin oesophagus he'd just reduced it to. "Listen, Christina," he said eventually, "we know exactly who Billy Harris is. We've known from day one. We know every pie he's got his fingers in, and how deep they're in, but if we start trying to pull them out, it'll mess things up for a lot of people."

I shook my head. "You've lost me."

"It's really complicated."

"No fucking shit," I said, and then I remembered the man I'd known, the bullying man-mountain who seemed only to be driven by the basest things, the same things that teenaged boys liked: fast cars, designer violence, leggy birds and ready cash. "But Billy's not a complicated man," I said, as if that could explain away the sticky situation Lewis had put us both in. "He's just a bad man."

"That he is," he agreed. "But there's far worse than him."

"I'm sure there is. But what's that got to do with me?"

He blew out his cheeks and drummed his fingers again on the table, but there was no music in it. It was simply the soundtrack to my impending doom, the tribal beat that brought King Kong to Fay Wray on Skull Island. I could almost see the ditch I'd soon be lying in.

"Well," he began, "your ex is sort of helping the police get to them."

If I was disorientated before, now I was just plain lost. "Get to them? What do you mean?" The drum beat of his fingers got faster. Maybe if I'd watched more episodes of *The Professionals* things would've clicked into place faster, but as I hadn't, Lewis had to talk me through everything he'd uncovered about my ex, about his lifestyle, and the network that fed it, and it was as he was talking that I came to understand just why the police had given Billy little more than a slapped wrist when he'd snatched Will from the garden, and hadn't even blinked when he'd smashed up one of my cars and defrauded me out of the other.

"So you're telling me that Billy Harris is an informer?"

"Yes."

"For the police?"

"That's right."

I tried to digest this but I didn't even know where to start. What did that even mean? Seeing me struggle, Lewis started to explain. Now that'd he'd managed to get the bad news off his chest he seemed to relax a bit more. He reached forward to take his first sip of coffee. It was mine that had developed the bruise colour this time. He then went on to tell me that Billy had appeared on the police's radar a good while ago. He was brash, he said, reckless, and cocky, and it was inevitable he was going to attract the attention of the law. They started watching him, observing him, and built up a dossier on him, "thick enough to put him away for ages." Why they didn't is because everything they'd learned about him screamed out that he was just a small fish. As with gangsters everywhere, it's always the small ones that make the loudest noise. The bigger fish are the quiet ones, they make no noise and stay out of sight, and yet they're feared more. So once they had enough dirt on Billy, they pulled him in and 'turned' him – if that's the right word for it. They thought Billy was the type of man who, to protect himself, would happily take a dump on others, and so it proved. Men who act like tyrants in their own homes, who beat up their girlfriends, and terrorise their children, are always cowards, and cowards will do anything to avoid going to jail. So Billy was the little fish leading the way to the big fish. And because of what that meant to the higher-ups in the police, they'd quite happily turn a blind eye to all the minor infractions he'd commit along the way. Every bruise on my face, therefore, my arms, legs or back, was just collateral damage in the reckless game of Cops and Robbers that Billy had been playing for years.

"What complicates matters," Lewis continued, "is that Billy's found out you're talking to me." He paused then, knowing full well the impact that was going to have on me. My hands were shaking now and my mouth was so dry it felt like a cat had shat in it, but I had no choice but to ask the obvious question.

"How did he find that out?"

He didn't know but his guess was that someone in the police – who he'd been speaking to in order to get some background on the subject – had let him know, probably to keep him sweet. My trying to get him off the streets was obviously working against the police's intentions, and that wasn't good for them.

"So what you're saying is, he knows I'm trying to get him put away?"

"That's what I've heard."

"And so …" I could barely get the words out. "he's looking to have me done in?"

Lewis knew he had to treat this delicately, and I could tell from the pained expression on his face that he wasn't happy about any of this. To him this was a loss, and he clearly wasn't someone who liked losing.

"What I reckon is, if *you* back down, *he'll* back down." He gave me a moment to absorb that, then continued: "Why we're in this situation now is because Billy doesn't want to go down for anything, but if something happens to you, something 'suspicious', he won't be able to avoid it. However, if he hears that you're not gonna push ahead with anything …" he leaned back in his chair, his face softening. "I'm pretty sure he'll lay off." That was some consolation, I suppose. To back it up, I had the knowledge that he hadn't found me yet. I know he could've if he'd wanted to. He had spies everywhere, one of them would've seen me out shopping, or driving around. I could very easily have been followed back to the house, or the bungalow, and done in. A botched robbery. A hit and run. Anything was possible. These thoughts were all written onto my face in the lines that made up my worried brow and Lewis, I could tell, could read every single word.

"What I've learnt in this job," he said, "is that sometimes you've just got to know when to let things go." Christ, I thought, if I didn't know that I wouldn't have made it out of my teens. "Just try and think of it this way: by having a no-mark like him on the streets, it gets worse people off them."

"But those people aren't hell-bent on trying to ruin my life."

"That's true enough," he answered, "but they ruin a lot of others and that's what's more important to the police. As I said to you before, they're only interested in the bigger picture."

A fly had landed on the rim of my cup. It was slowly crawling around it, taking all the pleasure it could from the few granules of sugar that hadn't made it into my untouched coffee. I'm glad someone was enjoying it. When I looked back up at Lewis I saw his lips were pursed. He'd said what he'd had to say. He hadn't liked saying it, but he'd said it. He looked a little anxious, and very sorry; anxious about how I'd react, and sorry that he'd let me down. Both feelings would fade over time, and in a few weeks, I knew he wouldn't even remember who I was, but I'd still have to live with the consequences of his failure. Whatever anxiety and sorrow he was feeling, therefore, was nothing compared to mine.

A "small fish" Lewis had described Billy as, in a small pond, but that's not what I saw, nor is it the man I knew. Billy Harris knew what pond he swam in alright, and how much space he had to move around in.

"Crafty old sod?" … Yeah, you got that right, 'Detective'.

THE ROAD TO CAMELOT

Phil travelled extensively, hopping between countries like most people do between isles in supermarkets. To make sure it wasn't all business I'd go along with him from time to time, and it was wonderful to start seeing the world I'd read so much about as a little girl without having to worry about my kids being taken and locked up in an attic whilst I was away. In fact, after the first month had passed without me seeing Billy Harris's monster scowl on the doorstep, or smelling his Brut aftershave as he pushed past me into the house, I started to believe I might actually be free of him for good. 'Lewis' must've been right, he'd obviously got on the case straight away and fed word back that I no longer had my sights set on trying to get my ex thrown in jail, and he, in return, must've put his machete back in the drawer.

Coming to terms with that meant I could stop jumping every time I saw a shadow, or heard a car engine rev too loud behind me, and the life-balance we settled into stopped feeling so precarious. The kids learnt to avoid getting under Phil's (and each other's) feet, and if they did, no one shouted, or raised a hand, or set off fireworks. In fact, it was a pretty frictionless zone all round, so much so that we barely ever had to decamp to the bungalow to give Phil some space. The only times we did was when his daughters were home from boarding school, and he wanted to give them his full attention. But it was no more attention than he gave my lot when he was with us, using what free time he had to help the younger ones with their homework or play games with them later on. Stephanie, we'd noticed, was struggling to tell the time on her own, and even as she approached her sixth birthday was having some difficulty with what the hands meant. To conquer this, Phil turned up one day with a massive clock and sat down with her at the dining table.

"This is the time in New York," he said to her, sounding like the world's friendliest teacher. "What time do you think it is there?"

"Err … eight o'clock," she chirped after counting out the numbers.

"Perfect," he said. "Everyone is just putting their coats on ready to go to work. Do you think they're happy?"

"No-oooo," she squealed, "everybody HATES work," and on they continued until it had all sunk into her head. It was amazing to watch.

He was even closer to Little Will, who pretty soon became like his shadow. Will would follow him round all the time, imitating his steps, often sliding into his dressing gown and slippers with his hands in his pockets so that he looked like Dopey in *Snow White and the Seven Dwarfs*. As for me, I felt I was slowly coming into my own too. With support from Phil I was able to get the wedding car business back on its feet, and in addition to that, I started to find more time to let the other part of me come through as well, the part of me I'd always shied away from – in public at least. It was getting stronger now, this sense of who I really was, and as I began to find the inner peace that had always eluded me, I also came to see that within the chaos of white noise that swarmed around the back of my mind there was a pattern there too, shapes, things I could make out that I'd never seen before. It was as if I was learning to see beyond the colour spectrum, into the ultraviolet range that exits out of the sight of most people. It was friends of mine who, over the years, had called this ability a 'gift', and those same friends who suggested that I might like to treat it as such. The best gifts, I knew all too well, are not the ones you put in a drawer and forget about, but the ones you can use to help you in life. So that's what I did, I peeled back the wrapping and took it out of the box. But it wasn't myself I'd be helping, it was other people.

Naturally, I'd known since I was a little girl that I'd had this 'gift'. Ever since that time I saw the old woman perched on my bed after the visit to the graveyard, I'd known I was more attuned to certain forces than most people. I didn't invite them in, but I didn't push them away either. They were just there, in the next room, sometimes with faces and sometimes not, and although they were strange to acknowledge at first, they didn't scare me, because that's not what they're about. It's only the unknown that scares people.

Some people who read this book will split their feelings about me on this issue. They'll accept all the normal stuff, all the abuse and the factual events, because they might be able to relate to that part – and God help them if they can. But they'll turn their noses up at the other stuff, the mystical, or 'psychic' bits, because, in the course of their own lives they'll have never experienced anything similar. That's fine, they know what they know, just as I know what I know. I'm not going to preach too much over the promise of another 'realm', or whatever you want to call it. In all honesty I'd probably have remained sceptical about it myself until I'd learnt more about my twin-sister. She was the lens through which I was able to look back thorough my own life, into my childhood, and once I did, I could see how some experiences were meant to be viewed. It was like seeing in 3-D. Add another camera just off to the side, and what was a flat two-dimensional space is suddenly given an extra dimension.

What many people don't know about themselves is that they too were once twins, just for a few weeks. A third or so of pregnancies begin as twin-pregnancies, but in those first few weeks one twin dies, or gets *absorbed* into the other – often appearing as a birthmark on the skin of the surviving twin. Who's to say where the psychic energy created by this short-lived human life goes to? Could it not be the voice that serves as a person's conscience as they grow through life, or sketches and colours their dreams when they're sleeping?

The first 'readings' I gave were back in Witley Close when I was with Billy Harris, but to call them readings would be to overstate their significance. Really, they were just chats, about as far from the 'cross-my-palm-with-silver' view of a psychic reading as you can get. Sometimes I'd just be sitting with a friend, having a cup of tea in their kitchen and, without even trying, I'd just pick something up, something about them or a family member. Out of the blue I might just ask: "You're not doing anything with a ladder, are you?" and they'd say, "You what?" and I'd have to explain, telling them not to go near any ladders in the next few days. They'd look at me like I was mad, but then, after I'd left, they might receive a phone call from one of their children that would set their hair on edge: "Mum," a son might say, "a tree blew onto the house last night so I need to go up onto the roof to fix it." It would always be something totally unexpected, something no one could've anticipated, and wouldn't make any sense until they'd put it into some sort of context, but once they did, they learnt pretty soon not to ignore it.

"Don't you dare go up any ladders!" they'd end up telling their son.

The school I got the children into was a good one. It wasn't a grammar school, but it had an excellent reputation, and the kids didn't come home from it each day wanting to punch things. Deryn, whose intelligence was starting to reveal itself more fully by the day now, seemed to exist in a different headspace than the others, and so, knowing how much she'd benefit from it, we decided to try and get her a place at the same boarding school that Phil's two girls were at: Howells in Denbighshire, where the actress Nerys Hughes had once gone to, and other such luminaries. We did make an application for a bursary, and were fairly positive that it would be successful, but at the very last stage it fell through. I never got to the bottom of why, but I've a sneaking suspicion that it had something to do with Nadia, who wasn't at all shy in voicing her displeasure at the thought of one of my kids going to *her* school. She was of a very similar age to Deryn, so they'd have been in some of the same classes, if not the same form, and I think this might have been too much of an intrusion for her. Both she and her sister, I was starting to learn, weren't at all happy with the prominent role me and the kids were beginning to play in their dad's life, "spending all his money" as I heard Nadia once put it. Either she said something to the school, or to her dad – who relayed it to the Head – but the bursary Deryn looked all but certain to get suddenly fell through. Deryn was devastated, as was I, because I knew what opportunities an education like that would've opened up for her.

By the time the lease was up on the bungalow, it was pretty clear that Phil and I were not parting ways anytime soon. As our affection for each other had grown, so too did his charity, and to that end he offered to help us move out of the bungalow and into a bigger place in Vicar's Cross. We still spent a lot of time in his house in Gayton, but because his girls were coming home more frequently now, at the weekends and during the holidays, we were having to decamp to our own place more often. The kids were growing too, and needed more space for themselves. We even got ourselves a dog, a beautiful Samoyed that the children fell head-over-heels in love with, Will especially, who was turning into a right little Doctor Doolittle as he got older. The three-bedroom-house I eventually found us was on Thackeray Drive, and it was as much of a step up as the bungalow had been from Witley. Will, for the first time, now had a room he could lie down in without having to bend his legs, the girls were able to get their own beds too, not having to clamber on top of each other to get to sleep, and I had a kitchen big enough to swing a cat around in – not that Will, the animal lover, would ever let me. As well as the extra space it offered us, it also opened up the gap between our old life and our new one, from the rag-tag bunch of nomads we'd *been* to the cosy family we were becoming.

During this time, Phil also purchased two more houses in Gayton, both on Chester Road, which I made it a bit of a mission to do up. The nicest of these was Bickerstaff House, and Phil's original intention had been for us, the whole family, to move into this one building when it was completed. The second one, just by the petrol station, he was planning to do up and sell on, putting the extra cash (which would've been substantial) straight into his pocket. When his daughters got wind of this plan they had a hissy-fit and did everything they could to scupper it. They weren't happy about their dad making any kind of commitment to living with us, even though the idea of marriage was now on the table, and they told him outright that they just wouldn't accept it. They'd always known how to play their dad, but as they were getting older, they were discovering new ways to manipulate him, and he felt he had no choice but to give them what they wanted. As I said before, blood is thicker than water, and Phil was no less of a slave to what ran between his veins and his daughters' than I was to what ran between me and mine. It wasn't that big a problem just yet, but I couldn't escape the feeling that it was going to be a huge one very soon.

When Nadia and Natasha asked if they could look after the dog for a few days my immediate reaction was one of suspicion. It was the school holidays, and they had come home where they lived with their father at the house. Short of things to do there (Gayton is hardly Disney Land) they'd asked when I popped round one afternoon, and felt I had no choice but to say yes. I knew Will wouldn't be happy, but if this was their way of reaching out to me it was only right for me to accept, as the benefits to all of our lives would be huge if the girls' iceberg attitudes towards me thawed even a bit.

"We'll look after it," they said, stroking him under the chin. "We promise."

As expected, Will hit the roof when he found out. His connection to that dog was very strong, spiritual almost, and he fretted that first night whilst parted from it. I chose to ignore his reminder that "They don't even like dogs," in favour of the view that they were making an effort. Samoyeds are quite exotic looking dogs. You can't walk past one and *not* notice it. They look like ghosts, with shock-white coats and palm-frond tails that hook back over them, and eyes that glitter like onyx. They were actually bred by the Samoyedic people in Siberia to help them herd reindeer, but the hunter-part of them has been totally bred out of them, meaning what you're left with now is the perfect family dog. They really can see into your soul, which is why kids – who are much closer to the spiritual world than adults – make such strong connections with them. *If* you're a dog person that is.

But Nadia and Natasha weren't dog people. They'd never had a dog, nor shown any interest in getting one, possibly because it would remove the focus away from them. What they'd also never had, judging from what happened, was common sense. Even a three-year-old would know to keep a door closed if you lived on a busy road and were looking after a dog, but that knowledge seemed to have bypassed the girls within 24-hours of taking possession of him.

We were in Bickerstaff when we heard the screetch of tyres. I felt a shiver run up my spine because I knew what was coming. It wasn't going to be good. Phil had wanted the girls to tell me themselves what had happened, that they had left the conservatory door open and that's how the dog got out onto the road, but they refused, so he had to break it to me himself. I was able to hide my tears but Will ran down the path to see Yogi dead on the road, he howled out in pain. It was Phil who'd had to peel the poor thing off the road and bring the body into the house. Even as he was doing that, with the blood still dripping from the fur, he was trying to work out how to tell me. "He just came out of nowhere, mate," the driver had said to him. "I didn't have time to react." The girls did apologise eventually, but looking back it's hard to believe they were ever truly sorry. In fact, knowing how much trouble they'd go on to cause between their dad and I, I'd go as far as to say that leaving the door open probably wasn't even an accident. They might even have thrown a stick into the road for the poor thing to fetch.

A year-and-a-half later, when the lease was up on the Thackeray house, we upgraded yet again. By this stage Phil and I were engaged – though we didn't make a big song and dance about it – and very much part of each other's lives now. The future seemed written, all we had to do was stand still and the escalator we'd stepped onto just before I'd jetted off to Florida with Mike would take us to our Happy Ever After. Yes, I'd kissed some frogs along the way, but I'd found my prince eventually, and Irby Road, where we moved to next, was to be our castle, our Camelot. Phil would still have his own place (his girls weren't ready for anything else just yet), but there was no question this was a huge step for all of us. I still wanted to maintain some degree of independence, however, so I insisted on paying for the new house myself. I didn't mind Phil's help – God I needed that – but I wanted the satisfaction of knowing that one day I would be able to think of it as my own. It wasn't a pipedream either. After I'd got the builders in to do their magic on the Witley house (the one Billy Harris had trashed), I'd been able to get shut of it for £35,000 – that's after forking out some, but not all, of the twenty six grand I'd claimed from the insurance. This money, I didn't even touch. Not a single penny. I asked the solicitor dealing with the sale to transfer the money straight into Phil's bank account.

Irby Road was my choice. Every house is lovely there, all of them are detached or semi-detached pockets of suburban loveliness. The asking price was £60,000 and Phil said he'd be more than happy to loan me the bulk of it, if I could throw in twenty grand myself. He talked about it being an investment and so, naturally, I took that to mean an investment in us, in our future together – after all, what else could he mean? The deeds, he explained, would remain in his name because it was far simpler that way, but I'd be down as a part-owner. Eventually, once I'd paid him off, he'd transfer the deeds over into my name and I'd be able to sit back knowing I had my own house. Trying to get my head around all the financial ins and outs felt a bit dizzying at first, as I didn't really have much of a head for finance, but Phil did, as did my friend Chris Clare who worked as a financial advisor. I brought him in to go over everything for me. He became very chummy with Phil and both agreed it would be no problem if I told the DSS that the Housing Benefit I was still claiming was being paid to a landlord – they didn't need to know that the landlord just happened to be my partner. To simplify things even more, Phil said it would probably only confuse the DSS if I told them I'd been put down as a part-owner of the property. "They'll only raise an eyebrow at that," he said, "and it's just unnecessary." I looked at Chris and he agreed. "He's absolutely right on that score, Chrissy," he confirmed.

"Whatever you say," I said. "You're the expert."

For two-and-a half years this is how we did things. Each month the DSS came in, I handed it over to Phil and topped it up with other money I had coming in from the bits and bobs I was doing. Every time the sun rose each morning, I was another day closer to owning my own home, my *dream* home, on Irby Road. As lovely as it appeared though, I knew it could look better. It still had someone else's fingerprints all over it. The wallpaper was theirs, the carpets theirs, the colour of the bathroom, the kitchen, they'd been decided by someone else, not me. As it was going to be my home, I wanted it to reflect me, us, my family, who *we* were. So, once we were inside and all the agreements had been made and signed, I rolled up my sleeves and got stuck in.

What I'd never had before – never even dreamed of having before – was an attic, and the opportunities this alone presented were stupendous. The first time I saw it I couldn't stop thinking about how I could've done with something like that when I was a kid. It beat the coal cellar any day. I knew at once Will would want it as his room, and then, as I spun around, amazed by how big it was, I thought I could probably get two rooms in there if I put a dividing wall in. So I did. I had a dormer window installed too, to let some light in, thinking a skylight would make the place still feel a little bit claustrophobic. I didn't stop for months. I worked around the clock and only took breaks to get the dinner ready for everyone. By the time I'd finished, I'd ruined ten tops and half a dozen pairs of jeans, but the money I'd put into Phil's pockets now amounted to more than half of the sixty grand we'd got it for. So I was getting there.

There were lots of amazing memories we were able to christen from this period, but my favourites were probably the 'duvet days' I used to spend with the girls. We'd snuggle up on the couch with a cuppa and some biscuits and I'd press play on the remote control, and the next two hours would be as close to perfection as any mum could ever wish for. Even today, Stephanie (who is 6'2" now) will still pop over for the odd duvet day, but our choice of films has progressed a little beyond *Cinderella* and *Sleeping Beauty*.

Will's love of animals moved into overdrive too during this time. Certainly, he adored whatever pet we had (we always had a dog) but he was keen to extend his interest onto other animals too. One day, after getting home from a reading I'd been doing at a friend's house, I decided to jump into the bath. After slipping off my clothes, I pulled the curtain back from the bath to turn on the taps and suddenly:

QUUUAAAAK!

A big green-headed mallard duck started flapping its wings – in panic, presumably – sending water and feathers spraying up everywhere. It was like the shower scene in *Psycho* only it was the Norman Bates character who got the biggest shock.

"AAAAAAAGGGGGHHHHHHHH!" I screamed.

"QUACK-QUACK-QUACK-QUACK-QUACK!" went the duck.

Not having time to even register what I was seeing, I ran out of the bathroom, and over all the *quacking* and *flapping* I didn't even hear the stampede of feet racing towards me from all directions. The kids found me half-slumped against the door pushing my heart back into my chest.

"Oh, good God Almighty," I panted, "what in the HELL was that?!

"Sorry, mum," Will apologised later when the colour had returned to my cheeks. "The poor thing had hurt its wing and was all dirty, so I thought I'd give him a quick bath."

As bad as that was, it was nothing compared to what I stumbled on a few months later. After doing Will's ironing, I went upstairs to put his clothes away (as expected, he'd settled himself into the now-converted attic). I'd been hearing the scraping sound for a while by this point, but had convinced myself that it was just Will playing some sort of game. He was fourteen now and at his most secretive, so he literally could've been up to anything. Besides, he'd brought so many pets home from so many different places (school, friends, the pond, etc.), that I really couldn't keep up with them all. On this one occasion I knew he was downstairs watching the tele. What I heard moving around in his room, though, definitely wasn't the school hamster. It had weight to it. Mass. I entered the attic slowly, put the clothes down on his bed, and noticed that the noise was coming from the eaves – the tiny triangular space between the roof and the floor that Will had covered with a curtain. I walked over to it, bending lower as I moved to accommodate the sloping roof, then got down onto my knees, and reached forward to the spot where the curtains seemed to meet. Holding my breath, I pulled them apart and —

— *CLANKKKK!!*

Something *launched* itself at me – something *HUGE* – something *looooong* – with a mouth – and teeth – *FANGS!* It moved as fast as Indiana Jones's bullwhip. Seeing my life flash before my eyes, I fell back in shock, instinctively reaching for my throat, assuming a big chunk of it must already have been torn out, but fortunately the panel of glass that Will had used to barricade the eaves had prevented the snake – the fucking *SNAKE!* – from getting its fangs into me.

"*WIIIIIIILLLLLLLL!*" I screamed, trying to scrape myself up off the floor.

"Oh, you found it then," I heard one of the girls say a few seconds later.

From head to tail the snake – it was a python – was ten feet long, and at its widest point fatter than my thigh. The girls had known about it for ages, but Will had sworn them to secrecy, figuring – rightly – that I'd hit the roof when I found out (I literally did!). As I tried to recover downstairs, pacing around the kitchen, waiting for Will to come down and explain himself, I went over what I was going to say to him. Hearing him approach, I got my finger ready to wag it in his face, but just as I was about to start laying into him, those same fangs appeared around the doorframe, then two, three, four feet of scaly brown and beige skin, and then Will himself, his face partly obscured by the fat elephant's trunk of a body, because he had the whole thing wrapped around his neck like Doctor Who's scarf.

"You better have a good excuse for this, young man," I said, backing away anxiously.

"Sssssh," Will whispered. "Go easy on Monty, he's got a really bad cold and I don't want you to scare him."

RUNNING OF THE BULLS

You get to a point, don't you, where you can't help but think about all the 'what ifs' in your life. I'm sure everyone's the same. I have hundreds of them to look back on now, maybe even thousands. What if *this*? What if *that*? I try not to dwell on them too much – I'm just too busy these days and don't really have time – but once in a blue moon, when my current partner is away working, I'll sit down on the couch with a cuppa, put a bit of relaxing music on – Enya perhaps – and allow a few thoughts to lower their sails and drift gently through my mind. This book was born out of those thoughts, examining all the what ifs and what-might-have-beens.

I don't think many people truly realise how precariously perched life is sometimes, how knife-edged the difference is between a happy life and a toxic one. No life is ever fully one or the other, but I'm sure most people, if they could, would choose one that was tilted more towards the former than the latter. And even though we're all faced with choices every single day of our lives, we never get a say in the degree of contentment that defines that life. That decision has already been made for us, by our parents, our teachers, and those around us when we're young and most open to influence. One bad decision leads to a thousand others. If I hadn't gone to that party with John Suckley. If I hadn't given Billy that cup of tea. If Ernest Golightly had been offered a different posting to a different air base. Or if my twin-sister had pulled through. If only the slightest thing in any one of these events was different, my life would be totally unrecognisable to the one I know.

Or I'd have had no life at all.

If she'd survived, I'd have spent my whole life searching for my twin-sister, trying to connect with her, just to know that I didn't have to shoulder all this misery alone. But would it have been as miserable if we'd remained together? Or if I could just have held hands with my mother, my *real* mother, just for a minute, and told her, as she lay dying, "I forgive you", how different would I feel now? How complete?

Another 'what if?', perhaps the biggest, began to form in my mind moments after I learnt I'd lost Phil's baby. He didn't quite reach full-term, but he was with us long enough to prompt thoughts about a long-term future together, one that added a degree of permanence to our relationship that we were, sadly, unable to give each other in the end – although that wasn't strictly down to us. Other factors contributed to that, other 'baggage'.

Losing the baby was a blow though, as anyone who's been through it will tell you. It totally knocked the wind out of our sails, and, after five years together, with external forces trying to wrench us apart, Phil and I really could've done with that wind. To take our minds off the loss we decided that what we should do was take a holiday – not a working one, but a *real* one, with all of us together, as a family, his kids and mine. We'd talked about it before, but for some reason we'd never really been able to get it sorted. I say 'some reason' but deep down I knew the reason, as did Phil. We were scared to. Because we were scared of what would happen if we put all our children together in one place for any length of time. But with the baby dying, and with the pressure building between us all, we felt we just had to give it a shot. If we couldn't make the holiday work then we couldn't make our lives work. That's a lot of pressure to place on what is supposed to be a nice, relaxing holiday, but the truth was, it really was that simple: we had to smash ourselves against a rock (in this case, the one near the southern tip of Gibraltar) and see if we were strong enough not to crack.

Once we'd landed at the airport, we hired a people carrier and all crowded in: Phil and his two daughters, and myself with Deryn, Will and Stephanie. Brina, who'd foreseen the difficulties, was wise enough to stay home. She knew that, even if the flight over was smooth, the actual holiday was going to be anything but. And she was right, the children didn't even want to acknowledge each other, let alone find things to do together. From the second we boarded the plane they did everything they could to put as much distance as they could between each other. It was like travelling with Liverpool and Chelsea fans. Thank God they were too young to drink.

We'd asked the hotel for adjoining rooms. We told the kids it was in case they needed to come in and see us about anything, but really it was so we could keep a closer eye on them. My lot were fine with this, and kept themselves to themselves – something they were used to – but Nadia and Natasha, pampered as they were, had no such intentions. Within fifteen minutes of arriving at the hotel, Nadia came bouncing into our room and sprawled herself out on our bed. I'd been hoping for a lie down, and thought Phil might join me, but she thought otherwise. As her dad finished hanging his shirts up in the wardrobe, Nadia turned to me and threw me a strange look. "*I'm here now*," it seemed to say, "and you are *not* getting your hands on my dad if I've got anything to do with it." What she really meant – as I came to understand in the days ahead – was: "Over my dead body are you getting your hands on our dad's money." What makes this so tragic to me even now is that both she and her sister had totally misread my intentions. I simply wasn't interested in Phil's money. I loved him as a person, not as a bank. His money couldn't hug me, could it? Or make me feel secure, and positive about life. His money didn't teach Stephanie to tell the time, or sit at the table every night and explain long multiplication to Will. *He* did that, *their* father. And he made me laugh. If I could've had him without the money, I would've. But what could a teenage girl, whose claws had been sharpened by her meddling mother *ever* hope to know about the complexities of the human heart? Maybe, in her million-dollar house in America right now, nearly two decades on, she's learnt this for herself. But who knows?

"Anyone fancy seeing a bullfight?" Phil asked, a few days into the holiday. He'd been looking through some leaflets he'd picked up in the lobby and had started flicking through them. I'd never been to a bullfight before, but I knew enough to know they didn't turn out too well for the poor bull. I was a bit squeamish about animals being killed, especially for sport, but I probably would've gone. But then I thought about how much Nadia and Natasha had been getting on my nerves since we'd arrived, and so thought it best to let them have their dad to themselves for a bit. So, as Phil took his girls to the arena to watch the bullfight, me and my gang went for a walk along the coast. The views were stunning. It was the perfect balance of nature wild and nature tamed, and the kids just ate it up. They'd never seen anything like this, and couldn't believe places like this even existed in the world. Such natural beauty was as alien to them as the rings of Saturn were to the Romans. But as jaw-dropping as it all seemed, there was something there that slightly spoiled the view, it was a hairline crack that stretched right across the horizon from one end to the other, and it was something that didn't disappear. Even after you closed your eyes.

One of the ways Nadia and Natasha used to get under my skin was to make suggestive comments. They would allude to the fact that because their dad always paid for everything, he paid for me too – and they weren't just talking about plane tickets. What made it worse was that I could tell these views weren't ones they'd cooked up themselves, but ones they'd had drip-fed into them by their mother. It started with my looks; for example, I always made an effort to look a bit glamorous when I got dressed up – short skirt, loads of make-up, nice hair – but the girls would always go for the obvious jibe, saying I looked like Julia Roberts in *Pretty Woman*. Yes, you can read that as a compliment – beautiful, sexy movie star, what's not to be flattered by? Well, the fact that she was a prostitute in that film, hooking up with someone way out of her league. *That's* what they meant.

One of the leaflets Phil had picked up in the lobby offered whale-watching cruises. He looked at it, saw the little map, and realised it wasn't too far away from our hotel at all.

"Who's up for it?" he asked us, passing the leaflet round for everyone to see. I was, certainly, and the kids were too, mine and his, so we decided that's something we could all do together. None of us had ever seen a whale before, and even if we didn't spot any, the cruise itself would give us a chance to relax and take in some of the amazing scenery.

Before we set off, Phil and I gathered the kids around us and gave them all a stern warning. "There is to be no misbehaving," we said. "This is a holiday. We're here to have a good time, so please just try and get on with each other." My lot nodded and agreed and so did Phil's, and then we all left the hotel and set off for the harbour.

For a little while there was great excitement between us on the boat. We all sat on seats in rows, turning our heads here, there, and everywhere, waiting for the water to break and Moby Dick to reveal himself. But after a while this got quite boring for the children and they turned their attention to the snack shop down below. We didn't want to give them anything too sweet, so we said they could have one packet of biscuits each. Five pairs of hands then assaulted the little biscuit rack as each child made their choice, then we all returned to our seats.

"We know they're out there," the captain said over the Tannoy. "Don't be shy now, come out and say hello to all these lovely folks." I presumed he was talking to the whales.

Within two minutes there was a disturbance, but it wasn't in the water. All heads turned towards the children as Will whined in distress. I thought for a second that he'd fallen in the water.

"That's mine," he yelled out.

"What's going on?" Phil asked. Fingers instantly started pointing and a cacophony of shouts rang out across the bay. Nadia, it turned out, had regretted her choice of plain biscuit and decided she wanted Will's chocolate ones instead. Being older, she decided she didn't need permission so just snatched them from him. Will didn't like this, and neither did Deryn or Stephanie, who leapt to his defence. It was like a scene in *Reservoir Dogs*. Within seconds all five were going at each other like cats in a sack, arguing over their biscuits. So much for a nice, relaxing afternoon. No wonder the whales stayed away, they could've heard this on the other side of the island. We were able to get to the bottom of it, eventually, and I told Nadia that she couldn't just take Will's biscuits off him because she didn't like the ones she'd chosen.

"I can take whatever I want," she snapped back. "It was my dad who paid for them." I was shocked enough by how she'd spoken to me, but she decided to go even further. She rolled her eyes up and down my body and then sneered so everyone could hear: "Just like he pays for everything."

I saw red.

"I'm not having any more of this," I said. "I am fed up of being treated like this by this little … " I wanted to say "bitch", but everyone was watching me, so I scaled it back to "upstart", and then walked away before I said something I might regret. No one bothered me after that.

A few days later it was the final night of our holiday and Phil and I thought we should really make one last concerted effort to have a slap-up meal together. All of us. He took his kids to one side and gave them the sternest warning he could, and I did the same with mine. "Unruly behaviour is simply not acceptable," we told them, "and we just won't stand for it anymore." It seemed so easy, and Phil and I could help the situation by sitting between them so the kids wouldn't have to sit next to each other.

Since the whale-watching cruise we'd existed in our own little bubbles, our own worlds; Phil went off to do things with his kids, and I did similar stuff with mine. It worked well, and we treated these decisions as if we'd just made them out of convenience, rather than admit the truth to ourselves: that we just couldn't work as a family. We came up with the idea for the meal therefore to address that fact. We needed to see once and for all. "If you have nothing nice to say to each other," we cautioned, "then just don't say it."

It started off very well. Drinks were ordered, and then starters, and everyone was getting along nicely. For a while, anyone sitting nearby might even have thought we were a perfectly normal family, just like all the others. The kids were occupying themselves and Phil and I were having a nice conversation, with his arm on the back of my chair. It was a snapshot of the life we could have if everyone just made a little bit of effort. But then I started to feel unwell.

That morning I'd run out of suntan lotion. I'd tried to make it last but after all the hot days we'd been having, I'd finally worked through the bottle. I'd had just enough to keep the kids covered but didn't have enough for me. I should've kept myself out of the sun, or put something loose on to cover myself, but I forgot. I didn't burn too badly, actually, so I thought I was okay, but just as we were sitting down to eat, I felt the first twangs of nausea. I said nothing though, and got stuck into my starter. The wine didn't help. Then the headache that I'd also been keeping to myself started to get worse, and by the time the main meals arrived, just at the point when everyone seemed to be getting along really well, I felt a wave of sickness sweep over me and I had to put my hand over my mouth. Seeing me, Phil took my other hand.

"You okay? You've gone really pale."

All the kids looked over.

"Are you alright, Mum?" Deryn asked.

I suddenly felt very weak and the idea of eating the tuna steak I'd just had placed in front of me totally turned my stomach. I thought I was about to be sick.

"I'm not really feeling very well," I told everyone. "I think I need to go upstairs for a lie down."

I hadn't seen Nadia bring her sniper's rifle, but just like that, she brought it up to her eye, quickly lined it up, and let off a round:

"Not pregnant again, are you?"

The shot went through Phil, through the kids, and straight into my gut. Given the reason we were here, and what Phil and I had been through to make it happen, she couldn't have said a more hurtful thing. But it wasn't just *what* she said, it was *how* she said it, like she'd been waiting all night.

"Right, that's it," I said. I stood up so fast I knocked the table and a couple of glasses went flying everywhere. "I am NOT putting up with this anymore.

Come on kids, we're going." All eyes were suddenly on me, and not just those around our table.

"But we haven't had our dinner."

"I don't care. Let's go."

Phil linked his fingers before him and sank his head down into his hands. You could tell he was thinking, *Did she really just say that?* But she did. Even Natasha seemed shocked. The kids squeezed themselves out of their seats, and I led them, in silence, out of the restaurant. By the time we reached the exit, we could hear the fireworks.

DOWN TO A SUNLESS SEA

"Ladies and gentlemen, please return to your seats and fasten your seatbelts, as we will shortly be making our approach into Manchester."

What the stewardess didn't tell us was just how bumpy our descent was going to be. In fairness, it wasn't her fault; nor could we blame the weather, because the turbulence that knocked us around the cabin during those last few minutes was all self-inflicted. It hadn't even been a long flight, just three hours, and for most of it the children had behaved very well. In quiet whispers Phil and I had talked about the future, slightly anxious in parts, but were able to reassure each other that nothing we'd experienced on the holiday was enough to send us crashing into the rocks. Sometimes we'd hold hands, and if we didn't quite clasp them together with the same firmness we once did, that was because we were familiar enough with each other now, and didn't really need to keep reassuring ourselves the way new couples did. We weren't teenagers after all.

"We're like a pair of old slippers, you and me," Phil said just before we came away.

"Hey, less of the 'old'," I answered.

Because the flight was packed, the children weren't able to spread themselves out as they might have liked. I caught Deryn rolling her eyes when I told her she'd have to sit with the evil stepsisters, but she knew better than to complain. It was for that reason that I thought of her as the sensible one. Before the tray-tables had even been returned to their upright positions, however, there was an escalation of voices behind us, and I had to call into question that judgment. Another disagreement. *Jesus*, I thought, *what could it be about this time?* Phil and I let go of each other's hands and were about to turn when I felt my seat tugged violently from behind. It was Nadia. She was grabbing my headrest in order to pull herself to her feet. Phil, blocked in by my legs, couldn't grab her to stop her, so he just hissed:

"Nadia, what are you doing, we're about to land?"

She ignored him and, with a face like thunder, squeezed herself into the aisle and began an angry march towards the rear of the plane. Phil had no choice but to let her go, so instead turned his attention to Natasha, who looked like she'd just bitten into a lemon.

"What the hell's up with your sister?" he demanded.

"Ask *her*," she said, jutting her chin towards Deryn.

But Deryn, sitting two seats away, was gripped by the same gargoyle expression. They were like a pair of angry bookends, one staring out the window into the battleship grey clouds, the other into the nothingness of the cabin.

"Well?" said Phil, doing just that.

"What?" said Deryn with all the surliness she could muster. So much for being the sensible one.

Eventually Phil was able to get to the bottom of it, but he probably regretted badgering them so much, as it was his own actions that had triggered the flare up. It turns out that he'd never told his daughters about our engagement. Hearing Natasha blab it all out, I had to bite my tongue, as it said so much about how much faith Phil had in us. He said he didn't remember *not* telling them, but that's the kind of response a politician would give about an extra-marital blowjob, and didn't really hold much water.

"I think we'd have remembered if you *had*, Dad," Natasha said, stating the bloody obvious.

By the time we landed there was still no sign of Nadia, but the second the wheels screeched onto the tarmac Phil was out of his seat and bounding down the aisle.

"Sir," came a 'more-than-my-job's-worth' voice, "you can't get out of your seat until we've reached — "

" — I need to see if my daughter's okay," he barked at the stewardess.

Looking back, I think Phil thought he could magic us all out of this mess. There was probably a little bit of denial going on (from both of us) that the bickering of our kids couldn't really escalate to a point that would see us having to throw in the towel. What we'd built up together, against the odds, was so strong that we really did feel indestructible. It would be like a woodpecker bringing down an oak tree. But as I watched him wrap his knuckles on the toilet door, trying to coax his daughter out, I saw just how fragile our foundations were. If magic *was* the thing that was going to get us out if this mess, we'd need more than Paul Daniels on the case. We'd need half a dozen Gandalfs!

Nadia didn't emerge from the toilet until the plane had reached the terminal. God knows what Phil had said to her through the door, or what she'd said to him, but when they returned, she seemed to have him wrapped around her little finger. He barely looked at me and totally snubbed my kids. It was hard to believe that just fifteen minutes before we'd been holding hands, talking about how strong we were, and how much we wanted to be together. Like a pair of old slippers, eh? Yeah, right. A pair of old slippers in the wheelie bin.

"We need our passports," I reminded him as we collected our things from the overhead lockers. Without even looking, he reached into his pocket and pretty much threw them at us. "There you go, Deryn," he said, "big, grown girl like you can sort yourself out from here."

"Don't you dare speak to my daughter like that," I jumped in, "It's that bitch there, that's caused this."

"Don't you call *me* a bitch," Nadia spat, suddenly full of more brass than a tuba.

I had to pull myself away to stop myself slapping her across the face. The cheek of the girl, and of *him*, talking to my Deryn like that, because *he'd* chosen to not to be truthful with his spoilt little brats. What the hell did he expect?

We collected our luggage separately, standing on opposite sides of the carousel. Amongst the families returning from their dream holidays away, we couldn't have looked a sorrier sight: a 'family' split in two, trying to avoid each other's eyes across the island of slowly rotating suitcases. Any thoughts of marriage then felt about as far away as the island from which we'd just flown. How ironic that the very thing he "didn't remember not telling" his daughters was the very thing that would now most likely stop that thing from going any further.

Once we'd collected our luggage from the carousel, we trundled in two groups over to the exit where a couple of limousines were waiting to collect us. In a show of mock-gallantry, Phil stepped back to let me and my kids into the first, which had been arranged in advance, with explicit instructions to take us back to the house in Gayton. *His* house. We slid in without a word and I'd just started to tell the driver to forget any instructions he'd already been given, and take us back to our own place on Irby Road. There was no way I could face Phil again that day, or his little coven of witches, but then Deryn interrupted:

"We can't do that, Mum," she said, "you left the car at his house."

She was right. And not just my car, my house keys too. I could've slapped myself for my own lack of foresight, but how could I have anticipated this? For someone supposedly gifted with strong psychic feelings, I swear to God, when it comes to my own life, I can barely see the hand in front of my face sometimes.

As we were driven back to Gayton, the kids slumped in the back playing I-Spy whilst I sat up front with the driver pretending to doze. I didn't want to talk, but my mind was buzzing with snapshots of conversations I'd had with Phil, turning over every word we'd exchanged during our time away. Were there any clues in there that signposted the way to what lay ahead? We'd even discussed 'waiting it out' at one point; all our kids were growing up now, it wouldn't be too long before the older ones would be out of our hair; before we even knew it, Nadia and Natasha would be so preoccupied with making a success of their *own* lives that they surely they wouldn't want to waste time trying to ruin *ours*. But to entertain that thought, even for one second, was to underestimate one vital element in their make-up: their mother. The Queen Bitch.

Phil rarely ever saw her now, or even mentioned her, but despite this, his ex-wife cast a long shadow over our relationship. Through the meddling of the children they had together, that shadow grew longer as time went on. I never met her, or ever heard her voice, but by way of Nadia and Natasha, I felt I got to know her as well as anybody else I'd met on my journey, and I can tell you this about her: she was as devious as any character from any fairy tale. Just as Kelly had been brainwashed by Billy into thinking ill of me, the girls had too; but whereas the effect upon Kelly served to keep her away from us, the effect it had upon Nadia and Natasha was the reverse. Phil, you see, was the goose that laid the golden egg, and she hadn't married him, and borne him three children (there was a brother too), just to see some other woman swan in and get her hands on *her* precious eggs. One of the ways she did this was to get the girls – her 'worker bitches' – to go into Phil's office when he wasn't around. They'd sneak upstairs and rummage through his papers, his files and cabinets, and photocopy anything that related to his financial situation. She was paranoid that Phil was making more money than he was admitting, and became hell-bent on making sure that what he was giving her for the children's upkeep was proportionate to his income. But no matter how much they kept agreeing on, she always wanted more, which is why Phil ended up no more a stranger to the family courts than I was.

After the limo had pulled up outside the house, I'd have given anything to have just sped away in my own car, but we had the ignominious task of having to wait around for 'Dad' to arrive with the key. The kids were bored and frustrated, so they kicked stones around to pass the time. Soon they were bickering. At least it wasn't raining. To anyone passing we might well have looked like refugees waiting in a camp, or evacuees in 1939, waiting to be collected at the train station. Sitting on my suitcase, I closed my eyes and tried once more to weigh up exactly where we were and what was at stake.

"I'm going to have one house here, and one in America," I remembered Nadia saying, not too long ago.

"Nothing in London?" Natasha asked.

"Oh yes," she beamed, "And a flat in Knightsbridge." I couldn't believe they were having this conversation – right in front of us – about what they would do with their dad's money once he'd died, but they seemed to derive a lot of pleasure from it. Too much.

"What cars are you going to get?"

"A sports one, like a Porsche or a Ferrari, and I might get a Range Rover too, just so I can look down on everyone."

"GIRLS," I said loudly, unable to believe my ears, "your father's sitting right next to you."

"He doesn't mind," piped Nadia. "Do you, Dad?" The thin smile on Phil's mouth resembled a throat after it had been slit, but instead of saying anything, he just simply shrugged. *Kids, eh?*

I heard the second limousine turn into the drive. *Here we go*, I thought. Doors opened and closed, and there was the crunch of gravel as Phil herded his brats over to the house.

"You need something?" I heard a few seconds later.

"My keys," I answered. "I left them here."

"Oh yeah," he grunted. "Give me one second."

He went inside and we waited. After a few minutes he returned and dropped the keys into my hand like I was his parking valet. Above us, smoke-trails from other planes crisscrossed in the sky. Other people setting off to start their dream holidays. God help them all.

"Thank you," I said, and then pressed the button to unlock the car. The kids heaved their suitcases into the boot, and I was about to follow them, but just as I stepped away, Phil spoke.

"You disrespected me in front of my kids."

I thought about what I could say, but went for the least aggressive option. Given the circumstances it was probably best.

"You disrespected *us*."

"It's unacceptable," he said, as if he was my teacher.

"I agree. If you want to apologise, Phil, I'm all ears."

But he didn't want to. He wanted me to. Even though we were only here because of his failure to be frank with his daughters. I knew the reason *why*, even if he wasn't yet ready to admit it to himself. What's weird is – and although I didn't know it then – I'd be here again shortly, not on this spot, nor with this person, but the words and the emotions would be almost identical. Only the stakes would be different.

"Well, when you're ready to," I told him, "you've got my number."

As I drove away from the house, I didn't know if we were over or not. I'd walked away slowly, back to my car, giving him a chance to come and stop me. But he didn't. He just watched me climb in and start the engine, then his eyes went up to the sky, and the smoke-trails. I knew that look. It's one you give God and it means "Help me for fuck's sake!" I'd used it a lot myself, but not for years now.

When I saw him again it was in the rear-view mirror and I was turning out of his drive. I was hoping to see a raised hand, Phil's middle-aged body trip-trapping towards me – "Chrissy, come back, I'm really sorry!" – but all I saw instead was the back of his head, then the door closing. I didn't know where that left us. Were we broken? If so, how badly? Thank God we had our own house, because without that we wouldn't have anywhere to go. I'd been right to plan ahead on that score, and with most of the money paid back to Phil it wouldn't be too long before he'd have to transfer the deeds over into my name. Once that was done – and not a day before – I'd be able relax, because the walls we'd be within would be our own. If we were broken, it wouldn't matter, just as long as those walls held. We'd be safe from the outside world, from arguments with exes, from other people's children, and all the horrible things the world could throw at us. Even the Big Bad Wolf wouldn't be able to get us.

For the next few days the phone sat on the table barely touched. If it rang it was because of friends, or family, who wanted to know how we'd gotten on. I'd look at it as I was passing, and wondered why Phil was choosing to ignore us. Surely, he'd thought about how he'd behaved and come to the conclusion that an apology would be the best way to go. Then he did ring, but instead of an apology, he just wanted to know when was best to come over to bring the dog food. I chose a time when I knew the kids would be out, and then we just sat at the table and talked. We were like strangers with nothing in common, struggling to fill the gaps in our conversation. Phil talked about work, which he'd thrown himself back into, but without much enthusiasm. I told him I'd done some more readings for people and had started charging for them now.

"Quite right," he said. "You give people a lot of comfort. It's only right they pay you for it." He'd never been against that side of me, and always encouraged it.

The biggest relief came from the fact that he was happy to let things continue on as they were with regards to the house. He'd called over each week to see us, we agreed, have a cuppa with me, then be on his way. We didn't need to get our hearts involved. And this is what we did. But as those visits began, and the time between them was filled less with thoughts of what we'd lost and more with thoughts of what we'd gained, the future we'd imagined together for so long seemed less and less real. When I saw him then, my heart didn't buzz with happiness like it used to, and I don't think his did either.

"I don't want this, Chrissy," he said to me one day after a few months, just as he was about to leave.

"Neither do I," I responded.

"Then what do we do?"

We sat with our mugs in front of us, both empty but still warm from the tea that had just been in them. I didn't know what to say. If Phil didn't have an answer, how the hell was I expected to have one? He was the problem-solver. That was his job: to prevent things from coming apart so that they didn't crash. *Well,* we *were crashing!* The obvious answer was right in front of us, but I knew I could never voice it. It involved his daughters and him making a decision, a tough one, but what right did I have to ask him to make it? He had to make it himself, and if he wasn't able to, then ... well, there were more fish in the sea, weren't there – for those still interested in catching one.

"I don't know," I answered finally, hoping he could read all this in my expression. But if he could, he said nothing.

Hearts die quickly if they stop receiving blood, and both Phil's and mine hadn't received any for ages. Not from each other. So, when he knocked next time and I saw the hollow look on his face, I knew what was coming. I'd sensed it anyway, but you didn't need to be Doris Stokes to see that one. I opened the door and he shuffled in, holding his breath, it seemed like. There was no hug, no kiss, just a mumbled "Hello", and even that was hard to make out. He had in his arms a big bag of dog food, a gift for the new one I'd got to replace the one his daughters had killed.

"I was just passing the pet shop and thought you might need some more," he said.

It was hardly a dozen roses, but I thanked him anyway. Dog food wasn't cheap.

I put the kettle on, waiting to hear the sound of the chair being pulled out from the table behind me, but the chair stayed where it was. I got two cups ready, mine and the one Phil always used when he visited, it was one he'd got from work which a contractor had given him.

"Chrissy," he began, "I've got something to tell you."

I stared into the spout of the kettle, watching the first wisps of steam start to rise. Will and Stephanie, I could hear moving around upstairs. They'd appeared when Phil had knocked, to see who it was, but I'd chased them away with a look.

"Before you say it," I cut him off, "I know what you're going to say ..." But did I really? If I tried to anticipate it, it might work to prevent him saying it, and I think (if I was being really honest with myself) that's what I wanted. Because I missed him, and I missed how he made me feel, and I missed the future we'd promised each other. And I missed his smell and his warmth and everything about him. "You've been thinking it's either me or them and you've chosen them." He looked at the ceiling, then at the floor, trying to find the right words. But he obviously failed to find any because instead of using any he simply nodded. He looked quite pathetic actually, with his eyes watering up like a toddler's, still clutching the bag of dog food. It looked like a limp shield in his arms. This successful man, this master of the universe, who sat atop a corporate juggernaut, with thousands of employees around the world, whose livelihoods lay in his hands ... here he was, in my kitchen, telling me he couldn't even master the beats of his own heart. That lay in the hands of his two teenaged daughters, who cared not one shiny shit about his happiness. Only about their own. Who said being a parent was easy?

"I have to."

No, you don't I wanted to say to him. To shout at him. *You really don't.*

He shifted his weight from one foot to the other and told me how sorry he was. I could tell he wanted to say more, but the words just weren't there. Behind me, the kettle stood silent. I hadn't heard it boil but it wasn't making a noise anymore. The two mugs sat there on the countertop, their handles touching, waiting to be filled, but they wouldn't be now. It was a while before I would take them out again, but by then what had been Phil's special mug would be just another cup, one of many that had been boxed up and put in storage where it would stay, wrapped in newspaper, for many, many years.

I didn't follow him to the door. I heard his car start up outside and drive away. Months would pass before I'd stop missing the sound of that engine.

UNIVERSAL ENERGIES

I fell into Reiki the way a child good at dribbling a ball falls into a football team. I'd never even heard of it until about twenty years ago, when Deryn came home one afternoon going on about this thing she'd started doing that involved the 'transference of energy' or something. "Oh, it's amazing, Mum," she kept telling me. Pretty soon she went on to take her Level One exam, which involved going away for a weekend to the countryside to do intensive sessions under strict supervision. "I can't believe what it opens up inside you," she said to me as she was getting deeper into it. "All the stuff it brings out."

We were still in Irby Road then, and by that point I was already coming along with my psychic readings. That meant people beyond my own small network of friends were now coming to me, actually travelling out, which forced me to reframe the readings a bit, i.e. make them a bit more formal. I was reluctant to see what I was doing as a business of any kind, but I did start charging for them, which had the effect of making the sitters (my clients) take it, and me, more seriously. People started coming from everywhere, not just on the Wirral, but across the water from Liverpool, and even North Wales. Some even came in minibuses and made a day-out of it. There were so many, I had to set up a booking system so I could fit them all in. And it wasn't just the kind of people you might expect either who'd come, 'witchy'-looking drama-teachers with shawls and sandals who burned incense day in and day out. I had solicitors, builders, sports personalities and even TV folk – producers, directors, and actors. Shobna from *Coronation Street* came, as did Sonia Greaves who became a frequent client, and eventually a close friend. She was the wife of Bob Greaves from *Granada Reports*, a veteran journalist who was a bit of an icon around the North West for close to four decades. Even if these people turned up a bit sceptical that first time (there was usually one in any group) they came a second time because so much of what I'd say would prove true in the intervening months.

One client I had was a lady who ran Carr Farm in Moreton, and because she liked me, she ended up giving me a room above the jewellery shop in the garden centre. Jackie, another friend, would invite me round to her place to do some readings as well. She'd set aside a room upstairs for me, getting it ready in advance with all the lighting and the candles and what have you, and then invite some of her friends round. As they had a good gossip downstairs, I'd take them off, one by one, and do a reading with each of them. £15.00 wasn't really a lot – that's what I charged for each 45-minute reading – but I said to everybody that if they didn't like what I told them, or how I told it, then they didn't have to give me a penny. No one ever refused.

It was one of Jackie's friends who suggested I try a bit of Reiki on her. We'd been talking and I mentioned that I'd been reading up on it, flicking through some of my daughter's books. I can't say it didn't intrigue me. "You should give it a try, Mum," Deryn had said to me many, many times. "You never know, with your skills."

The friend lay down on the bed – Claire, I think her name was – and guided me through what I needed to do. Unlike the readings I usually did, Reiki doesn't require the practitioner doing it to channel anything that isn't already present in the client. It simply involves the transference of energy – what we call 'universal energies' – through the hands, *into* the sitter, from the practitioner. Anyone at all can learn these skills but, like hypnosis, some will be more responsive to it than others. It's controversial only because of how the media portray it; they present it as a dangerous form of 'alternative therapy' which makes some people choose it over more traditional forms of therapy, and that's not really how you're supposed to look at it. Doctors would never prescribe a course of smiling to you, but anyone could tell you that if you smile more often you're going to live a lot longer simply because you're a happier person, and far less susceptible to depression – the gateway to all sorts of ailments.

I don't think anyone other than me was shocked by how quickly it seemed to work through me. Once I put my hands over Claire's body and focussed my mind on the task, I could immediately feel her energy pouring out. It was like nothing I'd ever felt before. We can all feel the presence of people around us, can't we? – no one would deny that – and that's because every single person has an *aura* surrounding them. It's like a bubble, and it extends around them in every direction by about six feet. The closer we are to someone, the more we can feel them, because we step *into* each other's aura. Once we're inside it, even if we can't see that person's face, we can sense what kind of mood they're in – whether happy or sad or tense or full of anxiety.

Even today, I'll start a session exactly as I did with Claire that first time: the client will lie down on a bed and I'll place my hands over their feet, about four to six inches away, and I'll make little movements above them – no physical contact is necessary. Slowly, as I move my hands, I'll start to pick up that person's energy, it'll jump from their body to mine. Then I'll progress up to the knee – gently – not forcing anything, just moving the hands around the body; and it's around this time that the sitter will 'let me in'. You're establishing trust now, perfect trust, between the two of you – you're picking up their energies, their vibes, and they're picking up yours. I'll then scan the area between the feet and knees, moving up and down a few times, extending further each time, up to the trunk, until I've truly established that vital connection between me and the sitter; and then, lastly, when the client is ready, I'll move up to the head. For obvious reasons this area is very important; it radiates energy like a candle, so you have to be very careful around here, drawing out the energy in concentrated areas, over the eyes – which will tingle – and the mouth and nose, and then I'll move down, slowly, scanning over the chin, tracing the line of the neck, never making contact, my hands floating over their body, surfing and absorbing the waves of invisible energy emanating from within them. Then I'll reach the *solar plexus chakra* – the third from the bottom, which is just up from the diaphragm – and I'll focus on that for a moment; then I'll let my hands drift down to the ground, or the *root chakra*, which sits at the base of the spine. I'm constantly drawing things out of the body, soaking it up into mine, all the negativity, and replacing it with the positive energy from within me. I've always thought of it as an "oil change for the body", and that's what I tell people. I'm taking away the negative energy and I'm putting good back in.

I don't think there's much of an argument to be made these days against the fact that stress can lead to cancer. Reiki – because it deals only in stress-*relief* – can create a cushion around the soul that shields it from much of that stress. The medical profession, of course, has very little time to hear any of this, but then the medical profession has billions of pounds riding on the fact that it *needs* people to have cancer, and therefore it *needs* people to have stress. I know that's a controversial view, but what can I say other than this is what I know. Of course it doesn't *cure* cancer, but without doubt, it limits the number of people who succumb to it.

After any Reiki session, a good night's sleep is always guaranteed for the client, because there is nothing left in the body to get snagged up on all the thorny issues of the day. It doesn't come without a price though for the practitioner. It's not like giving a massage, something I discovered the morning after I did my first session. Because of the transference of energy *out* of the practitioner and *into* the client, there is a great cost to the practitioner. The process is *literally* draining, because at the end of the day, you're just an object who's being *used*, a vessel that empties itself of all the good energy that exists inside it, and is left, afterwards, with just enough energy to make it to a couch to lie down on.

After that first session with Claire, I felt a compulsion to do more. As draining as it was, I felt no less cleansed than Claire did, and I knew it was something I could give a lot more of my time to.

"You see?" Deryn said, when I told her how it'd gone. "I knew you'd love it.

I started to practice after that, turning Deryn's earlier suggestion into an actual goal. I studied hard, went away to Altrincham for a few days to obtain my Level One certificate, then followed this up shortly after with my Level Two. One other thing it taught me is that you can never use Reiki for bad. It can only be used for good; the second you try to pollute its effects with any kind of negativity, it will rebound back on you tenfold, and God knows, I'd already absorbed enough negativity in my life.

But be that as it may, I was about to absorb a whole lot more.

I don't know precisely when it was Phil started seeing Dorothy, but well more than a year had passed before I first heard her name muttered. He'd been seen out with "someone else" at first, that's how friends put it; then, when he popped over one afternoon to collect his rent, he casually dropped her name into the conversation. He shook his head dismissively when I asked about her, as if she wasn't important. "Oh, she's no one," he said. I could tell she was though, and knew immediately that something would be changing soon. It was there in his eyes and, weirdly, his scent. People's scent changes a bit when they're in love, or going through a period of lust, the chemicals in their body alter and a different odour is emitted. Since Phil, I'd stayed away from men during this whole time. I still went out with friends, dancing and what have you, but if ever I found myself caught within the headlights of a man's gaze, I'd subtly move out of the way and let them fix on someone else.

Each Valentine's Day after we split, I kept receiving flowers. The first time I was quite puzzled about who they might be from, but when Phil next called round, he was only too happy to drop the hint that he was guilty as charged. He did the same for my birthday too, but with less mystery – and Christmas – throwing in a few presents for me and the kids. But after Dorothy's name first got mentioned the gift-giving suddenly stopped.

She was Polish. Maybe she'd been pretty once, but at 35, which she was when he met her, she had a pinched face which, over the years, must've squeezed out the qualities that made her attractive to most suitors. Phil, however, wasn't most suitors. Given how little time he had, I imagine he just went onto the internet, signed up to a dating service, and then just plumped for the first person who didn't seem like a psycho and was mildly fanciable. She was the opposite of me in so many ways, and I couldn't help but notice how awkward he seemed when he came round. Up until that point our conversations had always remained friendly, even jokey, but now they were as dead as our love-life had been in that last year. It was as if he was embarrassed by our history and all the intimacies we'd shared.

By the time it came to watching him stand up in court a few months later and trash me, it was hard to believe we'd ever shared anything other than hatred. As I sat there, listening to him explaining the situation to the judge, I didn't recognise him. This was 'Business Phil', 'Boardroom Phil', who lived in the sky between countries, hiring and firing people; it was not the man who played Grandma's Footsteps with my kids, and then read them *Where The Wild Things Are* before bed. I'd known for ages that his daughters were desperate to get me out of "their dad's" house, so the quicker I paid him back all the money I owed him and got the deeds transferred over, the better. But that day never seemed to get any closer, and now, as I heard speak him in that courtroom, wearing his smartest suit and flashiest silk tie, I watched it getting further away than ever before.

When it came my turn to speak, I fell apart. The more I said, the more I realised that the case I was making was held together with Blu Tack. Phil had told me, promised me, that the house would go into my name eventually. I told the court this, but I couldn't make myself sound as convincing as Phil, who was now saying that this wasn't the case, and never had been. So it was my word again his, and who was the judge going to side with: Posh Phil in his tailored suit, flanked by a team of pin-striped lawyers, or me, in my cheap frock, with my lip quivering and my hands shaking?

"And the agreement you made ... " said his barrister, looking right down his nose at me, "so you *claim*, was that you would be a part-owner of the property?" I nodded, my fists bunched nervously at my sides.

"Y-yes."

"'Part-owner'. What did you interpret that to mean?"

I poured out some words, but I sounded unsure, and when I saw Phil shaking his head condescendingly, the way politicians do, and the judge making the same action, my nerves turned into panic. I could feel everything coming apart around me. Phil had set me up. The tangle that had brought us here had arisen out of the issue with the Housing Benefit: they, it turns out, weren't at all pleased with the arrangement I 'claimed' I'd made with Phil, and even less happy about the fact that I'd listed him – my then-partner – as my landlord (after forking out twenty-five fucking grand for it!) under the assumption that I'd end up the full and rightful owner of the property. Honestly, he should have got Oscar for how clueless he acted when talking about our agreement. It was "clearly set out", he told the magistrates in Liverpool's Queen Elizabeth Law Courts, that the money I was handing over to him was just rent and nothing more. There had been "no discussion whatsoever" about me one day taking ownership of the house.

When Chris Clare was called to the stand I thought he was going to save me. Thank God I had a mate here who would speak up for me and expose Phil for what he was: a lying fucking toe rag. But if Phil was getting the Oscar for Best Actor, then Chris was getting Best *Supporting* Actor for his part, because the lies flew out of his mouth like bats out of a burning cathedral. He said he had "no recollection" of an agreement like that ever being discussed, and backed up Phil in every way. What he also failed to tell the court was the number of business deals he'd set up with Phil since I'd introduced them, and how his bulging wallet would suddenly shrink if he was to speak out against him. I thought I'd been very good at avoiding sharks when it came to befriending people, but there's always one that sneaks in, isn't there?

Whenever I looked over at Phil during the court case (he only attended one day of the three it dragged on for), he'd look away from me and *cluck* his tongue. It was heart-breaking to see what my former white knight had changed into over the last few years. *Yeah, sure, I'll rescue you, babe, but only if there's something in it for me at the end.* What could possibly have made him turn on me like this? And Chris? And all those others – oh yeah, there were a few – who took to the stand to speak out against me?

The answer could be summed up in two words: *Fucking Dorothy.*

From the second she arrived in his life, she did everything she could to get her feet under his table and her knickers next to his bed. She didn't have any children herself, so perhaps that's why Nadia and Natasha weren't quite so hostile with her – nothing to compete with. But seeing the matey relationship Phil and I still had together put her on edge for some reason, and she made it her mission in life to destroy it.

"The agreement we made, if any," Phil told the court, "was for the house to pass into the possession of my two daughters when they were of sufficient age."

"And my client was fully cognisant of that fact?" my barrister asked him.

"She was, yes," Phil answered. "Very much so." I honestly wanted to faint. He seemed so convincing. A man like that would *never* lie, would he? Not to a judge. Look how slick he seemed, how in control of his faculties.

As the days passed and the lies mounted, it looked increasingly likely that I might actually spend time in jail for this. The charge being levelled at me was fraud, and the sentence more than just a few weeks, all for something I was duped into. During a recess, I told my barrister, in no un-stark terms, that if a prison sentence was handed down, I'd have had no qualms about taking my own life. There was simply no way I could continue on, not when people thought of me as a criminal. All the maulings I'd endured, over the years, from those ravenous wolves who'd tried their best to tear me to shreds, and the one that actually managed it? Well, he was the quiet sheep who I'd given my whole heart and soul to.

Phil had changed the name on the deeds of the house to those of his daughters. He'd done it ages ago, I found out. There never existed on paper anything approaching the agreement we'd made. The house belonged to the girls and that was that. And as we entered the final day of what felt like the worst few days of my life, one thing seemed clearer than anything else: just how screwed I was. In my mind I kept seeing a prison cell, and the thought of it froze my heart. *Me* a criminal. I couldn't deal with that. And there was Chris Clare in his fancy fucking, pin-striped suit, with his silk handkerchief sticking out of his pocket, and his wallet bulging from all the deals he'd made with that duplicitous twat I used to share a bed with. Perhaps I should've called over to Phil so everyone could hear, and told him about all the times his new 'best mate' had tried to get me into bed, even while we were together; or the times he'd put his hand on my knee, or asked me out for a drink. "I won't tell Phil if you won't." If I'd let his hand wander any further up my skirt we probably wouldn't even be in this situation, but is that really the only way a woman can take control of her life? By spreading her fucking legs? Screw that. If that was the world then I didn't want any part of it, and I was already thinking of the easiest way to depart from it when the verdict was read out.

I didn't get jail. But I did get a good kick up the arse. The judge, in his summing up, described my plight as a "heart-breaking" one, and was able to recognise that it was my efforts, and mine alone, that had transformed the property from a run-of-the-mill town house worth sixty thousand quid, into the five bedroom palace that would soon sell for three hundred grand. He also seemed wise to the fact that prison would offer no benefits to anyone, not the DSS, not my kids, and certainly not to me, and when his gavel came down to dismiss the case, it sealed his final word on the matter: I had three weeks to get out. Though I'd narrowly avoided prison, even that was a kick in the throat. I had no back-up, nothing planned; that house *was* my back-up, that was why I'd poured my very guts into it.

But even six weeks was too long for one person:

"ONE WEEK!" Nadia shouted, just as the judge was standing, ready to leave. He looked up and followed the sea of heads that were all turned, in shock, towards her, then raised his finger.

"Do not push me on this, young lady," he said. Then he pulled back his bony hand and swanned towards the exit as everyone rose to their feet. A mark of respect apparently. I had none to give, his words had deprived me of all respect, for the system and for myself. Especially for myself. Two seconds later he'd vacated the room, leaving a huge judge-shaped hole in the court, but an atomic-bomb-shaped one in my life.

BABY, IT'S COLD OUTSIDE

Five pounds of spuds are not going to fit inside a two-pound bag. And by the same logic, the furniture from a five-bedroomed house is not going to fit into the back of a Minivan. I realised this, with no small amount of horror, when that same Minivan turned up to cart my stuff away on the day the judge had ordered us out by. A Minivan was all I could stretch to, and were it not for the kindness of a few close friends, I wouldn't even have had anywhere for it to be carted off to. Other friends and associates helped where they could, but in reality, most were just people I'd rubbed shoulders with over the past few years. "If you can take anything," I'd basically begged them, "just grab it, and I'll get it back off you later." Every single item, from the couch to the washing machine, right down to the smallest pot plant, rubbed in just much how I'd failed over the past three weeks. I'd done everything I could to avoid this happening, but I'd just kept running into one brick wall after another.

"Where do you want this, love?" a voice said from behind me. It belonged to a man who'd done some work on the house a few years back. He was carrying a lovely ornament I'd bought a while ago that looked great in the sitting room, but I barely knew him from Adam.

"Can you hold onto that yourself?" I said, fighting back the tears. "I'll take it back off you when I'm on my feet again."

"No worries, love," he chirped.

From the moment I arrived back after the judge's ruling, I was on the phone trying to stop this from happening, but it was like trying to stop the tide from coming in with a soup spoon. I rang up my bank that first day and asked what I needed to do in order to get myself a mortgage.

"Well, you'll need a deposit," the fella began.

"Okay," I said, writing it down on a pad. "And how much are we looking at for that. Roughly?"

"Roughly?"

"Yeah, you know, like, ball-park figure."

170

I nearly laughed when he told me, and I made him repeat it because that sounded like a lot of zeroes to me.

"No, I meant a *deposit*, not the full flippin' mortgage."

I broke it all down in my head: a £30,000 deposit meant *two thousand* readings. That meant 83-days, round the clock, one hour per reading, without a break. I couldn't supplement myself with Housing Benefit either because, in light of what had just happened, that was the first thing that had been snatched away from me.

I rang other places, housing agencies, private landlords, anywhere I could think of that offered the slightest whiff of security, but all I heard was the same thing over and over: "You'll need six months' deposit, and six months' rent in advance." Some were friendly, some were not. Each day the children would sit around the table in our soon-to-vanish home, and look down at their ever-shrinking meals.

"How did it go today, Mum?" they'd ask that first week. By the end of the second they'd stopped asking.

"What about this one, Chrissy?" someone asked. She was holding onto a lovely cabinet I used to keep the spare plates in. I had no idea how to answer. Having the space for a spare *anything* seemed a luxury I could no longer afford. Again, it was the same answer: "You couldn't keep hold it for a while, could you?"

I probably should've kept a record of who took what, but I wasn't thinking straight. I just assumed people would know to contact me when I'd sorted myself out. But a lot of these 'friends' were people I barely knew and the stuff they took I never saw again. Some of it I was able to store in a basement in Caldy, where a couple kindly offered to look after it for me, but other than that it was little more than a garage sale without any money changing hands. I could blame Phil's daughters all I liked for reducing me to this, but at the end of the day it was their dad who'd made all this happen. It was *him* who'd lied, to me *and* to the court; *him* who'd strung me along all those years, pretending he was someone he wasn't; and now, when the chips were down, it was *him* who was putting me out on the street.

As the last of the vehicles drove away, I tried to take some comfort in the fact that at least our furniture was safe, a claim I was sadly unable to make about *us*. Deryn was okay; no longer reliant on handouts from me, she'd recently found work in an office in Heswall; and, as luck would have it, one of the ladies she was working with had a house to rent, so she was able to bed herself down there, taking Stephanie with her. Kelly was still undergoing her brain-washing programme with Billy (yeah, even then), so I didn't have to worry about her being made homeless as she was married and living in her own home in Bromborough. And Brina had friends she could go and crash with too, so that was good. But things weren't so clear-cut with Will. He'd evolved in the past couple of years from Doctor Doolittle into Bear Grylls, and his interest in nature was morphing from a mild interest in pet animals into all things Grizzly Bear-ish. Not really a child now (he was fifteen when this happened) he'd recently bought himself a two-man tent and had taken to going out and sleeping in the woods, sometimes with his mates, but more often than not on his own. He said he preferred it to the house, which didn't surprise me given everything he'd been through. It unsettled me at first, I admit, but it was a bit of a blessing in all honesty, because it took some of the pain out of the decisions I now had to make. I wanted to tell him there was no way I could let him sleep rough – which is, technically, what I'd be letting him do – but what choice did I have? I just had to put my faith in God and pray that the caul that he'd been born with would finally bring him the luck I felt he was more than owed.

Some nights, Elizabeth, my next-door neighbour on Irby Road, was kind enough to offer me a place to stay, and if Sabrina found herself without a bed too on some nights, she'd join me. I also crashed in West Kirby sometimes at another friend's, Caroline's, but because I didn't want to show her or Elizabeth just how bad my situation was, I'd tell them both I had somewhere else sorted for the next few nights, so they didn't worry. Most of the time, of course, this was a lie, and I'd end up doing something I never thought I'd do in my life: I slept in my car.

These were pretty low times, believe me. I can still remember the mental anguish that flooded my mind as I tried to settle down and get comfy on the lumpy seats that were to serve as my bed for the night. They were not meant for sleeping on. But as the streetlights would flicker on, and the sound of the traffic faded to a distant hum, all I'd be left with was the sound of my own breathing and the still-fresh memories of the cosy life we'd all been living until recently in that lovely, warm house.

My Camelot.

Had it all been a dream?

To bounce up high from something, you need a hard surface against which to bounce. A pavement. A road. The forecourt of a block of flats. The bottom of a well. Logic dictates that the harder you hit it, the higher you'll bounce… Unless your brains get splattered in the attempt, of course. There's no question that on the nights I was forced to sleep in my car I was at the bottom of that well. The morning I finally hit it I can recall as clearly as thirty-seconds-ago. It was winter, and it was snowing, but I can't remember which side of Christmas it was – the nice one or the depressing one. The car engine I couldn't really afford to keep on, so I just slept under my coat and a pile of blankets, with my seat tilted right back, pressing into my arse or my side if I lay on that. It had been a tough night, very long, and I'd become even more familiar with the tiny dots on the fabric roof of the inside of my car. We'd had snow recently, lots of it, but there'd been a fresh blast of it in the night, some of which I'd watched fall. It blew into all the crannies on the windscreen, rounding off the hard edges of the wipers and expanding until eventually the edges met and the whole car looked like a big white wedding cake. I could've wiped the snow away from the windscreen by switching on the wipers but decided not to. I liked how secluded it made me feel. It was like being in a grotto. But just because something looks enchanting doesn't mean it feels warm, as the breath rising up in front of me kept reminding me. Fuck, I wish I'd brought more blankets, I was freezing my tits off now and just couldn't get my shivering under control. This must've been how Captain Scott felt in his tent on that last day. I just hoped the children were warm where they were, especially Will. I prayed to God he'd had the good sense to crash at a friend's last night, because a tent wouldn't have done him much good. Even Bear Grylls would've headed over to the nearest Marriot.

There was a sudden knock and some of the snow dropped off the driver's window just to my right. I saw a shadow over the car, a person outside, two of them maybe, and through the flakes of snow, my eyes were dazzled by a flash of fluorescent yellow. Another knock, more snow fell off, and then a voice.

"Hello?"

I wiped the sleep out of my eyes and wound the window down. The bright glare from the hi-vis jacket hit me like a slap. I saw a radio, a walkie-talkie, and a black truncheon.

"Have you been here all night, love?"

"Sorry?"

The sun was out, but low, and the figure stood in front of it, partially blocking it, but every time it moved, even slightly, the sun shot needles into my eyes.

"The lady in the house there – " he flicked his chin towards the house outside which I'd been parked all night, " – she says you've been here all night." I had to blink a few times to take in what he was saying. *The lady in the house, the lady in … ?* "Afraid you're not allowed to do that, love, it's a private road." Then it came to me. The 'lady in the house' must've been Dorothy. I was parked outside the house on Irby Road, *my own* house, half on the road and half on the pavement. *This'll take some explaining*, I thought. I began doing just that, trying to sound friendly and not combative at all, but I probably looked like death warmed up. The policeman nodded in that cold *'couldn't-give-a-shit'* kind of way they all seem fluent in, and then asked for my driving licence. I showed him it, and then he started wiping the snow from the windscreen.

"Any reason why you're missing your tax disk?" he asked, looking at me like he'd just discovered a dead toddler in my boot. He was right. It wasn't there.

"Err … no, I can't think how that's happened," I said, panicking. "It was there yesterday."

"You know, it's illegal to have your car out on the road without one, don't you?"

"I swear to God, it was there." I'd only renewed it a few months ago. I might be crap at picking boyfriends, but I wasn't about stuff like that. I started scrabbling round for it in a frenzy, because it was clear that this was all he was interested in now, but after watching me for a minute, pulling up the mats, and reaching under the seats, he stood upright and sucked in his breath. "Gotcha!" I could see him thinking.

This wasn't just a random stop, by the way. Dorothy had called the police that morning with the intention of getting me – and my car – removed from the area. Funnily enough, thinking back, I thought I'd heard someone earlier, a man and a woman outside the car, talking quietly. I thought I was dreaming at the time, but it must've been them, her and Phil, trying to see if I was inside.

Eventually, I had to give up. The disk just wasn't there. The hi-vis copper didn't miss a beat. He reached into his pocket to pull out his pencil, and as he started kicking the snow off my number plate to copy it down, I thought to myself, *Well, this is just fucking perfect, isn't it?*

He left me with a ticket and a warning: I had to get the car off the road within 24-hours or it would be taken off me. "Could be worse," he said, tearing out the ticket, "I could take the vehicle off you right now but that wouldn't be very charitable of me, would it?"

If I slit my throat there and then, I wondered, as he drove off, would they write-off the fine or would my kids have to pay it? Unfortunately, I didn't have a bread knife on me, so instead I clambered out of the car and crunched through the snow over to Elizabeth's. My hand was shivering so badly it took me a few attempts to ring her bell. I showed her the ticket and broke down in front of her as soon as she opened the door. There was also a fine for a thousand quid or something. Before I'd even finished the cuppa she put into my hands, she'd gone upstairs to grab Matthew, her eldest son, and once he'd thrown some clothes on, he came down to help me search for the tax disk. We turned the whole car upside down trying to find it, and after ten minutes Elizabeth told me to bring it into her driveway so that at least we knew it wasn't going to be hauled off anytime soon.

I climbed back inside to start the engine, and Matthew got down on his knees to scrape away some of the snow that had built up around the wheels so I could move it. Then, just seconds after he disappeared by the front left wheel, he called out. In his hand was a small piece of paper, coloured slightly, and circular in shape. There was a date in the middle, printed in strong black ink. The relief exploded out of me, and when my head fell forward it accidentally beeped the horn. Did I care? Did I shite. I just hope it woke up that bitch who was sleeping in my bed, in *my* fucking bedroom.

Shortly after this, I was giving a reading to another friend, Michael, a solicitor I'd gotten to know in better times. I'd been forced to up the ante on the readings since almost losing my car, which meant I was able to give a little bit of money to those who were able to help me out. Elizabeth's I was crashing at quite a lot now, and Caroline's too, but I was doing my best not to get under anyone's feet. "I won't be here long," I'd tell them, to which they'd just reply, "It's really no problem, Chrissy," but how could it not be? When working, I rarely mentioned my personal life to clients, but when the house was taken away from me, I had no choice. I had to tell people I was no longer in a position to do readings from home, so if they wanted one, I'd either have to come to them, or they would have to arrange somewhere. Michael, who felt like a big brother sometimes, picked up how out-of-sorts I'd seemed in recent weeks, and would often ask if everything was okay. When I spilled the beans (I didn't mean to, but he expertly whittled them out of me), he was amazed that I'd been able to keep my mind so firmly focussed on the readings, whilst my body was being pulled apart by wolves. He looked away for a moment, and I saw his brow furrow as he tried to chase down a thought. He must've caught it because he looked back at me with a glint in his eye.

"Didn't you tell me once that you'd made investments in a few things?"

"Did I?" His memory was better than mine.

"Years ago, after your ex trashed the house, you said you put some of the insurance money towards the refurbishment, but some of it you invested … Or am I going mad?" I had to ask myself the same thing. I trawled through my memories, going back years, but then, when he reminded me of Chris Reid a very good friend of mine whom I had known for years and trusted, introduced Chris Claire to me', it started coming back to me. Yes, the two Chrises *had* been friends, but they'd fallen out shortly after Chris (Clare) had duped me out of the house. The reason he mentioned it, he said, was because he'd seen some flats recently that he could really imagine me in, but – same old story – without a deposit, that's where that thought would have to stay: in his imagination.

Now it was my turn to furrow my brow. There was something in it, though, because a memory did emerge, of a conversation I'd had with the other Chris. There'd been so much going on in my life at that time, all of it dwarfed by fears of Big Billy turning up and slitting my throat, that I'd simply buried all memories of the conversation. I had met Chris, briefly, written him a cheque, and he'd gone off and done his thing with it, whilst I went back to checking over my shoulder every thirty seconds. The investments were all overseas, but I had made them, and it was quite a few grand, so unless something had changed, I should still be able to get my hands on them. It was just a few shares with Allied Dunbar, and one or two other companies that were on the up at the time. Chris knew I'd have some money left over from the insurance and, chancing his arm, asked if I'd ever consider investing it. "It'll just be sitting there in your building society going to rot otherwise."

When I got onto him again, after my session with Michael, I hadn't spoken to him for years, but he remembered me, and our conversation, and promised to look into it for me.

Thank God for people who chance their arm, because the very next day he was back on the phone.

"Good news," he announced, and I could see him, sitting back in a leather chair, putting his feet up on the desk, with a cigar in his mouth. The shares had actually crept up to sixty grand at one point, but various things had hit the market in recent years, and they'd taken a bit of a tumble. However, if I wanted to cash them, they'd still pay out a healthy £8,000. I had to sit down. *Wow*, I thought. Okay, it wasn't sixty, but eight grand was more than enough to drag me out of the swamp Phil had thrown me into.

"When do you think I could get my hands on it?"

"A couple of days," he said. "Maybe a week. You want me to start the ball rolling?"

Did I? Jesus, talk about a rhetorical question!

Within a month, I had a new place. I followed Michael's advice to the letter, and made an offer on the most suitable of the flats he'd picked out for me. It was way out of my range but, if my offer wasn't accepted, at least I had a few back-ups. But I didn't need one; my luck, which had been swinging away from me all year, now swung back with a vengeance, and by some miracle, my offer was accepted. Michael's main frustration, he said to me later, was that he wished I'd told him earlier, because he could've stopped me losing the house.

The new flat sat midway between the Dee Estuary and the River Mersey, in a place called Upton. It needed a bit of fixing up, but for me, that was more of a draw than anything. It just gave me more of an excuse to roll up my sleeves and to get stuck in, and I liked that. Out went the rough edges, and in came the smooth; out went the angry splashes of colour, and in came the muted hues of autumn, the candles, the incense burners, and the calming music. Of that, I'd soon be needing a lot more, because the chaos that followed me round like a starving dog wasn't quite done with me yet. In fact, when you're done reading through what comes next, you'll end up believing that everything that had happened to me so far was just a warm-up for what was to come.

"GIVE US A TWIRL, GOLDILOCKS"

He wasn't the first fella I'd danced with since Phil, but he was the first one I didn't mind walking back to the bar with after the song had ended, knowing a drink was on the cards. His eyes didn't look too hungry, and that was probably what made the difference – there wasn't a hint of anything Harvey Weinsteinish in them, but there *were* stories – long and interesting stories – and in the walk over to the bar I convinced myself that it would be no skin off my nose to hear one or two. But was he a man who would talk about himself constantly, or was he someone who would ask about me? The difference between the two would decide whether it was one drink or two.

"So, you've already met my mum, then?" Deryn said as we sat down on stools on the opposite side of the bar to her. We both pulled strange faces; mine said, "Ah, it must be destiny," but the comically arched eyebrows of this interesting Silver Fox expressed something else: "Surely you mean your *sister?*" I laughed when he said it, what woman doesn't want to hear that when she's knocking on the door of her fifth decade? Deryn winked at me. "He's a keeper," she seemed to be saying.

The Plantation in Chester certainly might not have been the world's sleekest nightclub, but Deryn worked there, and it was nice to drop in once every blue moon to see how she was getting on. Years had passed since I'd been to a club for any other reason, but nothing had changed, the women still wore skirts up to their knickers and danced around their handbags, and the men still stared at the women like vultures, trying to decide how tough they wanted their meat after the lights came up.

Wilf didn't seem like a vulture. More like a kestrel. He liked to swoop down after work, he said, to relax and wind down, and get his head out of business for a while. During that time, in the weeks leading up to the point I met him, he'd got to know Deryn a bit, and she'd told him all about me. She thought he might be just what I was looking for, despite me telling her repeatedly that I no more wanted a fella in my life than I wanted brain

178

cancer. I'd packed up Phil's mug two years before and didn't feel ready yet to put someone else's in its place. But I *was* ready for a laugh and a giggle, and when Whitney Houston came on, crooning about how much she wanted to dance with somebody, and I found myself bumping bums with this charming man, who didn't seem to care how he looked on the dance floor, I realised I might be ready for a boogie too.

"Here she comes now," Elizabeth's mum said when I came down the stairs, and swept into the lounge, like it was my coming-out party. "Give us a twirl, Goldilocks," she threw in, and I did, just to see the smile on her face. She always called me Goldilocks, because of my blonde hair and the ringlets I put in sometimes if I was going out – which wasn't that often. I'd done it for my first date with Wilf because I wanted to look my best when he called round to take me out for a meal. "God, look at them legs," she said. "You wanna be careful with them, Chrissy, or you'll take his eye out."

I was still living in Irby Road at the time, not yet having had my chat with Michael, and because I was back at a sensible hour, I didn't bother anyone when he dropped me off later.

"Have a nice time, Goldilocks?" Elizabeth's mum asked when she saw me the following morning.

"Lovely, thanks," I smiled, giving nothing away. But there was nothing to give away, other than how nice it had been to have a grown-up conversation again with someone who seemed very much into me. He knew a lot already from what Deryn had told him in the club before we'd even met. She'd sold me as an idea to him way before that first dance, but what she hadn't prepared him for was just how pretty I was (his words, not mine). This talk was making me blush, but it was still lovely to hear. What Deryn hadn't prepared *me* for (not that she could've known) was just how much money he had in the bank, but I got some idea when he walked me out to the brand-new BMW parked outside Elizabeth's house.

"This is nice," I said, with some understatement, as I slid inside. It was like stepping into something from *Star Trek*.

"Yeah, it's not bad," he answered. "I got it for a snip at ninety."

"Pounds?"

"Grand."

He started up the engine and I settled back into what must've been the comfiest seat I'd ever sat in, and we glided like a snooker ball across a baize table towards the restaurant. I couldn't even hear the engine, it was like a cat purring. The meal we had was great. It was a Chinese he took me to, the best in the area, and we had a full banquet, with enough food left over to feed an army if one happened to be passing. Wilf used chopsticks, probably not as well as he thought he did, but I stayed in my comfort zone and went for a good old knife and fork. Did Wilf enjoy the wine a bit too much? I don't think so. I certainly didn't notice, but then that's the problem with first dates, you're only seeing the magic trick itself, not all the wires and trap doors that go into creating the illusion.

"How's your duck?" he asked, deftly shovelling some crispy noodles into his mouth.

"Delicious," I said.

When he drove me back, he made sure to take me the long way home. Not because the roads were less congested or because he wanted to try something on, but because he wanted me to see where he lived. He could show off his ninety grand car all he liked, but it was just a toy compared to what we drove past on the detour he took me on through Frodsham.

"Just up there," he said, the streetlights glinting off his Rolex watch. "You can just see the outline of the house." I didn't need to peer because you couldn't really miss it. It was the kind of house artists painted pictures of, or fiction writers wrote ghost stories about (more about which, soon.)

"Veeery nice," I said, but inside my head was like, *Oh my God, you live THERE!* I knew the area, not well, but enough to know that the only people who lived there were the ones who'd done well in life – *veeery* well. But a second later, as impressed as I was, a strange shiver ran up down my spine. *Hmn*, I thought, *perhaps it was just the air conditioning in his car/spaceship.*

On the next date, a short time later, we went for an extra bottle of wine, and Wilf felt bold enough at the end to steal a kiss. It wasn't stolen, exactly, I helped him in no small way with the heist, and we both walked away with the spoils. When the third date rolled around – or maybe it was the fourth – what was stolen was bigger, and I became even more complicit in the crime, though there was very little guilt felt by either of us. We were grown-ups after all.

It was as we were advancing to this point, though, after the meal and the dessert that followed, that I should've noticed the little red flag going up in the back of my mind. I thought by now I'd know when one was being raised, but because I hadn't had to guard myself against one for so long, I didn't even notice it. Towards the end of the meal Wilf raised his finger and the waiter rushed over.

"Yes, sir?"

I thought he was going to call for the bill, but instead he asked to see a list of the spirits they had. The waiter nodded and went to get the list.

"Always good to finish off a meal with a nice kick of something strong," Wilf said, peering down at the list when it was brought over. "What do you fancy?"

"Just a Baileys for me," I said, wanting more of a tickle than a kick.

"Double?"

"Definitely not."

But it wasn't just a kick Wilf wanted, it was a full-bodied assault. "Give me the 18-year-old Glenfiddich," he said to the waiter. "And make it a triple."

"Certainly, sir," the waiter said.

"Oh shit," I thought.

Wilf didn't build the house he lived in, but he might as well have. It was rebuilt, to his specifications, out of junk, recycled junk, and looked quite spectacular now. Actually, that's not strictly true; it was rebuilt it out of the profits from his business, which was in recycling. He'd set it up himself, from scratch (the business, this is) and built it into one of the biggest recycling companies in the country, and his house – a sprawling, open-planned palace – reflected that. It was even featured in a magazine once, under the headline, 'Home of the Month', which caused him no end of pride. The business certainly put a few quid in his pocket each month, enough to a think a ninety grand BMW was a 'snip' – although I don't know exactly where the money came from, and never questioned its legality (ring any bells?). What was refreshing about Wilf, certainly in those early days, was that he wasn't all about the money. That was just a footnote, an accessory, and he only spent it because, as he kept putting it, "It's there to be spent."

It was a while before I first stayed the night. My scars from Phil hadn't entirely healed up yet, and there were still one or two left over from Billy. There was no way I was going to jump in too fast. But the slow start suited us both: things were still up in the air for me with my living situation, and Wilf was all over the place with his work. When I did finally stay over, I was never able to shake the feeling of unease I'd felt when we'd first driven past his house. Each time we went near it I felt it again. It couldn't be the air conditioner in the car *every* time could it? If so, why I did I still feel it when I stepped out and walked towards the house?

Frodsham, if you don't know it, is a very interesting town. Except for being known these days mostly as the birthplace of Gary Barlow, it barely registers on a map today, but it has a prominent role in history because of the significance of its river – the Weaver – where the much in-demand Cheshire salt used to begin its journey out into the world. Less well known is that James Bond himself lived there until he was a teenager, helping out his dad from time to time in the Ring O'Bells pub. At least Daniel Craig did before drama school and superstardom dragged him off to Hollywood, and forced a Walther PPK in his hand.

From the top of Frodsham Hill, under which the town has cowered for centuries, the view is spectacular, showing panoramic views of Cheshire and the duvet-spread of land and river that winds its way over to Liverpool. On Overton Hill next door, there used to perch an imposing helter-skelter, but that was pulled down in the Queen's Silver Jubilee year of 1977 after years of dereliction. In the shadow of that lay the Mersey View Hotel, a sad-looking nightclub now, but back in the day it used to play host to loads of up-and-coming bands, one of which went by the ridiculously-thought-out name of The Beatles. But before even that, *long* before, in fact, another group did a good deal of scuttling around there, but the collective name for what they were known as wasn't a group at all, but something for more disconcerting. They were known as a *coven*.

Frodsham had witches. Or, to put it another way, it had a community of people who *believed* there were witches amongst them. Nowadays, such women might purchase themselves a little crystal ball or some Tarot cards, and give readings up in a spare bedroom, but back in the old days, before there were nightclubs or helter-skelters to keep folk entertained, these women were subjected to all sorts of humiliating trials; and when they failed them (which they invariably did) they were put to death in the most appalling ways imaginable. Hung, drowned or burned at the stake, there was no method of despatching them that wasn't on the table, given it wasn't them being despatched but the Devil, who had taken control of their bodies. Chester, just 15 minutes down the A56, is awash with the blood of guiltless women who found respite only at the end of a rope in Vicars Cross, usually under the watchful eye of a stern witchfinder. People like Matthew Hopkins, the government-appointed Witchfinder General would get paid up to £25 to 'cleanse' a village of all its witches, so it was in their interest to find, and eradicate, them. Ellen Beech and Anne Osbaston, both from Macclesfield, were strung up in Chester for practicing what was described as 'the dark arts', probably meaning that one or two people who knew them got flu and died. Anne Thornton, who lived in nearby Eaton also suffered a similar fate, as did Mary Baguley from Wildboarclough, who was hung for bringing about the death, through 'witchcraft', of a man named Robert Hall. But these are just a handful of cases, and are only remembered because Chester was a major civic centre and had a better system for keeping records than Frodsham. I mention all this, not just because it's interesting, but because it plays an important part in what soon unfolded. If Billy's behaviour I can put down to the mistreatment he and his mother suffered at the hands of his abusive father, then Wilf's I might be able to put down to something far more peculiar – but I warn you now, you're going to have to take a big leap of faith with me to buy into it. I know I had to, and to this day, I still struggle to make sense of it.

If Wilf had mentioned his ex-wife when we first sat together in The Plantation with our glasses empty, I might well have thanked him for the drink and bid him goodnight. In all honesty, it probably would've depended on what his eyes did the moment he mentioned her: did he shift them to the side surreptitiously, or did he keep holding my gaze? These things, subtle as they seem, can make all the difference. It was weeks before he finally coughed out his first mention of her, but months before he'd shifted the "Oh, we're divorced" to the much more honest, "well, we're *in the process* of getting divorced." She was his second wife too, which he also held back for a while, as if he didn't want to admit that he'd failed twice at something. Trying, but failing, to be gallant about it, he'd hinted that the divorces were more their fault than his and complained that the money had complicated things enormously. "I've got to be very careful," he said. Divorces can be very costly to those with a bit of cash in the bank, and every action has to be thought through. Each date with another woman, for example, can end up being weaponised and end up on a solicitor's desk ready to strike you down with. It was almost a facsimile of the Phil situation, I thought, but I gave him the benefit of the doubt because everyone deserves a fair chance.

Those doubts were stretched nearly to breaking point though, when I finally started to stay over regularly. He asked me, on one occasion, if I wouldn't mind parking across the road, then leaving first thing in the morning, "just in case she turns up to collect her mail." It was an odd request, I thought, but he had his answer ready to go: "If she sees the car and realises someone's been staying over, she'll be banging on the door of her solicitor at nine on the dot." I had to trust him, what choice did I have? I just wish he'd been honest with me from day one, because at my age, I really didn't want to be creeping out of my fella's house at stupid-o'clock in the morning like some naughty teenager.

The one advantage it offered was that it meant I didn't have to spend as much time in the house, which still unsettled me. I didn't quite behave like little Damien at the end of *The Omen* when his dad dragged him kicking and screaming into Guildford Cathedral, but it wasn't too far from that. Something definitely stirred inside me each time I went near the house. I could sense a presence there, and it was not a happy one.

Usually, when I'd leave the house, I'd have a change of clothes with me, and I'd go straight to work, which I'd started doing again recently in the form of nannying. I'd done bits and bobs over the years, and soon let word get round that I was looking for something more full-time. Eventually, a guy in the garage I went to, passed my name over to a young couple he knew, Ruth and Richard, who ran a farm in Utkinton. They were after someone to look after their children four days a week, and knowing me quite well, he sang my praises to them. *Perfect*, I thought, after they rang me to arrange a meet-up. Four days. That would still allow me a full day to do my readings and my Reiki. When we did meet, I liked them, but I didn't warm to them as much as I did the kids, all five of whom seemed to take to me from the minute they met me.

"If they're happy, then we are," Ruth said, and we shook hands.

Once I got settled into my new routine, I'd head over first thing – whether straight from Wilf's place or my house – and begin the military-like operation of getting breakfast sorted for everyone. Often I'd stay there, depending on my shift, until they went to bed. I'd read them a story, which they all loved, and in no time, we got to a point where they didn't want me to leave.

"I can't tell you what it means to finally have someone we can trust," Ruth told me one day when she stopped for a minute to have a cuppa. She was always rushed off her own feet with farm stuff, as was Richard.

"Well, I can't tell *you* what it means to finally have a job I actually love," I told her. And I really did mean it. I enjoyed the routine it gave me each week, as well as the security, and it meant there wasn't so much pressure for me to pack my weekend with readings. When I was done each evening, I'd usually head straight home, but sometimes, if Wilf had called, we'd arrange for me to go over, and I'd either cook something or we'd drive out to a restaurant for a bite to eat and a glass or two of wine.

On one occasion when I popped over, I saw some vans scattered around the drive and some men in hardhats and hi-vis jackets just packing up for the night. Wilf came out and told me that he'd hired them to undertake some work on the house – an extension he'd wanted doing for a while. They seemed a pleasant enough bunch and I said hello, knowing I'd have to get used to them being around for a few weeks. But the next time I headed over there was no sign of them, their vans, or the extension.

"One of them saw a ghost" Wilf told me, when I asked him what had happened. I thought he was joking.

"A ghost?"

"In the lounge. Made him a bit jittery." He said that the builders had reported a few strange goings on since they'd started the work – which didn't surprise me in the least – but the ghost had been the final straw. "It was a bloke; a big, tall bloke," Wilf had been told, and he'd been spotted crossing the kitchen. The guy who'd seen it, a local fella, was really freaked out by the whole experience, and had managed to convince the others that the place was haunted. Whether they believed him, or just decided to offer an act of solidarity, the whole crew had immediately downed tools and took off. Although I expressed shock at the news, there was part of me that understood exactly where the bloke was coming from. Phil's own children, I later discovered, had reported hearing and seeing things too. The ghost, or 'entity', was definitely not from a good place. It had evil within it, and I don't want to sound any more unhinged than I might already, but I'm not entirely convinced it was human, even if it took a human form. People are often dismissive of Ouija boards, and quite rightly so, because people haven't got a clue how to use them, but in the right hands, they can do untold damage. All it would take is a well-connected person to try something a bit out of the ordinary, or even a bit reckless, and it's not impossible to bring something back into the space with you. What Wilf *couldn't* bring back after the sighting, into the kitchen, or any other room in the house, was a single contractor from the company the bloke worked for. That meant he had to start looking again, which required a lot of ringing round until he found a new company up to the task. Finally, he ended up finding a reputable firm that undertook the remainder of the work *without* taking on the unsettling dimensions of an M. R. James story.

When he'd purchased the property originally, Wilf hadn't given much thought to what might have occurred there in the past, but whoever does when they buy a house? A nice view is a nice view. Centuries ago, such views didn't exist solely for the purpose of allowing wealthy business owners to build their houses on, they sometimes had a far more sinister purpose, and that purpose, much as it dumfounds people in this day and age to even consider, was to enact the final part of the horrid business people like Matthews Hopkins were paid to undertake: the trials of women accused of witchcraft.

As I said before, much is known about the Chester witch trials, but almost nothing is known about the Frodsham ones, and I suspect, many others around the country. It's generally accepted that these things occurred, but not to what degree. As well as being sensational, they're also incredibly sad. I do believe in witches, not the way they're perceived, but I obviously speak from experience when I say that some women have gifts that not everyone is able to comprehend. What makes the stories so sad is that these women would've been just like me; sometimes they were young girls, other times they were old women, and they suffered appalling fates, simply because their behaviour didn't fit in with what was considered 'normal' for their times. But they were all real people with families, brothers, sisters, mothers, fathers, and their own children too. The loss felt by these women, the grief and sense of injustice they would've felt, as they were subjected to these horrendous trials, and then put to death, would have caused untold stress, and this stress really can leave a stain on the physical space in which it was created. It hangs in the air for decades, centuries even, and can affect people who spend time around it in different ways.

I came to learn about the Frodsham witches, not from the internet (about which there's next to nothing written), but from what some of the locals told me. No one knew everything, they just knew one or two bits, and I was able to weave together a fuller picture out of all the loose threads I was offered. On the actual site where Wilf's house had been built, I discovered, the witches weren't hung or drowned, but burnt at the stake, presumably to cast the evil out of them. It was done on that particular spot because it was more visible to the locals, and the more visible it was, the more people would get the message that it was wrong to indulge in the Black Arts. The Witchfinder would *always* find his witches because that's what he was paid for. If he didn't find any to 'cleanse' from the community then he wouldn't get his fee, and it wouldn't have been hard, if cash was on the table, to get people, *poor* people, to speak out against each other, whether they had any special gifts or not.

My guess then is that the 'ghost' witnessed by Wilf's builder was connected in some way to these poor women, these 'witches'. Perhaps he'd knowingly made accusations against one of them and had died consumed with guilt or loathing for a world that had treated him badly. Maybe his own wife had been accused. Or perhaps it was the manifestation of a number of spirits that had taken on a form the builder only perceived as male. Just like some people can make out more colours than others can on the colour spectrum, some people can do it with energy too, and in this case, the builder (who wasn't even aware he had this skill) caught a glimpse of one end of the energy spectrum, and didn't know how to process it. His untutored brain (just like my own, when I saw the woman on the edge of my bed) repackaged it into a recognisable form, the end result of which is what he described to his colleagues. These manifestations of energy, which is what they are, don't always take on this classic form, though. They can make their presence felt slowly, over time, and not just via a visible form. The energy can seep slowly into a person, over years perhaps, and change their characteristics, both physically and internally, to a point where that person barely remains recognisable to themselves.

If your scepticism about any part of that outweighs the credibility that I'm quietly hoping to put across in this book, then you might not want to read on beyond this point, because I'm about to take you into some very strange places.

"Do you fancy coming over tonight?"

"That would be nice. Do you want me to bring anything over?"

"Just yourself."

This is pretty much how the calls would go once Wilf and I had reached the position where we could start calling ourselves a couple. He'd ring at the end of the day, just as I was gathering up my stuff at the farm, and he was packing up his briefcase.

"Okay," I'd tell him, still getting used to having another man in my life. "Let me just go back and take a shower and I'll be right over."

As time went on, the phone calls would get earlier and earlier, drifting closer to four o'clock, and then three, and then two, and I would have to excuse myself for a couple of minutes to take them. They also started to become more frequent. I told Wilf it wasn't always easy to get away on the farm, even for a minute, as toddlers don't have batteries you can take out if you need to leave them for a while.

"Ah, they'll be all right," he'd say dismissively. "I just wanted to hear your voice."

"Yeah, well, you've heard it now," I'd say, pretending not to notice the gentle slur in his voice, "now I need to get back."

Later on I'd arrive at his, looking my best and smelling of soap, and we'd decide what to do. Meal out, or make something at home? Catch up on gossip or watch the tele? More and more the tele would win. One time as I was heading over, I was speaking to my friend Theresa on the phone. She'd called earlier and I rang her back just as I was setting off for Wilf's. He was away at a meeting and wouldn't be back until late, but he'd left me with a key. My plan was to let myself in, have a soak in the large bath, watch a film maybe, and then wait for Wilf. "Help yourself to a bottle of wine," he'd said. That sounded good to me. A big goblet of Shiraz in the tub with a load of candles around it, what could be better? But as I turned into Wilf's drive, Theresa made this strange shivering sound. She didn't know I was popping over to Wilf's, but I had been talking about him, and as the shadow of the house fell over the car it was like someone had just walked over her grave.

"You're going to his now, aren't you?" she said, all serious suddenly. Like me, Theresa had a gift, even more pronounced than mine, and it was never more in evidence than it was in that moment.

"How d'you you know that?"

She didn't answer straight away, but I could tell something had ruffled her. "Just be careful there, Christina," she said.

"I'm only coming over to have a bath," I laughed. "But if it's any consolation, I'll make sure I hold onto the handrails when I get in."

Once I'd parked up, I got my bag and headed over, but as soon as I opened the door, I knew something wasn't quite right. Even people who make no claims towards being psychic can sense when someone is standing right next to them. I mentioned it before; it's because you're entering into that person's *aura*, or that person is entering into yours. What greeted me when I stepped into that massive entrance hall, was that same feeling, but the aura I sensed wasn't white, which signifies purity or truth, it was dark, black almost, which means fear or distrust. All my instincts started telling me to turn round and go back out, but how the hell would I ever explain that to Wilf? Besides, I knew that nothing from the other side could physically harm me, and with that knowledge I pushed aside all the unease that was building inside me and walked through into the lounge. But whatever it was that was there with me didn't want to leave me alone; just as my shadow remained alongside me once I'd turned on the big light, the dark presence did too.

I decided to skip my long soak in the tub. The bath could wait.

But the wine couldn't. I went straight through to the kitchen and grabbed the bottle I was after, hoping that whatever force was following me around would eventually get bored and go and play in another room. The bright lights helped, and so did the TV, which I switched on once I'd crossed to the other side of the room. Perhaps my new 'friend' wasn't as much of a fan of *Coronation Street* as I was, but then it never was the same after Bet Lynch left. I parked myself down on the settee, put my phone down on the coffee table next to my wine and tried to relax, knowing Wilf would be back in hour or so.

It seemed to work. As I settled back and watched the complicated lives of those on the cobbles tangle themselves up into ever more absurd knots, I felt the sinister presence fade away. I drank my wine, big gulps at first followed by little sips, and when the adverts came on, thought I'd head back into the kitchen for a top-up. Silly me, I should've brought the bottle through. I reached forward to grab my glass and then, suddenly, there it was again: the *presence* – stronger this time, and even more malevolent. Every single hair on my body stood up on end, and at exactly the same time that I felt it, my phone rang and I damn near jumped out my skin. I might have even screamed.

"*Get out the house now!*" It was Theresa again. She spat out her words like a blast of machinegun fire: "You're not alone in there, Christina – *there's something in there with you* – I don't know what it is, but it's not good!" Theresa was about the most switched-on person I knew, particularly with regards to seeing things through her 'third eye' which is what we'd call the gift we both had, but the clarity through which she saw things made mine seem like it was all fogged up – and here was proof of it. I knew I'd be an idiot to ignore her, so instead of picking up my glass, I went for my bag and headed straight for the door.

"Just stay on the line for me, will you," I said over the pounding of my heart, "just till I get to my car."

"I'm not going anywhere," she reassured me.

Imagine someone walking directly behind you, someone big, massive, copying your walk, their arms and legs swinging in step-with yours, breathing down your neck, that's how I felt as I marched to the door, snatching up my coat as I went. But when I heard, or felt, something in my ear, like an actual whisper, all pretence of calmness left me, and I just bolted for the door.

"Are you alright?" Theresa wanted to know. She could hear panicked breathing, and the lock being fiddled with, and then footsteps on the tarmac as I hurried to my car.

"I think so," I said eventually, getting in and locking the doors, hoping the presence had been content enough to let me leave its home and didn't stalk me to the car. I immediately punched on the overhead lights and flicked the radio on too. Then I sat there, shaking, trying to get my breath back, and watched as the windows steamed up around me. The DJ on the radio then introduced the next song, The Righteous Brothers, who proceeded to unzip their *Unchained Melody*. But nothing felt as unchained as I did right then.

CYPRUS HILL

Except for the pillow fights, the dressing-up in bits of old curtain, and a total absence of Nazis named Rolf, I was starting to feel more and more like Maria Von Trapp with each passing day on the farm. The children were great fun to be around, and it was wonderful watching them grow and discover things in an environment that had, sadly, remained as out-of-reach to my own kids as it had for me: one free from violence, or even the threat of it. I often wondered how my own lot would've fared if they'd grown up in a family like this one, full of kindness and support. There'd be far fewer visits to the counsellor, that's for sure. One thing I did sense though, after a while, was a bit of tension in the air, not between me and the kids – who I adored – but between Ruth and I. I'd ask the children to do something and she'd override it – needlessly, in my opinion – as if she wanted to remind me whose kids they actually were. I didn't mind, they were her kids, but it might've rankled her that when it came to reading them a bedtime story, they would always say they preferred me to do it, rather than her. I think she thought I was getting too close to them. Her and her husband being farmers, they wanted to raise future farmers, and would sometimes have them out working all hours, to "toughen them up". But I was the opposite of that, a comforting friend, rather than a stern teacher.

One afternoon, a few weeks after my 'Amityville' experience at Wilf's house, my phone rang again. The children had just eaten their lunch and were sat at the table doing some colouring in, so I reached into my bag to answer it. *Strange for Wilf to be calling this early*, I thought, *I hope nothing's happened.*

"… don't s'pose you're able to … *hicc* … come and collect me, are ye?"

I'd noticed the slurring in his voice previously, but it was never so bad that he couldn't get his words out. This time I could barely understand him. He'd had a business meeting and the client kept insisting on "just one more", but by the time they'd polished off half the bar and staggered out to the car park,

Wilf saw two identical BMWs next to each other, both sporting his number plate. "Taxi for you, fella," the barman said, seeing him fumble for his keys. The problem was, I was the only taxi number he knew.

I didn't tell Ruth the reason I had to leave early, just that it was something personal, and it'd only be a one-off. She let me go, but I felt horrible having to lie to her like that. She was up to her eyeballs herself on the farm and had to drop everything so I could go and collect my pissed-up fella from the pub. It did not bode well.

When it happened again a few weeks later I told them the truth. I didn't mention that he'd gotten himself blottoed in the pub, just that his lift had let him down and he needed collecting. To them, there was no difference. I was still letting them down, and that was twice now, which wasn't what they were paying me for. Also, I think they might have suspected I was lying to them, which was awful. I told Wilf, once he'd fallen into in the car, that he really had to cut out this behaviour, because it was having a detrimental effect on my work. He sniggered. "Your *work*," he said, as if it wasn't important at all, but he did say sorry later that evening.

"You have to have a cut-off point," I told him. "You're a grown man, Wilf, you can't just get rat-arsed whenever you feel like it and expect me to come and collect you." His hands went up.

"I know, I know," he semi-apologised, "It won't happen again."

I never did visit the house again on my own. I'd still go round for meals and to stay the odd night, but I never felt comfortable in the place ever again. Whatever dark force it was that had chased me out that night must've known I wasn't as suggestible as others it had toyed with over the years; the builder for example, or any of the house's previous owners; or even its current one, who it had more time to groom for whatever malevolent purpose it saw fit.

One evening I turned up to find Wilf not at home. *That's bizarre* I thought, there's nowhere in the house you *wouldn't* hear the bell, and I rang it a few times. His car was there so I knew he was in, and also that he was expecting me. Uneasy, I walked round to the side of the house, looking through the windows and calling his name, but there was no response. I decided to give the bell one last try and then, when I walked back round to the front, there he was, standing at the door in his pyjamas. As if that wasn't weird enough, he also had on his face what looked like a mask, but then I saw that it wasn't a mask at all, it was his face. It had changed somehow, with his brow all sunken forward as if the muscles in his forehead had collapsed over his nose. He looked like a fucking zombie.

"Are you alright?"

"*Whaa?*" he said, but not to anyone in particular. His eyes chased after the source of the question but never quite seemed to find it. I'd never seen him like this before. I stepped inside the house, passing him, and walked through into the lounge. I couldn't smell any alcohol on his breath, but I found an empty bottle of vodka in the kitchen bin. He didn't seem drunk though, he seemed … well, is *possessed* too strong a word? I got him settled on the settee and put some coffee on, and as it slowly dripped through into the pot, I tried to pull him back to reality. But it was clear his mind was a long, long way away from Frodsham.

"I'm just feeling a bit down today," he confessed, once I'd got some coffee in him. I rubbed his shoulders as he sat there, slumped over. His muscles felt tighter than the links on a ship's anchor chain. Was it stress at work? That didn't seem likely, because he liked his job, loved it (so he told me), but I knew he'd mentioned a few times that he was growing bored with it. After an hour or so there was a glimmer of his old self again, so I made him a toastie and left him with a few more headache tablets, then drove home. I'd known alcoholics before, seen how they could become totally detached from themselves, and behave in ways totally alien to their own character, but as I said before, this seemed different. This seemed *worse.*

When I spoke to him again, days later, I brought up what had happened, but he told me he remembered nothing about it.

"It couldn't have been that bad," he said, making me feel like I was over-analysing it. I should've filmed it. However, just a few days later, it was already starting to seem like a dream. Maybe it hadn't been that bad. Maybe I was just projecting sinister associations onto his behaviour given what I'd experienced there myself recently. Maybe I'd dreamt the whole thing, as he suggested. Either way, Wilf and I soon drifted back to our usual routines, and things continued on, exactly as they were until, just after lunch a few weeks later, my phone rang again. I looked at the screen and saw it was him. *Here we go again,* I thought.

When I rushed to my car ten minutes later with my stuff spilling out of my bag to go and collect him, I still had the echo of the warning I'd just been given by Ruth ringing in my ear. If this was to happen again, she'd made clear, they'd have no choice but to look for someone else. I promised them it wouldn't.

Wilf had spoken about Cyprus early on in our relationship, but only as somewhere he loved to visit from time to time. Another year might have passed before he first mentioned packing everything up and moving out there. I thought it was just a pipe dream. Everyone has them, but the difference when you have a few bob in your bank is that you can bend your pipe dreams into reality. The boredom that had been creeping into him at work, and which he'd tried to push back by turning to drink, was getting on top of him, and after a couple of years of my being with him he decided to act on it.

"Why Cyprus?" I said.

"You ever been? It's amazing. Everyone's so relaxed out there, and the quality of life is second to none." We were at another restaurant, sitting by the window, and he nodded towards it. Inch-thick streams of heavy rain, blown by the howling winds, were streaking sideways across it like watery lightning.

"You don't get *that* for one thing," he said.

I could see his point.

It was Limassol he had his eye on, down on the south coast, but because there was so much space out there, he didn't want to just hop into someone else's place, he wanted to build his own. From scratch. To that end, he'd already started the ball rolling, and was now at the point where he just had to go out and choose a location.

"When are you flying out?"

"Monday morning."

He seemed happy at the thought, which was great, so clearly this was a good thing for him, but I didn't know what it would mean for us in the long term. We'd had a lot of ups and downs in the time we'd been together, with many more downs than I'd have liked. If it meant me stepping back so that he could live the life of an ex-pat in Cyprus that he'd always dreamt of, then that was what I'd do. I'd already been let go by Ruth and Richard, because Wilf hadn't been able to cut down his drinking. Despite his many promises, he hadn't made any attempt at all from what I'd seen to cut down the boozing, as the lunchtime meetings only seemed to increase; but always, when I went to collect him, there was never any sign of the person he'd supposedly been meeting. I started to wonder if these people even existed.

How Ruth and Richard got rid of me was a bit underhand, but I can't really blame them. They'd gone on holiday and said to ring them in two weeks when they were back, but when I did, there was never any answer. Finally, when I did get through, Ruth told me they'd got an au pair in, and were sorry they hadn't told me. But they weren't really. All the sorrow was mine, as it meant I wasn't going to see the children again. I'm sure they wouldn't have liked it either but, being farmers' kids, their parents would've turned it into a valuable life-lesson: "Don't get too attached to things!"

More nannying work followed, taking me here, there and everywhere, and one of the jobs I said yes to took me past Wilf's house, which still sent a chill up my spine whenever I drove past it. One afternoon, as I was driving past it on the way home, it wasn't a chill that overcame me, but something else entirely. A feeling of suspicion. There was car in his drive, but not one I recognised. What was especially weird about it was I knew he was flying out to Cyprus that day. *How odd*, I thought. Why didn't he tell me he was getting a new car? It wasn't until I got home that I remembered it wasn't a new car at all. It was his ex-wife's. Fair enough, I thought, but what the hell was it doing in his drive? There was nothing in the house that was hers. Had he bought it off her? Did she need to collect something? Or did she have to sign a document in relation to their divorce and couldn't face looking at him? But if that was the case, why in God's name was her car still there the *following* morning? It hadn't moved, not an inch. Nor did it budge the next day, or the next, or for the remainder of the entire week he was away. Was she living there while he was away?

He returned that weekend, tanned and full of beans, and as he opened his arms to hug me, I just came out with it:

"You took her with you, didn't you?"

His arms dropped like pigeons shot out of the sky.

"I've no idea what you're talking about."

"Don't talk to me like I'm an idiot, Wilf. I saw her fucking car."

"Oh, *that*," he said, trying not to miss a beat. "That was just a business thing."

"A dirty week away with your ex is business, is it?"

"I had to take her over there because we're still tied up in a few things together."

"What, like bed sheets?"

He sighed, exaggerating his frustration, like adults do with children, and told me not to worry my "pretty little head" about it. The thing was, I had no intention of worrying my "pretty little head" about *it* or anything else, but I would not be lied to.

"Look, Wilf," I said, "If you want to be with your ex, then be with your ex. There's no point us wasting any more time together if that's what you want." His face filled with alarm and he started to panic.

"Why the hell would I want her when I've got you?" Did he really mean that, I asked myself, or was he just taking the piss?

"Because you're a fucking bloke, and that's what blokes do!"

I don't know if I loved Wilf, but I did like him. There was the potential to love him, but that was about it. Anything else rested on the precondition of not behaving like a psychopath. Away from the drink, he could be wonderful company, but there was a darkness in him that I didn't like, and it was getting darker by the day. The question I had to ask myself during this time was simple: did I want to be around when that darkness started to fully consume him? Because I knew it would eventually. No one could hold back the night.

Just like that, he sold the recycling business, then moved out. The Limassol house had gone up quite quickly – in less than a year – and then he was in it, living, building his new ex-pat life, and the lifestyle that went with it. He'd been popping backwards and forwards the whole time, and when he was back, I'd see him. Sometimes it was lovely, other times not so, but I could tell he cared about me. He'd show me pictures of the house, and it was quite exciting to see it going up layer by layer. The place he'd chosen was beautiful, and he kept saying I was going to love it. I told him I'm sure I would, but there was no way I was going to go out there to live. He didn't like that, because I think he'd been expecting me to. But I couldn't drop my whole life just like that, simply because he was bored. *He* might not have had much of a relationship with his kids (he had four in total) but I did with mine, and they were front and centre of everything. The thought of not being there for them was too much. I owed it to them to be around.

I did visit. He begged and pleaded and badgered and cajoled, and eventually we made arrangements for me to go out, once he'd settled in. We agreed two weeks would be enough, even though he begged for more, and so I booked my flights. He met me at the airport, when I did finally arrive, and the first thing that struck me was how different he looked. He'd absorbed the laid-back atmosphere of the town and wore it on his now caramelised skin like an all-over tattoo. Gone were the suits and the stiff-collared shirts and ties, and in came the shorts and pastel coloured shirts and:

"Sandals?" I asked, pointing down to his feet.

"Well, you know what they say: When in Rome ..."

I'd been to Rome, but this was better. Prettier, at least. Everywhere you looked, once we got out of the airport, it was like a painting. Back in dreary old Blighty people ate their dinner on mats showing views like the ones we were passing – I think Olive and Ritchie even had a print in their hallway of one view we actually drove past.

The house itself was another surprise. I knew Wilf had tried to prepare me for it, but seeing it was another matter. Situated near the top of a high valley, the five acres that made up the property seemed even bigger because there was no one else's property it touched. Inside it seemed even bigger, like Doctor Who's TARDIS, and when I first went to the bathroom I thought I was going to need a map and compass to navigate my way back to the lounge. There were so many rooms on so many levels, with balconies looking out from each, showing views of hills that rolled and tumbled into one another. There were other houses there, you could see their roofs, all pastel and terracotta, but if you wanted to walk round to one, you'd be best off taking a rucksack. By the time I'd had my shower and we'd reached the swanky restaurant Wilf was keen to show me I was starting to wonder if two weeks was going to be enough.

"Cheers!" Wilf said, happy to see my smiling.

"Cheers!" I replied. Our glasses kissed. "This is ..." I tried to think of what to say. "Impressive," was all I could come up with, but it didn't feel enough.

"Told you you'd like it."

He insisted I went for the most expensive cocktail on the menu, and so I did, but it looked more like an expensive bunch of flowers than it did a drink.

"You don't mind if you only stay a week, do you?" he then said as I was enjoying my first sip. Assuming he must have more on his plate, workwise, than I'd thought, I said it was fine, but I was disappointed, nonetheless. Still, I was keen to know what it was he was tied up with over here, so I asked what was more important than me?

"Actually, it's my ex," he said. "She's coming over."

The kick of vodka in my cocktail abruptly turned into a sharp jab in my gut. I hadn't seen that one coming.

"Oh," I said. "Any particular reason?"

"Just business stuff. She won't be here that long."

"Can she not stay in a hotel?" I asked, thinking it a sensible question. But he prickled.

"She *could,* but … well, there's just a lot for us to go through, and if she finds out you're here, she'll … " He kept talking but I stopped listening to what he had to say. He might as well have started speaking Greek to me.

Here we go again, I thought.

Here we fucking go again!

THE DEMON ON THE MOUNT

Christmas is a time for miracles and, as Wilf reminded me that winter, New Year a time for new beginnings. That was the approach he used to get me back out again, and he only started using it once he'd exhausted all the other ways. By early December, I'd grown bored of hearing his pitiful ramblings down the phone – sober one minute, pissed the next – pleading with me to go back out. He wore me down eventually and I ended up agreeing, but only if he promised to sort out all the arrangements. The children, mostly grown by then, were all settling into their lives and had made their own plans that Christmas, so there was little to keep me at home. Instead of sitting there on my own, with my little bottle of Baileys, watching all the Christmas specials, I thought why not at least go somewhere where I wouldn't freeze my tits off, and where there'd be someone who might want to pull a cracker or two with me? After all, there was no actual evidence Wilf had even done anything with his ex, and if he really was interested in her, why didn't he spend all his time calling her instead of me? This, and other stuff, was all flashing through my mind as I sat across from him in Limassol's swankiest restaurant, choosing what to have for our pre-Christmas dinner.

"Whatever you fancy," he said. "You just take your pick."

In the days leading up to me coming out again Wilf had been on a full charm offensive. A changed man, you might say. Once my no's had turned into an eventual yes, the pestering calls stopped, and when we did speak he sounded lovely, in control, which to me was the best Christmas present he could've given. There would be some jewellery too, he promised, but none of that mattered as much as seeing him return to his old self. Even more impressive was the fact he didn't spend the whole meal asking for drink after drink to be brought to the table. We shared just the one bottle between us – a gorgeous Argentine red, if I remember – and watched from the patio the pale winter sun bedding itself down for the night over towards Egypt. It did get a bit chillier once it had gone, but there was no need to rush out and turn ourselves into the little boy from *The Snowman*.

"Now That. Was. Delicious," I said, laying down my knife and fork at the end of the meal.

"Worth coming out for?" Wilf asked, taking his last sip of wine.

"Absolutely," I said. He took my hand across the table, and it felt good. I'd missed that. The closeness. The warmth of his hand. He raised the other one and I tensed slightly, waiting for him to ask for another drink, but instead he surprised me:

"Bill, please," he said. Now, I know that would've been hard for him, but as he'd said so himself many times over the phone leading up to this: "New Year, new beginning."

That worked for me.

But as he was about to remind me: it wasn't New Year yet.

It was getting dark now, and Wilf drove us back along the main road, through the town, on our way to the house. One hand was on the wheel and the other was around me, holding my shoulder. *Yes, Wilf, I really was here*. It would be nice to get back whilst we still had the evening ahead of us, rather than feel pressured into doing something. Drinking for the sake of drinking. The TV wasn't great in Cyprus, but we'd find something we could watch. It was only as we pulled into the car park of one of the hotels we were passing that Wilf suggested we make just one slight change of plan.

"Just a quick one," he said, shooting me his most boyish smile.

"Can't we just go back to the house? I was looking forward to us just relaxing together."

"There's loads of time for that. I just wanted to show you this place first. You'll love it."

I held my breath. He could tell I wasn't happy.

"Come *on*," he said, rubbing my shoulder. "Just the one. It's Christmas." Certainly, everyone else seemed to think so, you could tell by the glazed, kiss-me-under-the-holly look they had in their eyes. They all seemed so jolly, and merry, but all were looking forward to having a great Christmas away from home, and on the beach, if the weather played ball. I climbed out and followed Wilf, who followed the crowd, who followed the Christmas music into the cosy lobby of the beckoning hotel.

"Just one," I reminded him.

"Just one." He pressed his hand onto my lower back and guided me in.

Three hours later the glasses still hadn't been cleared from our table. During the first drink we'd gotten around to talking about the future, our future, and our relationship, and how we both saw it. Wilf went to the toilet just as we were about to leave, but returned with more drinks. I rolled my eyes, but his cheeky grin convinced me there was more mileage to this conversation and we should let it run its course. Half an hour later, the waiter, seeing our glasses nearly empty again, brought more drinks, and the first sign of worry started to appear on my face. We still had to drive back, I remembered, but when I pointed this out to Wilf, it didn't seem to bother him. He sat forward and took my hand.

"You *do* love me, don't you?" he asked.

"What kind of question is that?" I replied, uneasy. I remembered when Billy used to ask me the same thing. Normally he'd have had his hand around my throat at the time, and I'd be pinned to the wall, leaving me no option but to tell him what he wanted to hear. I thought it best to adopt a similar line now. Just to be safe.

"Of course I do."

"So why won't you come out?"

"I am out. Here I am. Hello!" He smiled, but the smile didn't hang around for long.

"To *live*."

"Wilf, we've been through this ..."

And we had. Many times, which is one of the reasons I used to avoid his calls. He didn't want my answer to involve my children, but that was the only answer I could give, and after I'd given it for the seventeenth, eighteenth and nineteenth time, another few glasses had appeared on the table, and he was sliding off his seat. It was getting out of hand, and suddenly that 'New Year/new beginning' conversation was starting to feel a long, long time ago. When he raised his hand to call to the waiter again, I put my foot down and insisted we left right then.

"AGH, YOU'RE A FUCKING KILLJOY, YOU ARE!"

My heart sank, but as it did, every single head in the bar lifted, and swung towards us. That was our evening gone – and probably the holiday.

"Ssssh, will you. Christ, you're all over the place."

"I can't have any fun with you."

"Not in that state, you can't." He slipped off the chair again. I noticed people smirking, and I wanted the world to swallow me whole. *This can't be happening,* I thought. It was all going so well. He wiped the spittle from his mouth and then turned round to tap the shoulder of the person sat behind him, a nice-looking guy in his thirties who was out with some friends.

"Eh, mate," Wilf drooled, barely able to stay upright. The guy turned his head.

"Wilf, *no!*" I hissed.

"Do you like *her?*" He jabbed his finger directly at me. The guy looked at him blankly. His friends did too. "Well, you can fuckin' have her if you want." The guy blinked, confused, and Wilf stood. "She'll fuckin' shag anything." And with that he staggered off towards the door, bouncing off the walls like a blind seagull. The poor guy and his friends looked at me with pity in their eyes and all I could do was shrug and apologise. He knew I had no money on me. My purse I'd left at home at his insistence ("You're not going to need it, are you?") and all I had with me was my phone – for emergencies – in case the kids needed to reach me. When I got to the door I saw him crossing the car park, fumbling in his pocket for his keys.

"You can't seriously be thinking of driving back," I shouted after him.

Ignoring me, he pulled open the door and fell inside the car across the seats. I raced after him.

"Then let me drive, I've only had a couple."

"Fuck off," he said. "You can stay here —" He flicked his chin back towards the bar. "With *him.*"

"Don't be bloody stupid, I don't even know the bloke."

He dragged his legs inside the car and then tried to get the key into the ignition. I couldn't believe he was seriously contemplating driving back in this state – he could barely sit up right. But if I got in the car with him, I could at least make sure he kept the wheel straight and stayed on the road. Once we'd turned off the main thoroughfare we'd soon hit a quiet road that led all the way out to the house; it was, after all, in the middle of nowhere, and if I remembered correctly, what junctions we'd pass would be virtually empty at this time of night. I was able to get around to the passenger side before he'd even been able to start up the engine, and then, once I was sat down, I just crossed my fingers and prayed.

Strangely, his driving was better than his walking, and he was able to steer us out of the car park, and the town, without clipping any other vehicles. But just because the driving was uneventful, that doesn't mean the journey was. The insults started almost immediately, and it was clear from the stream of invective that he lashed me with, that he'd been bottling this up for a long time. Every slur he could think of he hurled at me, from the playground-level 'slag' and 'slapper' to the more grown-up 'whore' and 'prostitute'; and as we crawled through the moonless landscape, I had no choice but to swallow them all down and resist punching the bastard in the face.

Either side of us there were snakes. The whole area was filled with them. Wilf had seen dozens during the time the house was being built. "They're not small things either," he'd say on the phone. In fact, the large whip snake could be up to three metres long. There is also the blunt-nosed viper, which is far more dangerous, and people have been known to die from being bitten, but they only really attack you when you disturb one. I was so tense during the drive back that I hadn't been thinking about snakes, until I noticed the car slowing down mid-way between the town and the house. *God*, I thought, *I hope we haven't run out of petrol.* I looked at the symbol – nope, it was three-quarters full – and then I looked at Wilf and saw that, once again, his brow had collapsed over his face, just like it had back in Frodsham that time. As there was no moon, his face was lit only by the soft LED glow of the dashboard, which only added to the strange countenance his face had taken on. In profile he looked quite scary, every inch a child's drawing of a demon. It was quite terrifying.

He brought the car to a stop and then switched off the engine.

"Get out," he said, almost growling.

In front of us, two blades of yellow light stretched out ahead, but the inky darkness swallowed them whole. It was into this void that Wilf's expression was fixed.

"Don't be stupid," I said. "We're in the middle of bloody nowhere."

Saying no more, Wilf pushed open his door, stepped out, then marched around the front of the car, crossing through the yellow beams, until he came to my side. His hand reached for the handle but before it got to it, I grabbed it from the inside.

"Open the door," he said flatly.

"NO!"

"OPEN THE FUCKING DOOR!" He screamed it that time, and started yanking at the handle.

"I'm not getting out."

He cursed, punched the glass, then stumbled round back to his side. I should've closed the door, but I didn't think. I was still too shocked. What was he going to do? I was trembling now, convinced he was going to hurt me. But instead, with anger boiling out of him, he got back into the car, started the engine, and carried on driving. I could hear him mumbling to himself as he ground through the gears. I don't know what he was saying but it included a lot of swearing – f-words, c-words – and words in other languages. In fact, it sounded like he was speaking in tongues at one point. I just prayed we didn't see any oncoming traffic, as he seemed so full of rage right then that I was convinced he would've steered us right into the path of anything just to get back at me.

By some miracle we did finally make it back to the house, and when the two yellow beams flitted across the pale walls, I'd never felt such relief in my life. What I really needed now though was to pee, as I hadn't been since we'd left earlier that day. But as I was gathering up my stuff, Wilf shot out the car and locked it. I heard the two beeps. I pulled the handle, nothing happened. I banged on the windscreen, shouting through it, but it was useless. Wilf knew what he'd done. He had no intention of glancing back. After he entered the house I could trace his route around it from the lights he switched on: hall first, then lounge, then corridor, toilet, bedroom – and sometimes I could see his shadow moving around in front of the blinds. He didn't look outside once. I sat in the car with my mouth open, wondering what to do. He was punishing me, that was clear, but for how long would this farce go on? All night? Till he was sober? What if he fell asleep? Still, it wouldn't be the first night I'd ever spent in a car, would it? At least it wasn't snowing this time.

After half an hour I remembered my friend, John Parry, back home. He ran a car dealership in Chester, and specialised in fancy cars like this. He also knew about Wilf, and understood that he could be a bit of a sod sometimes, but I don't think even he could've expected the predicament I presented him with. He sounded groggy when I rang him, but I'd forgotten it was well past midnight when I rang, and some people had to be at work in the morning. Once he'd shaken off his tiredness (and incredulity), we got down to the serious business of trying to get me free.

"There'll be a button you can press to unlock it," he told me, then set about trying to describe where I might find it. As I didn't know the exact model, he couldn't be sure. "I think it's a key symbol you're looking for," he said. "It should be clearly visible." But it wasn't, and I felt like a blind person trying to make a cup of tea in a stranger's house.

Then I had another thought: what if I found a way out, and then, as I made my way over to the house, Wilf locked it again whilst I was still outside? I'd be trapped then, between the car and the house, with all the snakes and God knows what else around me. I'd have to pee in the drive and leave the door open, and then, just as I thought this, I heard a loud knocking on the glass next to me. I jumped out my seat. *Jesus!*

"Get out the car," he said, dead-eyed. I told John I had to go and quickly hung up the phone. Fortunately, Wilf hadn't noticed I'd been on it.

"No," I said. "If I get out the car you'll lock it and I won't be able to get back in again."

"Why the fuck would I do that?" he asked.

"I don't know," I answered. "Why would you lock me in it in the first place?"

I did end up opening the door, but only after I'd thought through a sensible strategy. It was a simple one: open the door and then just run to the house as I fast as I could; once inside, head up the stairs and get myself parked on the loo. It worked, within thirty seconds I was on the toilet and peeing like a horse. The relief was indescribable. I was still shaky from all the tension and had a bit of a cry, partly out of shock, but partly too out of self-pity. How on earth had I allowed this to happen? There was no hope for us now, that was certain. I needed my freedom and Wilf needed help. Serious help. In the two years between Phil and Wilf the amount of arguments I'd had with people was literally zero. I hadn't felt threatened, or sad, or depressed, or suicidal – only a bit lonely, but was it worth going through all this just to prevent the odd wave of loneliness washing over me every few months?

I wiped myself, then flushed the toilet, but I'd forgotten that, in my rush to get the loo, I'd not locked the door. As I turned, I saw Wilf appear. He was standing in the doorway, back-lit by the hall light. His face was still contorted like some Habsburg freak, and his hand was curled around the handle of something which hung down by his knee. Something that glinted in the light.

"You don't love me, do you?"

I nearly collapsed on the spot. What he was holding was a carving knife, its blade as long as my forearm. I'd seen some scary sights before, but this was something else. It was like a scene from *Halloween*, and I knew that if I ever wanted to see my children again I would have to handle the next few minutes with more delicacy than I'd ever handled anything before in my life. One word out of place and I would end up as the tabloid headline Billy was never able to write.

"Of course I do, you daft sod."

"You don't act around me like you used to."

"We've been together four years, Wilf. Who does after that time, eh? It doesn't mean I don't love you." He started to tap the blade against his leg – *tap-tap-tap* – but he still seemed lost inside himself. I thought of my kids, and what I'd give to be curled up on the sofa with Stephanie watching *Sleeping Beauty*, or finding a frog under Will's bed. "I just prefer you when you haven't had as much to drink, that's all." A tear appeared in his eye. The first chink in the armour perhaps. "You're still the most wonderful person I know. Why do you think I came all this way out here, eh? It wasn't for the sunsets."

He looked around the bathroom. His eyes full of suspicion. What was he looking for?

"What are you doing up here?" he said.

"Having a pee, what does it look like?"

Trying to break the tension, I moved towards the sink and pumped some soap into my hands. They were still shaking. "Ooh, this is nice soap," I said, sniffing my fingers, "where did you get it?"

He ignored the question, as I thought he might, and his cold, dead shark's eyes, floated back to me and stayed on me. *Tap-tap-tap* went the knife against his leg.

"Get downstairs," he said, "I don't want you up here."

"Can I dry my hands first?"

As I reached for the towel, I remembered how I used to make silly Miss Piggy voices for the children to temper the violence erupting out of Billy sometimes. This was all too familiar, only this time I wasn't pinned to the wall or lying in a heap on the floor. As Wilf's empty eyes moved over me, I kept thinking of them. Every move I made, and every word I said right now, was for them, even Kelly, who I missed so much.

What made Wilf like this? Alcohol – yes, but what else? Just how much of Frodsham and its crazy goings-on had he brought with him to Cyprus? I know it's mad for most people to think thoughts like that, but knowing what I know, I couldn't stop asking myself that very question. What I didn't even know then was the history of Limassol – the actual area where Wilf had built his house. "It's got loads," he'd said, but he was just talking about the town and what had happened in the last couple of centuries. I wouldn't know it for a good while, but by the time the twentieth century had even arrived, Limassol's history wasn't to be thought of in terms of *hundreds* of years, like in Frodsham, but in thousands; and considering it involved the Ottoman Empire, the Crusades (Richard the Lionheart stopped off there on his way to the Holy land, to whip up some support), and had its fair share of sword fights, it was a bloody and chaotic one.

We made it downstairs eventually and I was able to get the TV on without being stabbed to death, which was a huge relief, but during the whole fifteen-minute period that took to get through I had to act as if the knife in his hand wasn't there, and we were just going to sit together, like an ordinary couple, on the sofa, and watch TV like we always did. A normal, happy couple. All the while, I kept having to reassure him that he and I were absolutely fine, hunky dory, that nothing had changed, and yes, I *did* still love him. I've no memory of what was on the TV, but the news came on at one point, I remember, and that was followed by some dreadful American soap where the actors did a lot of over-acting (I knew how they felt!). Then, at about two in the morning, or maybe it was three, I saw Wilf's eyelids start to flicker, his inner battle to stay awake finally buckling, and as the tension in his face fell away, the jaw slid back into place, and his jagged brow unknotted itself. I watched him for a minute, sitting upright, still holding the knife, but tottering like a Jenga tower with most of its lower blocks gone. Then the knife slid from his hand and dropped onto the floor and the 'tower' toppled sideways onto a cushion.

I took off his shoes, and went to fetch a blanket for him. Then I picked up the knife and went into the kitchen to make myself a cup of tea, strong, with two sugars. By the time I'd drunk it, I could hear him snoring.

SHIELD OF THE GODS

The calls would start about five o'clock. Most times I wouldn't hear them because I'd have my phone switched off in my bag and it would go straight through to voicemail. But sometimes I'd forget to turn it off and I'd hear it ringing. Once in a while I'd answer it, because after the calls started, they just wouldn't stop.

"Oh, hi love, how are you?" he'd begin. "Had a good day?" I might hear some liquid – vodka presumably – swilling about in a bottle, and the odd sip from it sometimes, discreetly taken, but if I ever asked if he was drinking, he'd just deny it.

"Nope," he say. "Haven't touched a drop."

The calls would continue throughout the evening, and his mood would sink lower with each passing hour.

Since my last visit I'd been clear with him: we were finished, over, kaput; but have you ever tried to finish with an alcoholic? Each time he'd ring, I'd remind him of the facts, but he'd just ignore me and carry on in one of two ways: either he'd say he missed me and ask me to come out one more time so we could give it another try, or (if he'd had more to drink) accuse me of shagging other men and start flinging shit at me. There was barely any mention of my last visit. When I told him about the knife, and how scared I'd felt, he waved his hand as if it was nothing. "Agh, you're over-reacting," he'd say. "I'd never hurt you in a million years."

There's an easy answer to the question of why I didn't just change my number: I did. But, being a crafty sod, he'd get round that in just a day or two. He'd ring around my friends, having come up with a reason for needing my number. Theirs he'd have gotten ages ago by promising gifts from Cyprus, items that were hard to get in the UK, or things he could get much cheaper over there. "Give us your number," he'd say to them, "and I'll let you know how many I can get." This even extended to my clients, a few of whom he'd met. I'm sure they enjoyed the Armani jeans he got them for peanuts, or

208

the bulk-bought Dolce & Gabbana tops he also brought back, but it probably wasn't worth the hassle of a one-o'clock-in-the morning phone call he gave them when he couldn't reach me. *"Where the fuck is she?"*

The calls would continue through the night until by about two-o'clock in the morning, at which point his body would collapse in on itself, the drink pushing him into a void that would stop him from hurting himself, or others. He'd wake-up the next morning, get some coffee on, and go about his business (whatever that was); then, as the afternoon lurched blindly towards the night, the Cirque Du Wilf would re-erect its tent once more, and the whole shit-show would begin again.

"Hi love, how are you? Had a good day?"

Frodsham might earn a place in the Domesday Book thanks to the importance of its river, but Limassol can be traced right back to Ancient times. There are some graves on the island that have been dated back more than four thousand years. Of more significance to my story is the Roman soldiers who were stationed there two-thousand-years later, just after Jesus' time. There'd been no massive battles there, so it's hardly important enough for Mary Beard to do a documentary about it, but the Romans did have a base there for a good while, and kept having to send out soldiers, new recruits, to replace the ones who were already there. It was those ones who witnessed the awful massacre of 240,000 Greeks by the Cypriot Jews in 117 AD – one of a series of Jewish uprisings that took place across the region during what became known as the Kitos War. The Romans stationed there, mostly young conscripts, were overwhelmed and had to call for back-up. Eventually a big section of the Roman Army did arrive and fought off all the Jews, who were then banished from the island for centuries, meaning they were no longer able to work or take up residence there. Obviously this isn't stuff I would normally know, but I read up on it a bit just to try and make sense out of what happened later on, when I did let my guard down and allowed my arm to be twisted one more time.

Yes, I know, you probably think I'm mad, bonkers, crazy, mental, but as he'd done last time, Wilf had managed to wear me down yet again, not just with apologies, but with enough promises to make me start seeing possibilities again. That's the thing with successful people, they don't get to where they are by luck alone, do they? They get there because they know how to sweet-talk people. They don't recognise 'No' as a legitimate answer to anything, and so, if they see a weakness, they capitalise on it. That's why they're successful; those that can't do it are the ones more likely to fail. Anyway, three or four days into the holiday (let's go ahead and call it that) things were going swimmingly. I'd managed to get a promise from Wilf that he wasn't going to drink while I was out there, and because we'd avoided fancy meals at restaurants, he'd been able to get through it. I was actually proud of him, and we were having a great time together, going out in the day, being tourists, and if we stopped off for a drink anywhere I'd make sure it was never anything stronger than a double espresso.

On this one particular day, I said I'd cook something if Wilf didn't mind picking up some ingredients whilst he was in the town stocking up with supplies. He'd be gone a couple of hours, he said, and that was fine. It would give me a chance to catch up with people from home. I would've had a little swim in the pool outside, the one directly beneath the spare bedroom window, but I'd never learnt. We didn't do it in school, and there was no way Olive and Richie would ever fork out for some lessons. I rang the kids first, had a chat with Deryn and Will, and then I rang Elizabeth, my saviour from Irby Road. She'd become like a sister in recent years, and was only too well acquainted with what had had happened during my last visit. She was keen therefore to know how things were progressing with Wilf, worried that I might end up buried in cement and 'disappeared' in the foundations of some new building project.

Even now, more than a decade later, she still speaks about what happened next and gets a shiver when she thinks about it. She didn't actually witness the event herself, but she heard it, and remembers only too well my reaction to it – though in truth it was my silence she was listening to, followed by my dumfounded retelling of what I'd just experienced, sort of like a live-commentary.

About the day itself there was nothing peculiar: it was a typical afternoon, the sun was out, the sky was dazzling, like Blue Curaçao, and on the horizon, wherever you looked, the air rippled from the heat. I sat on the sofa, nattering away to Elizabeth with the patio doors open, telling her how nice Wilf was being, and she sounded pleased.

"You just keep those bottles hidden," she said, and I laughed.

I didn't scream when I sensed the movement behind me, but I did react. Elizabeth says she heard me gasp, but I don't remember. She thought Wilf must've appeared out of nowhere and had given me a fright. *What did he have in his hand* this *time,* she remembers thinking – *a knife, a machete, or something worse?*

"What is it, Chrissy?"

She had to ask it a few times, she said later, before I finally responded, but that doesn't surprise me because it had happened by then, and I'd had to process quite a lot of information in those few seconds. It was the wall behind me, you see, the plain wall which was just plaster over brick. There was no art on it like there was on some of the others, and it was out of this that he appeared.

He was massive, six feet tall, but made all the bigger by his armour, which bulked him out like the Hulk. Some it was leather, but there was a gold breastplate and bits of metal on his arms and shoulders too. His helmet, also gold and framing his face, was adorned with red fur, on the top, like a Mohican, and in one hand he was holding a shield which had a picture of something on it, an eagle, or some kind of bird. He came out of the wall like he was stepping out of the shower, then walked towards me, not marching, just kind of casually. The top of his boots I could see, but not the bottom, because they disappeared *through* the floor, as if it was the real ground he was walking on, not the cement floor the builders had put down just recently.

"Chrissy ... . ? What is it?"

That must've been when I gasped, when I first saw him, but I didn't feel scared because, unlike in Frodsham where there was always that atmosphere of danger, the sensation I felt this time wasn't one of oppression at all, or cruelty, but one of kindness, and that kindness was in the soldier's eyes too.

"... Are you okay? Speak to me ... "

He looked at me as he marched forward, his eyes flitting down for a second, all warm and comforting, and then he nodded as if to say "Hello".

Maybe that's when I gasped.

I'd like to think I responded, but I have no idea. Then, after acknowledging me, he altered direction, just slightly, and carried on without stopping. I watched him twist, the red fur bouncing on his head, his massive arms swinging, and his shield gliding smoothly through the air, and then, just as he'd appeared out of one wall, he vanished through another on the far side of the room.

" ... Are you still there, Chrissy? ... "

Go on, admit it, you think I'm certifiable.

If you're tempted to put this book down now and tell yourself that you suspected I might be a bit crazy from the first page, then it's fine. Really. But please bear in mind, I'm not writing this book to convince anyone of the supernatural. It's just that, if I was to talk about my life (as many people have asked me to) and *not* mention any of this, it would be wrong. I'd be lying to you. Try thinking of it this way: if I wrote about what I saw in my dreams, nobody would question it, no matter how strange or bizarre they were; however, if I witness something equally as strange or bizarre, but am fully awake and cognisant when I do it, they *will* question them. And yet the only difference between them is my state of consciousness at the time. Strange or not, though, the only reason I'm mentioning any of this now is because there's a part two to all this which I'll get to in a moment.

"Chrissy, you've got me all worried, please speak to me."

I'd forgotten all about the phone. About Elizabeth, back home in the Wirral, talking to me, worried about me, wanting to hang up so she could call the embassy and get the police out to see if I was alive or sprawled out in a pool of blood on the floor. I spoke slowly to her when I found my voice again.

"You're not going to believe what I've just seen ..."

"Christ, Chrissy, I thought something must've happened to you."

I told her I was okay and then, very, very slowly, as I played the whole encounter back through my own mind, I told her what I'd just seen. She said she had to sit down to take it all in. I told her I *was* sitting down, but I still wasn't able to take any of it in.

"Do not get under that duvet."

"Hmn?"

I span round, expecting to find Wilf there – *Why was he whispering?* – but he wasn't. Nor could he have been, unless that was someone else I could hear pottering around downstairs.

Did I imagine it then?

No, of course I didn't. I knew what I'd heard, and I'd long-since learnt that to ignore such 'warnings' (which I believed this to be) was to do so at my own peril. What the nature of that peril was exactly I didn't yet know, but if the evening carried on in the same direction it had started to veer off in ... well, I had some idea. That was why I'd told Wilf I had a really bad headache and needed to go to bed early. He wasn't happy about it, as I knew he wouldn't be, but he didn't reach for a bread knife so that was a bonus. I was getting nervous though, because he wasn't doing what he'd promised he was going to do and that annoyed me.

"It's my house, I can do what I want," he'd said. I didn't argue with him, I just forced out a little kiss and made my excuses – and it *was* an excuse – then headed up. I'd also need to come up with another one to explain why I'd chosen the spare bedroom to sleep in and not the main one we always shared.

I hadn't told him what had happened earlier. I was planning to, but when he reappeared after his jaunt into the town, I could tell he'd already had a little tipple and that put me on edge. I cooked the meal, pasta and fish with a nice red sauce, and we sat and watched TV for a bit. When Wilf went to the toilet and returned with a bottle of wine, I had to bite my tongue.

"It was a gift," he said. "It would be rude not to try it."

Not wanting to antagonise him, I had a glass – one tiny sip again to every huge gulp of his – but when I noticed the slurring I knew I was on borrowed time and I didn't want to be the red flag to his angry bull. It was time to get out of the arena.

Heeding the warning from moments ago, I lay down on the duvet (not under it) and got myself as comfortable as I could, but I can't say I wasn't anxious. The fact that there wasn't a lock on the door didn't help. As I lay there, I played the voice over in my head again and again. It was a definite warning, but a warning from what?

Some hours later, I had my answer.

I must've dozed off because I woke with a start. What was that I'd just heard? A noise? Where did it come from? Outside or inside? I was lying on my side facing the shuttered window with the door behind me. The swimming pool was outside my window, about ten or twelve feet below. I don't know what time it was, but it felt middle-of-the-night late, two or three am. Maybe even later. If it hadn't been for the hall light coming in through the open door it would've been pitch black and I'd —

Hang on, the *open* door? That couldn't be right because when I came to bed earlier I'd made sure it was —

Another sound.

A rustling. Behind me.

Something was moving, touching the bed. I could sense it, hear the breathing. The breathing was laboured, with a slight rasp to it.

I turned slowly, my heart galloping now, and saw a grey shape next to my bed; it was crouching low, to the side of me, by my chest, an arm on the bed next to me. I blinked a few times, trying to bring the shape into focus, and then it spoke.

"… Why are you in *this* bed?"

Discovering it was Wilf didn't dampen down the fear. In fact, it added to it, and I was forced to pull off the shelf the excuse I'd made up earlier:

"I just thought I'd give you some space, love," I said. "I knew I'd be tossing and turning all night, and I didn't want to —"

He sniffed. He sounded like he was crying. Or *had* been.

"You didn't want to sleep with me … Did you?"

It wasn't rising yet, but I could sense the hot magma swirling about within him. How soon it would rise depended on just how much he'd had to drink.

And how I handled what I was about to say.

"I just thought we'd both benefit from a good night's sleep, that's all. So we could do something nice tomorrow."

I couldn't see him yet, not properly, but I saw his head sink down. For a moment he said nothing, but I could hear more sobbing.

"You don't love me … I know you don't."

I took a breath. Here we were again. I had to be very, very careful.

"Don't be silly. Of course I do."

"You don't … Or you'd want to sleep with me." I could sense it rising now. The magma. It was coming up fast.

"I've just got a really bad headache, love. I think it might be a migraine."

As we talked, and Wilf got louder, my eyes adjusted to the dark and I could see that his face had changed yet again. I was back with Mr Hyde, and knew at once we were both in for a rough night. But just how rough I had no idea until a minute or two later when, without a word, or any warning, he grabbed the edge of the duvet and tried to lift it over my face.

"Wilf … what are you … WHAT THE HELL ARE YOU DOING?"

It was obvious, but I asked because I wanted him to tell me he wasn't doing what I knew he was trying to do. But he was. I swiped at his hands, and clawed at his fingers, holding back the urge to scream. He probably hadn't realised I was lying on it at the time, and that's the only reason I'm here now – because he couldn't get enough of the duvet over my face to suffocate me. I thrashed wildly about beneath him, watching him bite his lip as he struggled to pull it up, but not succeeding.

Then the screams *did* come. I started to hit him now, weak pathetic punches, against his head and chest and his arms and his hands, but he didn't seem to feel anything. I was hyperventilating now, calling out – *actually* calling out – for Archangel Michael – waiting for him to start laughing. Surely he was going to start laughing, because this was so ridiculous, so pathetic, so crazy. What the actual fuck were we doing here? Thank God he was so far gone, or I wouldn't have been able to get my knee raised up between us. When I finally did, I pushed out as hard as I could and he went flying back against the wardrobe, crashing into it and nearly knocking it over.

We both took a breath. My instinct, as he recovered, was to race to the window and jump out before he could come at me again, but then I remembered the swimming pool outside. if I jumped, I'd drown. But instead, he just disappeared round the doorframe again and vanished.

I lay on the bed with my knee still raised, panting and shaking, with the duvet still partly covering my face. Had that really just happened? Was that really Wilf, or was it something – or someone – else? Was it that thing from Frodsham? Collecting my thoughts, I sat up, trembling, and switched the light on so I could think more clearly . There was a set of drawers in the room, if I could move those in front of the door that would give me some security, or at least a notion of it. Perhaps I should follow Wilf downstairs and try and talk to him. If I could get a coffee inside him that would help surely. We could sit on the sofa and, like we did last time, wait for this to pass. Because it *would* pass. Wouldn't it?

But I didn't get a chance to decide about anything because a second later, as I was just about to stand up, there he was again: he flew around the doorframe like a giant Swingball and came straight at me. It wasn't a scream he let out as he raised the claw hammer above me, but it was something primal, and it put the fear of God into me. I just had time to acknowledge that these were to be the last few seconds of my life, so I raised my arms above me, but not nearly high enough to protect myself. I quickly conjured up an image of my children, all of them, Kelly too, and sent out some love to them, and hoped they would get it, but the blow I was expecting didn't come.

He must've stopped himself, I thought. He must've considered what he was about to do, and pulled his arm back; but when I looked up, I saw the look in his eyes. He was as confused as I was. The claw hammer was still raised, still above my head, just two or three inches above my eye, held there in space as if he was trying to bring it down on me but ... but for some reason couldn't. Something, or someone was stopping it. Then I felt a sensation again, like a warm breeze blowing through the room, and I remembered how I'd felt something similar when the soldier, the centurion, the thing with the gentle smile on its face, had passed through it earlier that day.

Could it be?

Could it possibly be ... ?

We did make it to the couch, though not for another 20 minutes or so. During that time, we said very little. Wilf had disappeared after the attack and I didn't see him for ages. I don't know where he went. When he returned, he ordered me downstairs and I went, following obediently. He still had the claw hammer in his hand, but looked at me as if *I* was the evil one, having conjured up a spirit to bedevil him.

It's a fine line, they say, the difference between love and hate, and I'd never been more aware of that fact than when I sat down on the sofa next to him and saw him break down. He was like a little boy. In *Cat on a Hot Tin Roof,* I remember, Paul Newman's character talks about the *"click"* he reaches when he starts drinking. This was definitely the same with Wilf, only his "click" was far more destructive, and had an actual physical form when it took control of him. The fact that I felt tremendous sympathy must've been where the love came from. The hate was easier to spot. That existed in the form of the claw hammer that he'd placed on the coffee table in front of him, ready to snatch up at a moment's notice.

"Can I put the tele on?" I asked.

He nodded. I didn't want to watch it, but I thought it might help distract us both from what had just occurred. It was a local news programme, an attractive lady and a handsome man, both in light suits, talked earnestly about the state of the world, but we didn't hear what they were saying because I turned the volume off. No doubt it was still going to hell in a handcart.

Wilf shook his head, he was in his own world now, his own little no-man's-land.

"What's wrong with me?" I heard him say.

I had a hundred answers, but I kept them to myself. Now wasn't the time.

I played back instead what had just taken place in my own mind. It had all happened so fast, but when I slowed it down and ran it again – the entire scene – I was convinced that I'd felt a presence there, the sense of some other force in between Wilf and I when he'd come at me with the hammer. I could feel the aura. I looked at the plaster wall behind me, the one that had featured so prominently in what had occurred earlier that day. Surely they were connected. The nod he'd given me, the centurion, that was a sign. *It's okay*, he was saying, *I'm here*. And then the warning later. Was that him? Or was that someone else? My twin-sister, looking out for me, perhaps? Wishing me to live more of the life that she'd been denied five decades before?

There are no easy answers to these questions, I know that; not answers that would satisfy most people. I know in time an answer will come, but whether it's here in this life or not, that doesn't matter as much to me now as it once did.

The television remained on for the rest of the night and we both just stared at it. If it had been white noise we'd probably have carried on watching it with just as much interest. Eventually Wilf's Mr Hyde left the room and a sleepy Dr Jekyll took his place, and when he did, I picked up the hammer and hid it out of sight. As I searched for a good spot, one he'd never find, I reminded myself that this was the second time I'd done this in barely the same amount of months. If it happened again it would be down to my own stupidity. But how many more times could I rely on the good will and grace of those who inhabited a world that ran alongside this one, but wasn't quite this one, to save me?

LOCKED-IN SYNDROME

"I'm going to go in, Chrissy," he said. "I'm going to go in and get dried out."

"Okay."

"No, really. I am. You're too important to me. I just can't risk losing you."

I paused for a moment to take in what he was saying. How serious was he? I tried to look for clues in the way he'd said it, but then became conscious of the aching silence. I filled it with a second "Okay."

"You don't sound convinced."

"It's a shame it's taken you so long to realise that."

"I know, I know, I know, but I have now, and I'm just really sorry for how I've behaved."

I could feel the hurt in Wilf's words, and the regret – there was no question he felt genuine remorse – but what I had to ask myself was: did he feel sorry for how he'd behaved, or just the fact that he'd now lost the only person left who had been there for him these past few years?

I was back in England when we had this conversation. Actually I'd been back for a long time, six or seven months by then, and had even been out to see him again, but if I wrote about that I guarantee you'd lose the will to live. How many times can I keep saying everything turned to shit and keep it interesting? The only thing different that time (and it was the last time) was that he'd moved out of the house and gone into a penthouse apartment in the town centre. "A stepping-stone back home" he'd called it. He'd had enough of Limassol, he said, but part of that might've been due to a business thing he was involved in going totally pear-shaped. I don't know the ins and outs of it, but I know it resulted in him being forced to kneel down at the edge of a pit with a gun pressed to the back of his head, thinking he was about to be executed by some ex SAS soldiers. About the time in the penthouse when he locked me in the room, and I was convinced he was about to set fire to the whole complex he remembered nothing. Nor did he remember anything about the claw hammer attack the time before. Not a single shred of it. So he claimed anyway. And when I told him about it, as I had all the other times, his response was the same:

"I would *never* hurt you, Chrissy. Not in a million years."

I was gone that same day. I'd forced him, while he was sober, to get me a seat on the very next flight out. But then it was back to the same old routine. The calls, the pestering, the hassling of my friends, my family, my clients; some told him to fuck off and leave them alone, some told him to fuck off and leave *me* alone, which I was grateful for, but they knew, as I knew, that it wasn't really him doing the calling, it was the drink, the Demon Drink, with 'demon' being a much more apt word in this case than sense would normally allow. That was why it meant a world of difference to hear him talking about going in to get dried out. It was the first time he'd ever acknowledged he even had a drinking problem. Up until that moment it was everyone else's.

"I need someone to support me through it though, Chrissy" he said, "because it's not going to be easy."

No prizes for guessing who he wanted that someone to be.

The Limassol house got snapped up in about ten minutes. Nowhere in the marketing materials, however, did it offer a full account of all its many unique features: massive kitchen, large swimming pool, Roman Centurions that walk through walls and stop nutcases from smashing your head in, but that didn't seem to bother anybody. Wilf was only too pleased to get shut of it; it had been a nice project while it lasted, but it hadn't worked out – whatever 'it' was supposed to be – but now it was time to shift his attentions to another project, one closer to home, and he felt a need to involve me in it. He'd already proposed, a few times by now, feeling that because I hadn't yet abandoned him there must still be something between us, something we could strengthen even more. But it just wasn't an idea I could even entertain.

One way of keeping me involved in his life was to ask that I keep an eye out for a suitable house for him. He knew I enjoyed looking at properties, and probably felt that if I found somewhere for him, I'd be more likely to feel a connection to it. He wasn't wrong. The Wirral might not have the best reputation elsewhere in the UK, especially to those who only think of it in terms of Birkenhead, but there are some very lovely places around, with properties that reflect that, and these were the kind of places that Wilf despatched me to. Even though I was now pushing fifty, it wasn't hard to remember just how much I'd once pined to live in a big house when I was little, cowering in the coal cupboard, and wishing for a turret up which I could run to hide from my abusers. That yearning to be Guinevere, it never left me. The deep longing to be plucked from my life and to find myself in a tale worthy enough to be remembered, and perhaps mythologized, by future generations, who recognised all the romantic aspirations that swirled around inside me. But as my suitors mounted, and proved themselves unsuitable Lancelots, I came slowly to realise that I'd fixed upon the wrong myth. If my life resembled anyone's from those old Arthurian legends, it wasn't Guinevere's, it was the even more tragic tale of the Lady of Shalott, cursed to view the toings and froings of life outside her castle window only through reflections in a mirror. If ever she succumbs to temptation, so the legend goes, and looks *directly* at the world outside, she will fall ill and die. But Sir Lancelot, who she falls in love with from afar, rides past her window one day and she just can't bloody help herself, she flies to the window and fixes her eyes upon him, unleashing the full effects of the curse.

My own fate was sealed when I agreed to go with John to that party when I was eighteen. The moment I walked in through that door and took from his hand the drink he'd just poured for me, that was the moment I looked from the tower and saw the world for what it was: a bruising and fearful place, full of too many people who thought only of themselves. I have being floating ever since, close to death, drifting downstream towards Camelot, where my body might one day be recognised for the beauty I'd like to think it always had inside it.

I did see a house, one that caught my eye; more than caught it, in fact – it positively seduced me. It was on Grammar School Lane in West Kirby. It needed a fair bit of work doing on it to make it suitable enough to meet Wilf's exacting standards, but it had a lot of rooms, and space enough to accommodate every single wish a modern man with a few quid at his disposal could demand from a home. I couldn't wait to tell him about it.

"What's the number?" he asked, "I'll make an offer and we can both move in there." This, after me talking about it for barely thirty seconds.

"We?" I said. I hadn't seen that one coming. I'd actually just bought my own flat, so there was no way I was intending to pack up my stuff yet again. But it was becoming increasingly clear this was Wilf's intention all along. I'd certainly help him work on it, as it would be a nice project for me, but nothing more than that.

He gave me the nod and I went ahead and spoke to the estate agent, and after a little bit of back-and-forthing, I was able to get eighty thousand off the asking price. That alone tells you something about the kind of house we were talking about, and I did get a little bit excited about it, but not enough to consider turning my life upside down for. However, when we were talking, I accidentally let it slip that the flat I'd just moved into needed a new bathroom and kitchen, and before I could stop myself, Wilf's eyes lit up with an idea that, he suggested, would help us both out.

"Okay then," he said, "this is what we'll do to make it easy for ourselves: I'll come over and live with you in the flat while they're fixing up the house, and I'll pay for the new bathroom and kitchen." It wasn't exactly what I was thinking, but eleven grand – which is what the new bathroom and kitchen would set me back – was a good deal of money, and if I was to cover it myself it would mean I'd be stretched for the next few years.

"It's less than I'd pay in a hotel," he said, with only the slightest hint of exaggeration. I was uneasy about it, but I agreed, once I'd reminded him about his promise to get dried out.

"Yeah-yeah, don't worry about that," he said. "I've got a meeting with them in a few weeks."

It worked. The kitchen and the bathroom both got installed, and totally transformed the flat, and as it was being done, Wilf's house got finished too. We somehow made it through without incident. There was bickering, but at no point did it escalate to a point where a knife or a claw hammer were being reached for. Even better, the vodka, the whisky and the beer all stayed in their bottles, and the bottles all stayed un-purchased on the shelves in the off license down the road. He really was trying.

During this time there was nothing physical going on between us – I was still too bruised – and we kept separate rooms. But as soon as his own house was fixed up, and he finally moved in, I noticed a slight, but discernible crawl back to the person I'd known previously. He had no job, so was living off his savings, but he was bored; bored without me, and bored without a series of daily tasks to sink his teeth into. I think this is why he allowed himself to slip back to the person neither of us wanted him to be. It was like watching a baby polar bear on a tiny ice floe drift further and further away from the land, and as he got further away, be become more and more desperate.

"Why don't you come round tonight?"

Two years had passed since he'd last asked that, the 4pm or the 3pm question that always heralded the slow unravelling of his mind. It was hard to believe how much had happened since. But I was tougher, and my friends were tougher, and we were all wiser to his crap. None of us were going to stand for any more of his babbling bullshit. The best way for me to avoid it was to be firm with him and not put myself in a position that would see me vulnerable around him: all I had to do was not spend the night.

But as wise as I was, the fates were wiser, and they conspired to let him put a noose around my head one final, and very nearly fatal, time.

I can't remember what it was I had to drop off at his, but I drove round early one night straight after work to do it. I was in my Jag, which had always been reliable in the past, but when I got back in, after having a cup of tea with Wilf, it wouldn't start. I was outside for ages turning the engine over, hoping it would catch, but no joy.

Shit, I thought, *this is all I bloody need right now.* The garage had closed at five, so I knew I wouldn't be able to get anyone out to take a look at it until tomorrow. It was annoying enough already knowing I couldn't get back, but doubly annoying because how the hell was I going to get to work in the morning?

"What's the problem?" Wilf asked from his door. He'd heard the empty coughs of the engine, but he was certainly no mechanic. Even if he was, would he have helped, or just seen this as an opportunity?

"Don't worry, I'll get the garage out first thing," he said. But their 'first thing' was nine o'clock in the morning, the *next* morning, an hour after I was due at work. "Not a problem, I'll run you in myself," he said, once I'd voiced my plight to him.

Okay, so maybe not a problem for you, I thought, *but it was for* me, *because it meant I'd have to stay the night.* I knew I didn't have a choice, but it would mean I would have to walk willingly into the lion's den and bed myself down for the night, without even a catapult to arm myself with if things turned rough. But if I was vigilant, I said to myself, and made sure he understood the terms, then there was no reason it had to descend into tragedy. The second there was any funny business, any at all, I'd be out the door and flagging down the nearest taxi.

But there was no funny business that night. Still on his best behaviour, we had a very pleasant evening and Wilf's personality came down on the side of Dr Jekyll, which meant he remained his witty, charming self. He was even up before me the next morning to get the breakfast on, and it wasn't hard to remember that morning all those years ago when Phil had done the same. After I'd showered, he then drove me to work and sorted out the car once he'd got back, promising me it would all be taken care of by the time he collected me later that day. Unfortunately, that promise wasn't his to make, and when he turned up at the house I was babysitting in, he had to break the news to me.

"It won't be ready till Friday," he announced.

"Bugger" I said, unable to help myself.

"They had to take it in because it needs new parts, which they've got to order."

That was the last thing I wanted to hear, but before I'd even summoned up enough dread to ask how much, I was going to pay by cash but Wilf wanted the English money so I gave it to him and he paid for the repair by cheque. *Thank God for that*, I thought; but any relief I felt was now outweighed by the realisation that I was going to have to stay at Wilf's for the rest of the week, as a taxi to and from work would probably set me back more than the Jag would cost to fix. I would just have to extend my trust in Wilf over a period of a week rather than just a single night, and pray that he didn't let me down in the process.

As I was processing all this, I suddenly noticed we were taking a different route back and hadn't stopped to think why.

"Which way are you going?" I asked, the memories of that white-knuckle drive to his house in Limassol still ripe in my mind.

"Don't you want to pick up a few things from the flat?"

"Oh yeah," I laughed. "I suppose I'll need one or two more outfits."

The 'thing' happened on the third night …

We'd gone to mine on the first – *after* he'd told me about the garage – and I'd packed up a bag with all my stuff in it, just some essentials really, with an outfit for each day and some not-sexy-at-all underwear. As the evening wore on and we got closer to going to bed, I discreetly placed my bag by the door, directly beneath my coat, with my car keys positioned clearly in sight on top. I told Wilf it was just to save me time in the morning, but in reality, it was in case I had to flee the house at the drop of a hat. Bear Grylls would be happy, because everything I'd need to survive a nuclear war was in it. The following night was as pleasant as the first and we had another lovely evening, but I still made sure my bag was by the door in case he kicked off again and Mr Hyde put in an appearance. Both mornings Wilf made me breakfast as I got ready, ran me in to work, and then collected me, and after dinner we watched tele till our eyes got heavy and then went up to bed. Not for a second, as I got into my pyjamas, or brushed my teeth, or fluffed up my pillows, did I relax. The whole time I felt as if I was skating around on a frozen lake during the last few days of winter. At any moment, I thought, it was going to crack, and the only thing that would decide whether I drowned or didn't was just how close to the edge I was when I heard it.

When it did finally crack I was in the middle. I could see the edge, but the centre was closer. And so was the danger. I'd just said goodnight to Wilf, and told him I was heading up. Usually that was the signal for him to follow; he'd turn the tele and lights off and follow up straight away, but this time he just looked at me and said, "'Night, then."

"Oh," I said, taken aback. "Have you got work to do or something?"

"No, I'm just going to stay up and watch this for a bit."

Why that answer was strange is because there was a TV in the bedroom, and he could easily have watched it in there. I wouldn't have minded. I told him this, but he said felt like staying up for a bit.

I should've checked that I'd put my bag by the door just then, but for some reason the thought never crossed my mind. I went into the bathroom that led through to the bedroom – it had once been a garage before Wilf had converted everything around – and could be reached by a single step up. Through that you'd reach the long hallway that ran directly down to the lounge where Wilf was still sitting, so, in effect, the bathroom was one end of a dumbbell and the lounge was the other, with the hall serving as the handle connecting them.

I had a wash and brushed my teeth, then went to lie down for a bit, in my pyjamas, with the tele on, and after about half an hour I felt myself drifting off. I knew I needed one last pee, so I thought I'd just go quickly. But when I was in there, I thought it odd that Wilf hadn't popped his head in to see how I was. In fact, he was being very quiet. Just to check he was okay, and hadn't had a heart attack, I thought I'd pop my head out and shout down the hall to tell him I was about to go to sleep. I could see the couch and the back of his head, but it looked like it was slumped forward.

Oh God, I thought, *that didn't look good*. I could hear the TV on, but he clearly wasn't watching it.

"I'm just going to sleep now," I called gently, not wanting to wake him if he was asleep, but prodding him in case he wanted to join me.

His head started to turn towards me in slow-motion, but from the way his brow had collapsed into itself again and pushed his chin forward, I could tell

Mr Hyde was back amongst us and it would be a while before I saw Wilf again.

"What are *you* doing up?" he said in that voice again, the one that was his but not really his. That was when I remembered, with a stab of panic, that I hadn't put my bag by the door. It was behind me, still in the room, and not only that, it wasn't even packed, my stuff was strewn all over the place. I knew the door would be locked. He always locked it, and since his episode in Limassol with the ex SAS soldiers, he'd been totally paranoid about doors and windows being left unlocked, because that's how they came to get him: they just turned up out-of-the-blue, dragged him into the back of a truck and drove off with him still inside.

Locked or unlocked, though, I still had to get out, and so I mumbled the first thing that came into my head:

"I, err … I just wanted to get a glass of water."

"You know where the taps are."

I nodded, not wanting to disturb him, thinking I'd just go and grab the water, and then … and then what? I had two choices: head back to the room and wait it out, praying for him to fall asleep, *or* find a way of trying to sneak past him to get to the door, so I could get the hell out. Then, just as I entered the kitchen and was starting to think that might be the better option, I saw him next to me. I jumped out my skin.

"You'll need a glass."

"I was just getting one."

I grabbed a glass and filled it at the tap. My hands were shaking. He watched me drink, closely, as if he'd never seen anyone drink a glass of water before, the just carried on staring at me. I knew, like last time, that I needed to keep the mood light. I couldn't let my unease let the situation move beyond my control. I lowered the glass.

"Shall we go back in and watch something?" I asked.

"No. I want you to go back to the bedroom."

"I'd rather watch something."

"You can watch it in the bedroom."

I was going to say more but there was something in his tone that convinced me that wasn't the right thing to do. The more I stuck my head out to try and recover the night, the easier it would be for him to get the noose around it.

I took my water back to my room, sensing him right behind me, ghosting my every step, head bowed, mouth slightly agape. It really was very creepy. I got to the door and turned towards him.

"Are you going to stay up for a bit then?" I said.

"Mmghn," he mumbled. I gave him a smile and went to close the door, but he did it for me. I was still in my clothes, as it happened, which meant I wouldn't have to get changed, but if I was to try and find a way of sneaking out – as I now felt I would have to – then it would be best if I had my stuff all packed and ready to go. I threw my bag up onto the bed and as I started filling it, I heard the strangest sound outside my door. It was like something being dragged, something heavy. I didn't dare investigate because I didn't want to set him off; the less contact the better, a fact I was, at that very moment, stitching onto my brain so forcefully that this time I'd *never* forget it. I wanted him gone from my life, forever, but first, I had to get myself gone from this fucking prison. The scraping sound went on for quite a while, thirty seconds at least. What the hell was he up to? I could hear him on the other side of the door, breathing heavily. I wish he'd go the fuck away so I could sneak out.

After five minutes, he still hadn't gone back to the lounge, so I sat on the bed, drumming my fingers on my bag. I let my eyes drift over to the TV. Shattered now, the flickering images worked at making me sleepy, and I must've dozed off because the next thing I knew I had a horrible taste in my mouth and the TV was showing something else, about planets or something. I walked to the door but couldn't hear anything. *Now's my chance*, I thought, so I grabbed my bag and went to the door, turned the handle and …

CLANK!

The door opened about a centimetre, but no more. I pushed harder, but there was no give on it; I rattled the handle – as if that would help, but it just wouldn't budge. That's what the scraping sound had been. There was a large plant in the hallway and ladders; he must've shifted it and placed it directly outside the door, trapping me inside. If his behaviour before hadn't unsettled me, this certainly did. What the hell was he planning *now*?

"Wilf?" I called, still with as much softness as I could muster.

But there was no response. I wrapped on the door, hoping the banging might rouse him, but again, nothing. Then I shouted. Still nothing. Grabbing the door handle I pushed as hard as I could against it, but it wouldn't shift.

"WILF!" I screamed. I was getting scared now. Really scared.

There were three windows in the bedroom; two big ones, and a tiny one that had no function whatsoever, other than to let a sliver of daylight into the room. It was tiny, but even so, Wilf normally kept it locked, "just in case".

Bad sorts can always let a small child into a property, who then goes round to the back and opens a door to let others in. I knew it wouldn't be open now, but I tried it anyway and, weirdly, discovered that it was. I didn't miss a beat. I grabbed a chair and pulled it over to stand on, then did what no middle-aged woman should ever have to do. Thank God I was such a slight build, "as skinny as a rake" one or two friends had said, because that meant I was able to squeeze my head and shoulders through, and then heave myself through. As I scrambled to get myself onto the ledge, I knocked a couple of ornaments off which smashed onto the floor. I couldn't allow myself to feel too much remorse though – it was better than my skull.

That still might have been damaged, however, if I'd landed poorly after dragging myself through; that, or my neck might have snapped. But as ungainly as my landing was, nothing was damaged – except for my dignity – when I dropped like a worm onto the ground outside. I'd forgotten my bag, but that didn't matter, at least I was out, and it couldn't have been too late as I saw lights still on in a couple of the houses across the road. It was just after midnight when I'd last checked, and this felt not much later.

I wasn't really thinking much beyond getting to safety, and some inner sense told me to just head for the nearest house with a light on. So that's what I did. The first one was three or four houses down. I saw a few moths circling in the glow of the porch light outside and, following pretty much the same instinct as them, ran towards it. The gate was open, so I just limped through, looking like some scream-queen from a cheap horror film, and knocked on the door. God, I hadn't realised how badly I was shaking – look at my hand. Was I cold or was that just plain fear? Plus, I was still in my bloody pyjamas.

More lights came on. A trail of them that led from the sitting room to the hall, to where I was standing outside. Then the door opened. It was on a chain.

"Yes?"

I didn't know the neighbours at all, but it didn't take me long to convince the couple who lived there that I wasn't there to rob them. They saw me trembling, heard my voice catch in my throat, and finally took the chain off.

I almost fell into their hall.

SPIRITS, BE GONE!

The picture the policeman sketched out for me about what would've happened had I not fled the house was fairly horrible. Maybe he'd just read too much Enid Blyton when he was a kid, or watched too many episodes of *Quincy*, but it sickened me to my stomach. They'd found Wilf on the sofa, he explained, sprawled out, paralytic, next to a couple of bottles of vodka. One of them empty. Around him were a few pills – paracetamol, I think – the rest of which they reckoned he must've washed down with the vodka. As the scene was described to me, in lurid detail, I couldn't help but cast my mind back almost thirty years, to when the police told me what they'd discovered at the home of my wannabe rapist. The one from the phone box. There were clear echoes of that here, but this was far more sinister. It looked very much like Wilf had been planning a murder-suicide thing; his intention, they believed initially, was to come for me, suffocate me while I slept (something he'd already attempted in Cyprus), then return to the lounge and polish off the last of the pills and vodka.

"The alcohol takes away the guilt," the policeman said, "and that embold-ens the perpetrator to act in a way he wouldn't usually."

But it wasn't even that simple, as I'd find out a few hours later.

It was the husband who'd rung the police, once I'd finally coughed out my story to the kindly couple who let me in. I'd mumbled and babbled out to the pair of them a little bit of the back-story that led me, like all those moths, to their porch. They stared at me, swapped a quick glance, then, once they'd digested all the misery of my plight, the husband trotted off to the phone, and the wife popped the kettle on.

"I know what you need," she'd said. And she was bloody right.

I don't remember if they arrested Wilf then, but they did drag him straight off to the hospital so he could get all the crap pumped out of him. Only, it turns out there was no crap to get pumped out of him. The pills were a prop. He'd hardly taken any at all, barely enough to stop a headache. It was all just part of the grim show he wanted to stage. Only the Devil knows what he was thinking in his addled 'Mr Hyde' state, but it seems the suicide part wasn't quite what it looked like. Pills were found in the toilet, you see, lots of them, so they think Wilf had flushed most of them away, or attempted to. What they eventually concluded, therefore, was that they reckoned Wilf wanted to get shut of me, but only make it *look* like he'd tried to take his own life. So, instead of it being a murder-suicide, it would've been just plain old murder, the attempt on his own life being marked down as a failure. Perhaps he was even going to try and make it look like it was a pact we'd settled on together, to divest himself of any responsibility for my death. But that's only if you believe Wilf was even in charge of his own actions at the time, because who the hell knows what was driving him on?

However, Archangel Michael beat him to it, because that window, that tiny window in the corner of that room ... I know it should've been bolted shut. It was *always* bolted shut. Just like all the others. Wilf was obsessive about stuff like that. But there it was, just when I needed it to be unlocked, unlocked it was.

It was the middle of the night when the police drove me back to my flat. I felt sorry for the couple whose night I must've ruined, but I hope the fact that I'm so eternally grateful to them offers them some consolation. They helped save my life. And yet, despite that, it still needed another intervention, because not even half an hour later, after the police had left, I got a call from them. They'd just picked Wilf up again, they told me. He'd discharged himself, still drunk, from the hospital, and was on his way to see me. They'd found him at the end of my road, and he still had the Devil in him. I think this is when most of his dark intentions had spilled out. They were so disturbed by what he said, and his tone, that they carted him straight back to the hospital and asked a security guard there to make sure he didn't leave. I was so disturbed by what they told me that I rang Stephanie (who really wasn't happy to be woken up at mad o'clock) and begged her to come round. God love her, she did exactly that. But it didn't stop me shaking all night, waiting for a sinister shadow to appear at the window.

In the end, they weren't able to bring any charges against Wilf, not even for barricading me in the room. By the time the police had arrived, and had managed to get inside, he'd moved the cupboard away from the door, and they only had my word – and their own fevered imaginings – to work with. What they had their *own* word for was how to keep him away from me in the future: *'Injunction'.* It wasn't a new word on me, to be truthful, I'd used it before, numerous times, for Billy Harris, but with him it had proved about as effective as a chocolate fire guard. He totally ignored it, and didn't I just learn why, soon after? But much as I tried, I couldn't for the life of me imagine Wilf wearing the jacket of a police informer. He was intelligent and smart, but there was nothing about him that would make you think he could wrap the entire Cheshire police force around his little finger.

In the meantime, the security guard did as instructed, and stayed with him in the hospital which, bizarrely, I could actually see from my flat. In the morning, after giving him a stern dressing down, the police advised Wilf to stay away from me. As it was only an informal warning he took as much notice of it as a dog would a piece of raw chicken, and the very next day, almost immediately after being discharged from the hospital, he turned up at my door "to see how I was doing". Echoing the police's warning, I told him through the door to get stuffed and, not 24-hours later, after a quick trip into town, I had an order from the court, saying exactly the same thing, only in far scarier language. Wilf, in turn, responded by sending me a bunch of roses and a bottle of Champagne. One ended up in the bin, the other down the sink, where he was more than welcome to join it.

I didn't know then that good things lay just around the corner. I'd been in a tunnel my whole life, one built by others, so didn't know precisely when I'd be thrown to the left or flung to the right, I just had to sit tight and react accordingly. Eventually I learned to lean into the turns, even the sharp ones, to make them seem less violent. But every tunnel has an end, and even though I couldn't see it, it was just up ahead around the bend. My new life.

Wilf wasn't cruel the way Billy and John were. The obvious explanation for his behaviour is to say he was just a victim of a condition that has always plagued our society; from Buzz Aldrin, the second man on the moon, to Dudley Moore. People turn to alcohol for so many reasons: some because they're too poor and it's an escape from the opportunities they regret not taking, and others because they're too wealthy and it's an escape from the guilt they feel at their own success. What both have is a void at their centre that they think they can fill with alcohol. Over time they eventually discover they can't, but by the time they realise this it's often too late, because by then, after their lives have fallen apart and their families have left them, it's the void that's controlling them, not them that's controlling the void.

It's interesting that they call strong alcohol 'spirits'. It got the name because, in Medieval times, alchemists in the Middle East became fascinated with the vapour that was given off during the alchemical process when they making medicines. They collected it and used it to treat people, but because of the form it took they believed it to be the 'spirit' of the original material they used. They must have seen how it changed people when they took too much of it, how it altered their personalities and made them behave in ways they wouldn't normally. As I've said already, when sober, Wilf was the nicest man in the world, but when that 'thing' got inside him, that spirit or demon or whatever the hell it was, it made him unrecognisable, in both his actions and even his voice. If only he could've stayed away from the bottle, we might have had a good life together, and *he* might've been the light at the end of my tunnel. Instead, he was just another hazard, one of far too many placed on the tracks to derail me. I did well to get around him.

But even then, even with the injunction in place, and an army of people around me ready to tell him to fuck off to hell, there was still one more hazard to get past. He'd got his solicitor to place it there and it revealed itself in the form of a claim that I owed him £11,000 – the money he gave me to have the kitchen and bathroom redone. He said I'd promised to pay him back every single penny for it and that I'd failed to. It was as laughable as it was untrue, but one of the many things I've learnt in my life is that nothing is ever too laughable if it's got lawyers behind it. They certainly weren't laughing when they heard that my defence rested solely upon a verbal agreement we'd made, in which I'd said he could stay at my flat whilst his own house was being worked on.

Once again, I went knocking on the door of another friend, Brian, another solicitor, who refused to watch me trampled on by some big bully who could afford to arm himself with posh men in posh pin-striped suits. Fortunately, this time it wouldn't be a total trampling, because there was more than just my word. There were documents.

"You negotiated everything for his house on Grammar School Lane," he said, going through my defence. "You got eighty grand *off* the asking price *and* managed to wrangle another twenty thousand *off* the building work ..." as he talked through all this to clarify it in his own mind, I could see a little glimmer of hope floating, like a cloud, on the horizon. He pulled out a rope and, just like a cowboy, expertly lassoed it.

Eleven grand was PIN-money for Wilf. He could burn through that in a couple of days if he so wished. But to me it was food on the table, and the bricks and mortar around me. Wilf knew this, and that's why he was doing it. It was straight out of the same playbook that Billy and John had been reared on: *If it doesn't love you … destroy it!*

Yes, I could get the money, but I'd have to sell the flat to get my hands on it, and that would make me homeless again, and there was no safety net this time, no money hidden away inside some long-forgotten shares. They'd all been cashed and were in the walls around me. There was only my life left to me now, and I didn't feel quite ready to cash that in just yet.

Fortunately for me, Brian felt the same, and in no time at all he was able to get proof, in writing, that I'd done all I claimed I'd done to secure the Grammar School Lane house. He'd also got the builders to confirm that I'd negotiated the twenty grand off their fee, and used all this to build our case with. He then tapped out a letter to Wilf's solicitor saying that we could either settle now, and I'd pay him £4,500 (the limit to which I could then stretch), or we could battle it out through the courts for the requested eleven; *but*, if Wilf lost the case – which he more than likely would – we'd hit him for a hundred grand in damages – the same amount I'd saved him in the first place.

He went for it. Early the next week we heard back from his solicitor. He'd settle for the four and a half, even though what he ended up taking himself (after his solicitor had bitten off his fee) was little more than he'd stuff into the knickers of a lap dancer on a lonely night out.

In the years since, I've often wondered if Wilf regretted taking this route. All I ever wanted to do was help him, so that I could help *us*, but he was unable to meet me even one tenth of the way there. He did send me flowers, anonymously, like Phil used to, asking me to give him another chance, and another, and another, saying he would never hurt me, "not in a million years, blah-blah-blah," but the only thing that seemed likely *not* to happen in a million years was for him to do what he long-ago promised he would: go to rehab and get dried out. He never did go. But maybe it wouldn't have mattered anyway, because, when you weigh up everything that led him to where he was right then – twice divorced, with four kids who barely ever said a word to him – it might not have been the spirits that resulted in him being dumped on the trash heap in the first place.

Not *those* spirits anyway.

232

A MESSAGE FROM THE OTHER SIDE

I know there's no such thing as a Happy Ending. Not a real one. Not the way we're raised to believe they exist. It all depends on where you finish the story. End this one with Phil whizzing me away from Big Billy in his people carrier, and I'm Walt Disney's Sleeping Beauty. But end it on my wedding night, after drunken, lecherous, "Where's-my-fuckin-dinner?" John ordered me to put "put up the bans", and I'm more like the one in the 17th century original, where poor Beauty gets raped repeatedly by the king, and impregnated with his child. All while she's sleeping. Yes, it's compelling, but it's certainly not something that CBeebies would be rushing to adapt for their next Christmas panto!

I'm ending my story here though because this is where I am. It feels happy enough, and that'll do. Not everyone made it into the story, but that doesn't mean they didn't play an important role in it. If I'd written it five years ago, maybe I'd have brought different things out. If five years into the future, maybe different things again. Our story changes as we go along, and how we think of it changes too. There's a good chance that my own grandchildren, or even their kids, will read my story one day. This version of it anyway. They'll read about Big Billy and Wilf and Phil, and even John Suckley, which is weird. To them I might not seem any more real than Sleeping Beauty does to me right now, or even Guinevere, whose ultimate fate wasn't much better than Beauty's (depending on what version you read). "Who's that?" one of them might ask their mum, pointing to a faded picture she finds in the back of an old photograph album. "Oh, that's your great nanna," my granddaughter will answer back, marvelling at my big hair. "Her name was Christina. She wrote a book about her life, once upon a time." "Really?" my great-granddaughter might ask, amazed. "Yeah. I think I've got a copy of it somewhere," her mum will then say, trying to remember where it might be. She might even know a little something about what came after the book appeared – my final years, the time and date, etc. Even where I'm buried.

But, of course, they'll just be details. This, what you're reading now, this is the real me. The one that's worth remembering.

I do think about what might come next or, 'crossing over' as I like to think of it. Not so much about *how* I will cross over, but about how happy my spirit will be when I eventually do. How settled. I don't want to leave behind anything negative, you see, some part of me that will end up sitting on the bed of a little girl who, years later, ends up being traumatised simply because I wasn't able to cross over peacefully. I see it so much in what I do. I can feel it in others, those who still feel slighted in some way, by their time here. It was never long enough. They never achieved what they wanted. Someone hurt them. Probably the best way of guaranteeing I don't leave anything negative behind would be to tie up all the psychic baggage I've been dragging around with me since the moment my twin-sister and I were pulled out of my mum – her dead, me alive. I've picked up most of it, I think, and tucked it all away, but the one thing I just can't access is that part of me that connects me to my dad. Not Richie, who died years ago, but my real one, who Patricia ('Dodo') met in Malta when he was stationed over there. Ernest Golightly, or Ernie, as he might be known to his friends in the States. When this book is finally finished, I'd like to send him a copy. You see, even before a word of this thing was typed, before I'd scribbled down a single note, or put any thoughts on tape, that was the one thing on my mind. I read somewhere once that J.K. Rowling knew the end of *Harry Potter* long before she'd even started the first book, the Philosopher one. Well, that's how I've always felt about this. That's the image I've got in my head. I can see him opening it. I can. Sitting by the window. His face all tanned, his thinning hair as white as a seal cub's. He's opening it on his lap. It's sunny out, the sky's blue, and there he is, peering inside and seeing the cover. "What the hell?" he says to himself. I know he has a family, a big one, and his children – in their fifties, I would guess – have spread far and wide. Probably done amazing things. I don't want anything from him. Nothing that a few words couldn't satisfy. I'm not sure his family could ever understand that. A single word would do, a handshake would be better, but a hug … that would be best. A hug with my dad. My *real* dad. It hurts that that I never got the chance with my mum. That I met her, spoke to her, looked into her eyes, but never knew it was her. God, it makes me sick with hurt. I can still see her now, too. Standing there in the shop. Across the counter. Her hair black. That smile. Elizabeth Taylor. "You're better than all this, Christina."

Am I, Mum? ... Am I really?

I put them together sometimes. As they must've been. Shy. Nervous. Dorothy and Ernest. Dodo and Ernie. I imagine the few moments of happiness they shared, and the loneliness my mum must've felt to have risked her marriage on something she must've known in her heart couldn't last. Or perhaps she'd genuinely hoped for more. Maybe *he* had. It breaks my heart thinking about it. But if she hadn't risked it, if she hadn't looked for that escape, if he hadn't, for the fleeting joys they must've given each other all those decades ago in Malta, then I wouldn't be here. This must be why ghosts are so central to who I am as a person. Because ghosts made me.

I'm in a good place right now, but I still have my little fears. The same fears I've always had. They still send a ripple of panic through me from time to time, often at night, when I'm drowsy and forget where I am. They revolve around the idea of not having a roof over my head. The insecurity that comes with all that. Of having barely enough money to live on, and not knowing how I'm going to get more. Of not knowing how I'm going to fill six plates with food, and very often failing to. Unless you've experienced it, you can't know how paralysing it is.

"You really don't need to worry about this," my partner says to me now. I can pass the message on to my rational brain, and it understands the words, but they mean nothing to the unconscious part of me, the part that still remembers what it was like to be woken in my snow-covered car by the police and told to move on before they forcibly removed me. Things can change so quickly. That's why I've never stopped working, even if it's only for PIN money. I still do my readings, my Reiki, car boot sales – I do a lot of those now – and I clean. Right now, I go in and clean at a big country house nearby, which I love doing. It's a Grade II mansion house (one of a number of stately homes I've worked in), built in the 17th century, but I probably best keep my mouth shut about any spirits I've sensed there, in case the people who own it read this and start asking me too many questions. But I could tell you a few tales, alright, not just from there, but from all the other places. They would blow your mind.

A good many of the people I've written about in these pages have crossed over themselves now. Olive and Richie, they're gone, as are most of my brothers and sisters. I don't want to waste any more ink on them, especially Raymond, but it doesn't hurt to tell you he's no longer with us. When I was told, I simply said, "Oh, right," and then carried on with what I was doing. He's with the insects on the wall now, pressed in deeply to the plaster.

Big Billy's on his last legs too. The cancer that entered his system a short time back has been slowly sucking the life out of him. How he's made it this far, I've no idea. "The Devil saves his own till last," a friend of mine once said. Most of the children don't speak to him at all now, seeing him for what he is, but Will and Stephanie will still make the effort. It kills me that they do, but what can I do about it? He is their real dad after all, and I think I've made it abundantly clear throughout these pages how I feel about blood connections. If I was Stephanie, who still has a good relationship with him ("He makes me laugh, mum.") I'm sure I'd be exactly the same. If there is any doubt about how bad he was in the past, though, or how terrible things got, they can just read this book. No doubt they'll do it through gritted teeth. They know what they know already, so there'll be no major shocks, but any gaps they might have, this should help fill them. Even if you're lucky enough to know your parents, to grow up with them, you don't know everything, do you? Their past is like a foreign country. I hope reading this thing doesn't open too many wounds for them. It's opened a few for me writing it, that's for sure, but then, that was my choice. It's been cathartic, certainly, and if it can do something similar for them, that's just a bonus. All through my life I've watched people punching through walls to get rid of the stress that's built up inside them. This book is my version of that. This is me punching through a wall, but the benefit is, I don't have to pay for the wall to be re-plastered, and I didn't break any nails in the process.

Phil caught Dorothy in bed with another fella. I know that will surprise literally no one. Did he really think it was for love? Surely to God not. He's still going, anyway, pushing eighty now. To this day, l wonder what it was she had over him. Even his own mother wondered it. She told me once. "It's like she's got him under some kind of spell," she said to me. Well, it's broken now. She broke it when she spread her skinny legs for some other bloke. I don't see him anymore, although I did not too long ago, at a car boot sale. "You still owe me money for that house," I said to him. He almost laughed. His daughters are out in America, living the good life, in the million-dollar apartments he bought them. They've got good jobs – as Accountants, I think, working with celebrities like Elton John – but that's what a private education will get you. Shame there wasn't enough decency spread between the pair of them to let my daughter benefit from the same. Deryn would've done well as an Accountant, or even as a Lawyer. Kirsty Bertarelli went to Howells and she's the richest women in the country now. Of course, the dog-murdering little witches turned on Dorothy too eventually, but you probably guessed that. If they thought I was a gold-digger, me, who had no interest whatsoever in their dad's money, imagine how they reacted when Dorothy moved in with her Grave V Gold Digger's Kit.

Was it all worth it? Of all the questions I knew I was going to ask myself at the end of this book, this is the one I kept putting off. But as I've been writing it, I've been thinking about it more and more; my life, each and every incident – the ones I've included, and the ones I haven't (there's still loads I haven't even touched upon) – and my impression of them has altered greatly. If the purpose of life is to leave the world in a better situation than the one that greeted you when you arrived, then, yes, I've done that. I've done okay. I don't feel any bitterness, not towards anyone. Even Raymond. Those that were horrible to me, those who made me their enemy, and tried to fill me with hate, they were the ones who ended up suffering. Not me. Certainly, there were times I thought about ending things myself, but I always found something to pull me back. There's value in that. When you *know* there is something else after this life, it takes the fear out of everything, and when you know you can live without fear, then you can really start to live. That's where I am, now. Living. *Really* living. With five amazing kids, some grandkids, and an amazingly supportive man who, honestly, couldn't do more for me.

So, 'yes' is my answer. It was all worth it.

Like I say, there's only one thing missing, but once I've printed this out and done all the other things I need to do for the publisher, I'm going to pop it in an envelope and send it to him in America. I've got an address for him that Deryn managed to track down. She's good online. Not like her mum. It'll either get to him or it won't, and if it does, and he reads it, who knows? There might be another chapter still to come.

You have to live in hope, don't you? It's worked for me so far.

EPILOGUE:
TAXI TO THE FUTURE

I nearly deleted the email straight away when I first saw it, just like I had all the others from that address. If I'd known how to send things straight to my junk box so I didn't even have to see anything like that, I would've done it years ago. But I didn't. So there it was. Just sitting there. An email from Dating Direct. I'd signed up years ago, after a friend recommended it, but then, after a couple of 'what-the-hell-was-I-thinking' dinner dates, I'd never gotten round to leaving. Far too bloody complicated. Anyway, I'd washed my hands with fellas a long time ago, so to say I had any interest in what any one of them could've said to me at this stage in my life would be just plain ridiculous. Mentally, spiritually, and sexually, I wanted nothing from anyone, and I knew, no matter how much they tried to charm me, or make me laugh when we first met, all it came down to – all it *ever* came down to – was me ending up cowering somewhere, covered in bruises and praying to Archangel Michael to make it all stop. So, I did the most sensible thing I could. I moved my curser to the email, right clicked on it, saw where the delete tab was and … *opened the email!*

We met in a car park in Mickle Trafford. It felt safer to meet in public. That's just what you do, these days. Far too many weirdos about. We both got out, put on our bravest masks for each other, and said a quick hello. Then, once I'd sensed how normal he was, I climbed into his car and we drove to Chester, to a Steakhouse not a million miles away from where they used to hang the witches. I wasn't thinking about them, though, as I tucked into my steak with peppercorn sauce, but I might've mentioned them later. Wayne seemed interested. He *was* interested. In everything, as it turned out, even the Reiki, which he asked loads about. He seemed curious, about everything, and was full of facts. It made him seem youthful. He certainly looked it, anyway.

He had to fly out to California the next day for a thing he had on, a conference, I think. If ever I forget the date, Wayne's quick to remind me, because it's locked in his memory. Not because the conference or the flight was memorable, but because the date itself (*our* date, not the calendar date) ended up being the most expensive date of his life. We talked for the whole evening, four or five hours at least, and it was so wonderful and so involving that neither of us remembered the car park we'd left his car in closed up for the night at 11pm.

"Oops," he said.

His flight out was the next morning from Manchester, but it says a lot about Wayne that he didn't fall to pieces when he saw the locked gates that stood between us and his lonely- looking car.

"Is there anything you need in it for the flight?" I asked him.

"Everything."

Almost before he'd finished answering, his hand was up in the air and he was hailing us a black cab that just happened to be passing. He'd thought fast, and responded, and we travelled back to Mickle Trafford, giggling like two school kids in the back of the taxi. It felt good. Yeah, I liked this. Someone I could have a laugh with.

"You're more than welcome to stay the night," I said, as I climbed out to pick up my own car. "I've got a big spare room." He declined, politely, because he really didn't want to travel to California in the same clothes he'd just met me in. Understandable, I suppose. I watched him driven off in the cab, the clock still ticking, guessing as to the look of delight on the driver's face as he tapped Wayne's Warrington postcode into his Sat-Nav. He must've thought it was his lucky night. He'd be doing the journey again, of course, in just a few hours, because he had to get *back* to Chester to collect his car from the car park, so he could get what he needed from it, and then whizz over the airport . It was a round trip of well over fifty miles, and ended, (so he told me when he returned), like a scene in a comedy with him racing to get to his terminal before they closed the gate.

"Hold that plane!"

Wayne calls it our anniversary, and I'm happy with that. When January 31st next rolls round in 2022 – when all this dreadful Coronavirus stuff has gone the way of the exes – it'll be our seventh one together. "Happy Anniversary", we'll say to each other, and then we'll raise our glasses in a toast. "Here's to whatever comes next."

Lightning Source UK Ltd.
Milton Keynes UK
UKHW011254190821
389108UK00002B/46